IMAGES
of America

WAUSEON

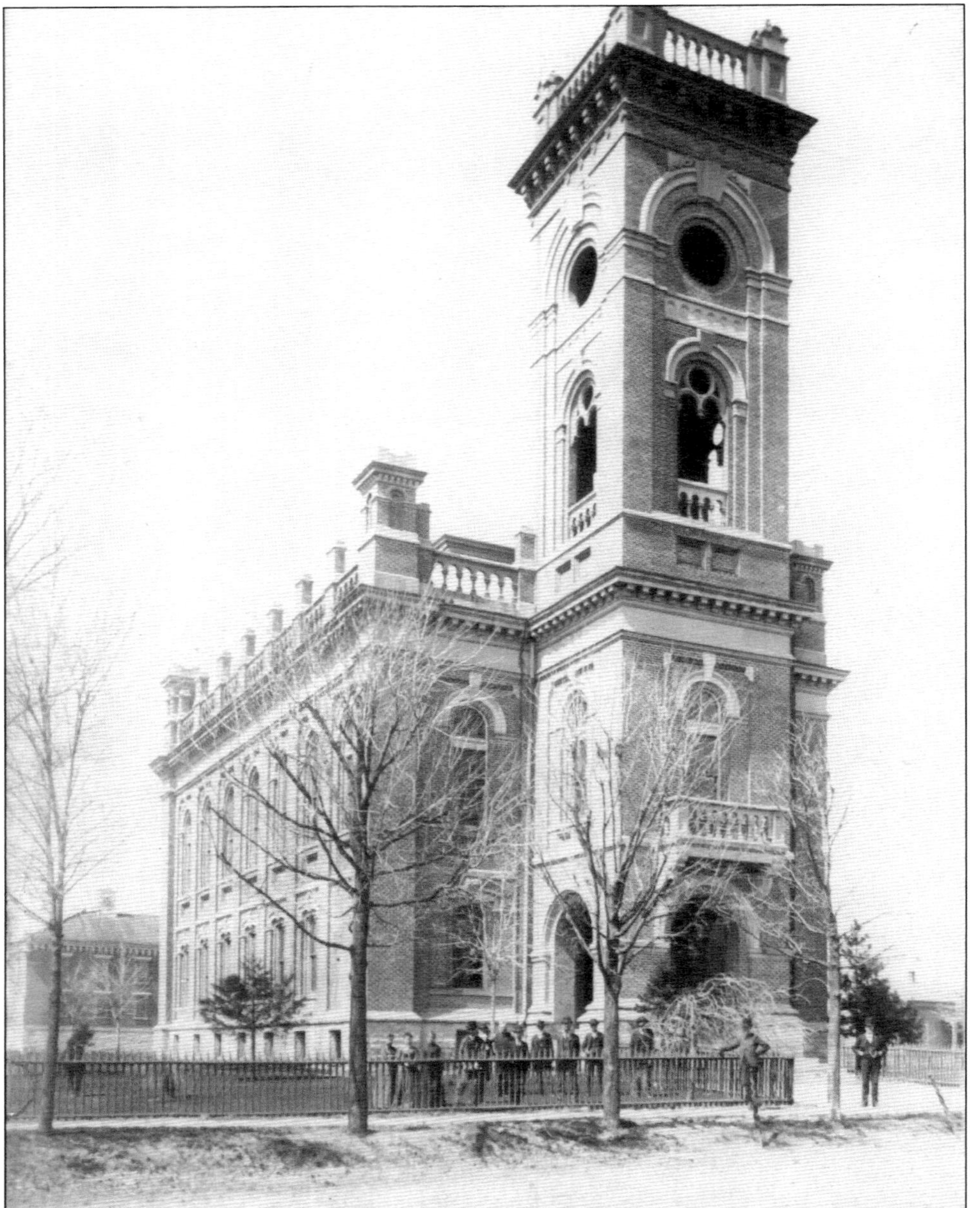

Once Wauseon became the county seat, the county needed a new courthouse. Located on property once owned by early businessman E.L. Hayes, the courthouse was built in 1870. This scene is from that time, prior to installation of the clock. The clock was installed in 1891 and powered by 1,400 pounds of weights. (Courtesy of the Fulton County Historical Society.)

ON THE COVER: Within 25 years of its founding, Wauseon had become the county's retail and business center. Pictured is a mixture of original wood-framed and brick businesses along the still unpaved South Fulton Street in the late 1890s. (Courtesy of the Fulton County Historical Society.)

IMAGES
of America

WAUSEON

Robert Krumm

ARCADIA
PUBLISHING

ISBN 978-1-4671-1257-4

Published by Arcadia Publishing
Charleston, South Carolina

Printed in the United States of America

Library of Congress Control Number: 2014938650

For all general information, please contact Arcadia Publishing:
Telephone 843-853-2070
Fax 843-853-0044
E-mail sales@arcadiapublishing.com
For customer service and orders:
Toll-Free 1-888-313-2665

Visit us on the Internet at www.arcadiapublishing.com

This book is dedicated to those who collect, protect, and share the artifacts that tell the tale of our community's rich history.

Contents

Acknowledgments

This book could not have been written without the cooperation of John Swearingen Jr., the amazingly knowledgeable director of the Fulton County Historic Museum, and museum volunteer Mish Arlo. Mish spent long hours scanning many of the photographs appearing herein.

Thank you to the staff of the Wauseon Public Library for your research assistance, the associates at Tomahawk Printing, and Rob Huffman, founder of Priceless Photograph Preservation in Ann Arbor, Michigan.

This book contains pictures and postcards taken from the private collections of James and Mona Sauder, Hal and Jayne Bailey, Joseph Horwath, Floyd Franks, Richard and Nan Zimmerman, Carol Krieger, Kevin Nelson, the Wauseon Rotary Club, and the Wauseon Fire Department. Local historian Gene Vanderbunt added greatly to the chapter on local railroads. Also, much appreciation goes to Rich Batdorf and INTV Channel 5 for assistance soliciting photographs.

Seldom in life does the cavalry arrive in time to rescue anyone, but Arcadia Publishing has numerous professionals who did, including my editor, Jesse Darland, who kept me on track and on deadline.

I am indebted to my parents, Edwin and Nancy Krumm, who shared their interest in history by taking their children on many field trips to Ohio historical sites.

Finally, immense appreciation goes to Sharon, my wife and best friend. I owe her both apologies and gratitude for indulging me when I "zoned out" with research and writing. She is the most patient and supportive person I have ever known.

Unless otherwise indicated, all photographs are provided courtesy of the Fulton County Historical Society.

INTRODUCTION

The history of Fulton County and Wauseon began long before the first settlers found their way here. Prior to white settlement, there were thousands of years of human activity.

In the beginning, what is now Fulton County was settled by the Paleo-Indian people, living in the area as early as 13 centuries before the birth of Jesus Christ. These natives crafted stone tools, many of which are still being unearthed in the Wauseon area today. They slowly developed sophisticated cultures, built dozens of burial mounds (several of which are untouched and protected by local landowners), and developed into successful hunters and gatherers, harvesting wildlife, growing crops such as corn (farming, it is believed, was taught to them by early French trappers), collecting wild honey and berries, and collecting maple tree sap to produce syrup.

The early Native Americans hunted small game, birds, elk, and bison. The Indians had to be totally self-reliant, producing everything they ate, wore, or used for cooking and shelter.

Most of the remains of buffalo in Ohio are associated with later cultures, which thrived between 1000 and 1650 AD. There is speculation that a drought in the west forced the migration of some herds to the east. The earliest actual account comes from French explorer M. de Vandreuil in 1687, who wrote, "Buffaloes abound on the south shore of Lake Erie."

By the time whites began settling here, an estimated 3,000 Native Americans inhabited the area. With the encroachment of settlers, the peaceful natives lost many of the skills they needed to survive. Within only a generation, Indians became reliant on the tools, clothing, and weapons of the trappers and settlers. For example, they learned firearms were far more effective and efficient at hunting game and far easier than crafting bows and arrows.

By the late 1830s, two factors led to huge challenges for the Indians: the new settlers competed with them as hunters, and compounding this, the dense forests were being cleared for construction material and land for farmers' fields. The once abundant wildlife was becoming more and more scarce.

Sadly, many of those that were still in the Wauseon area in the 1830s and early 1840s would have to beg for food in order to survive. Settler Mary Hibbard recorded in her diary on November 29, 1840, "I cannot think it right to force them [the Indians] to leave their native woods and plains, to which they seem so attached, and go to a strange land. They were a harmless people, never disturbing the whites, unless first misused by them—getting their living principally by hunting, picking berries and sometimes making baskets, which they exchanged with the whites for bread or potatoes." Hibbard also noted the Indians frequently came to their farm "hungry and asked for victuals, for which they seemed very thankful."

It should be noted that not a single drop of blood was ever shed between Native American Indians and white settlers in Fulton County.

By the mid-1700s, a few Frenchmen had begun engaging Native tribes in the fur trade, exchanging beaver and otter pelts for cheap goods such as beads, blankets, and simple tools such as hatchets and knives. After the American Revolution, the settlement of the Northwest Territories, which encompassed the Ohio Valley, began in earnest. From all directions, settlers were moving into the area.

First to arrive were missionaries, who created settlements in central Ohio to introduce Christian beliefs and horticultural techniques to the indigenous Indians. They were soon followed by vast numbers of farmers. Ohio's population increased rapidly, chiefly by migrants from New England, New York, and Pennsylvania. Southerners settled in the southern part of the Ohio territory, traveling by boat, canoes, and log barges along the Ohio River. Yankees, especially in the Western Reserve, near Cleveland, supported modernization, public education, and antislavery policies.

The tribes' days of peaceful existence were coming to an end. Along with only a handful of other tribal members, they began feeling the pressures resulting from white settlers invading their hunting grounds. At first, the Indians tried to coexist with the newcomers, but they quickly became dependent on them, finally agreeing to leave their hunting grounds to be relocated farther west.

The Battle of Fallen Timbers in 1794 and the Treaty of Greenville in 1795 set the stage for a few hearty homesteaders and entrepreneurs to begin moving into the area. Their appearance led to the establishment of permanent settlements throughout the region. Waterville was established in 1818, Defiance in 1822, Adrian, Michigan, in 1826, Toledo in 1833, Napoleon and Delta in 1834, and Bryan in 1840. The first settlement in what became Fulton County, at Lauber Hill, took place in 1833.

By the end of 1801, Ohio's population growth turned into a raging river, reaching 45,000 people. To put this into prospective, this is more than Fulton County's present-day population.

Congress determined that the population was growing rapidly and Ohio could begin the path to statehood. The assumption was that the territory would have in excess of the required 60,000 residents by the time it became a state. Congress passed the Enabling Act of 1802, which outlined the process for the territory to seek statehood. Residents convened a constitutional convention. They based their new constitution on numerous provisions from other states and wholeheartedly rejected slavery. On February 19, 1803, Pres. Thomas Jefferson signed the act of Congress that approved Ohio's boundaries and constitution.

During the American Revolution and again in the War of 1812, the local Potawatomi (a subgroup of the larger Ottawa Nation) allied themselves with the British. The natives feared American settlers would continue to occupy their land if they did not receive assistance from the British. The Potawatomi natives did not have a large presence in Ohio, and throughout the late 1700s and early 1800s, they signed numerous treaties forsaking any land claims in Ohio.

Spurred by the young nation's success against the British in the War of 1812, settlers began moving into western Lucas County, which, in 1850, split off into Fulton County. In 1832, the tribes living in northwest Ohio agreed to sell their land to the federal government, accepting a small restitution for signing the Council Oak Treaty and agreeing to be moved to Kansas.

What is now Fulton County was part of the Great Black Swamp, basically an area of dense woods and wetlands. The swamp was an extensive, glacially fed wetland area in northwest Ohio and part of extreme northeast Indiana. It existed from the end of the great glacier (c. 10,000 BC) until the later part of the 19th century, when settlers dug ditches to drain the water.

While development of the young state proceeded rapidly, the swamp's dense habitat created a formidable barrier to both development and travel. The area to be known as Fulton County was crisscrossed with numerous Indian and wildlife trails. Yet, it remained difficult for settlers to traverse. To overcome this obstacle, a corduroy road was constructed from Fremont to Perrysburg in 1825.

The corduroy roads were made by placing logs adjacent to each other and perpendicular to the direction of travel. This required significant labor and muscle power to fell and cut trees to the proper length, between six and eight feet. The roads were not perfect, but they provided a temporary solution. Often, the logs shifted or sank into the muck, resulting in hazards to horses and wagons. Toll fees of 10¢ were usually assessed to travel these roads.

Early Wauseon settlers used this type of road construction, too. In the 1990s, while widening Shoop Avenue during the administration of Mayor Jerry Matheny, construction workers uncovered rotting remnants of logs buried several feet beneath the road's asphalt surface, which had been used for a wooden road.

Settlement of the region was also inhibited by endemic malaria. Early settlers called the disease "swamp fever," or "ague," and suspected it was carried by "bad air." Early Wauseon newspapers carried advertisements promoting cures for the fever. Malaria continued to be a chronic problem until mosquito breeding grounds were drained.

Because of these obstacles, Fulton County was the 87th of Ohio's 88 counties to be established. Also, the impassibility of the swamp was a factor in keeping blood from being spilled during the so-called Toledo War in 1835–1836. Also known as the Michigan-Ohio War, this was a boundary dispute between the State of Ohio and the adjoining Territory of Michigan.

The "war" resulted from an erroneous latitude calculation by surveyors, leading to a misunderstanding of certain geographical features, specifically the southernmost points of Lake Erie and Lake Michigan. Both Ohio and Michigan claimed ownership of a 468-square-mile strip of territory along their common border. The disputed area included Toledo and a stretch of land about 15 miles north of present-day Wauseon.

In 1835, Michigan petitioned for statehood, including the disputed territory within its boundaries. Riled by the attempt, Ohio congressional delegates stalled Michigan's admission to the Union. Ohio's then governor, Robert Lucas, and Michigan's 24-year-old governor, Stevens Mason, were unwilling to cede jurisdiction of the area. They mobilized militias, sending them to positions on opposite sides of the Maumee River near Toldeo. The single military confrontation of the "war" ended with shots being fired into the air, resulting in zero casualties.

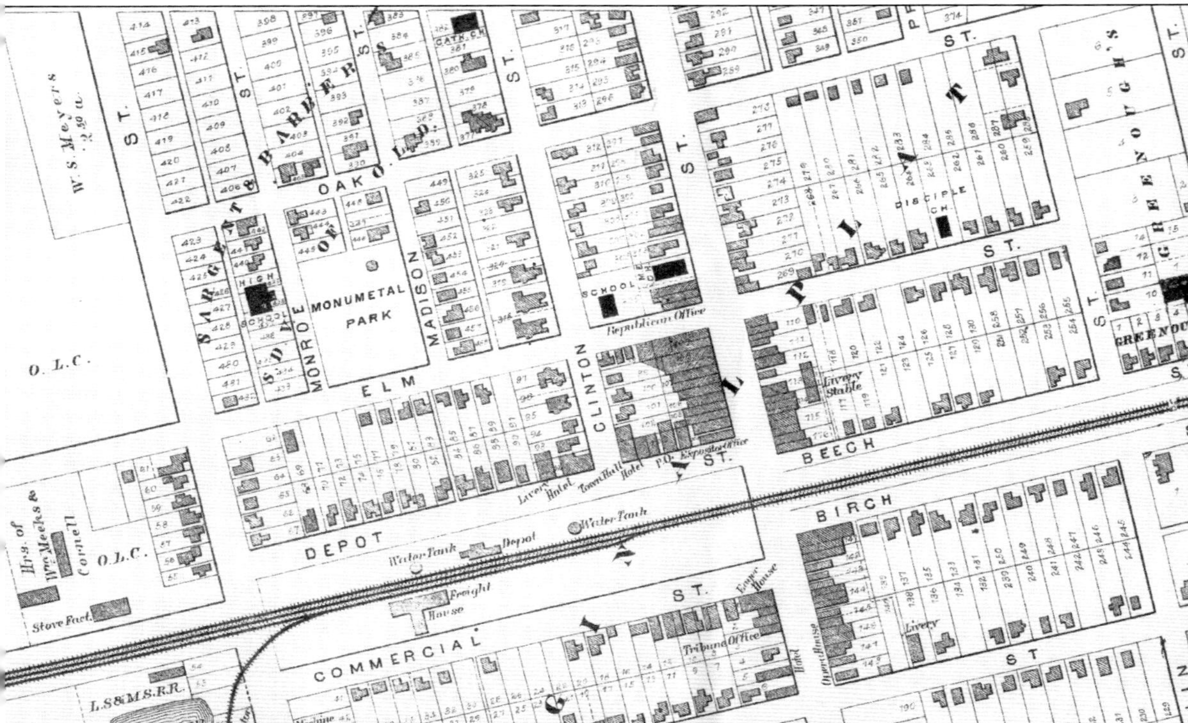

By the mid-1880s, when this map was drawn, the original Wauseon village site had expanded far beyond the original 160 acres. This is a portion of that map showing the area encompassed by the 1855 plat.

One

Formation of Fulton County

It is believed that the first white settler in the area was John Grey, who arrived around 1824. Grey was a fur trader who never took title or cleared any of the land. Grey's log structure served as both a home and a trading post. He eventually left the area, fearful of hostile Indians.

The first two permanent settlers in the area were Eli Phillips and a noted hunter, Joseph Bates. Phillips later claimed he was the only white settler in the area, with his closest white neighbors living in Michigan. Bates moved here from Williams County in 1833. He, too, had a good reputation and was known to be well versed in the area's geography.

Lucas County was established in 1835. Within a portion of its borders was the future Fulton County. The area was established as a single township, York Township.

In 1838, the federal government reached a treaty with the Pottawatomie Indians and purchased their land, giving them a tract in Kansas. Local settler Dresden Howard was appointed to relocate the area's Indians there. Despite grandiose descriptions of the wonderful opportunities they would experience in their new home, many Indians were reluctant to cross the muddy Mississippi River. Some remained hidden deep in the Black Swamp, while others fled to Michigan or Canada.

Twelve years later, Fulton County was formed. The county's northern border forms Ohio's boundary with Michigan. The county is basically a rectangle 26 miles wide and 15.6 miles from north to south, encompassing 407 square miles. An 1840 census registered a population of 303 whites. By 1920, the population had expanded to 4,778.

The county seat was originally the city of Maumee, and then it was moved to Toledo. All land deeds and other important judicial affairs required at least a full day of travel there. A discussion began that this area should become independent. Several leaders, including Delta businessman Nathaniel Leggett, lobbied for an independent county. Their efforts came to fruition on February 28, 1850, when the state legislature established Fulton County.

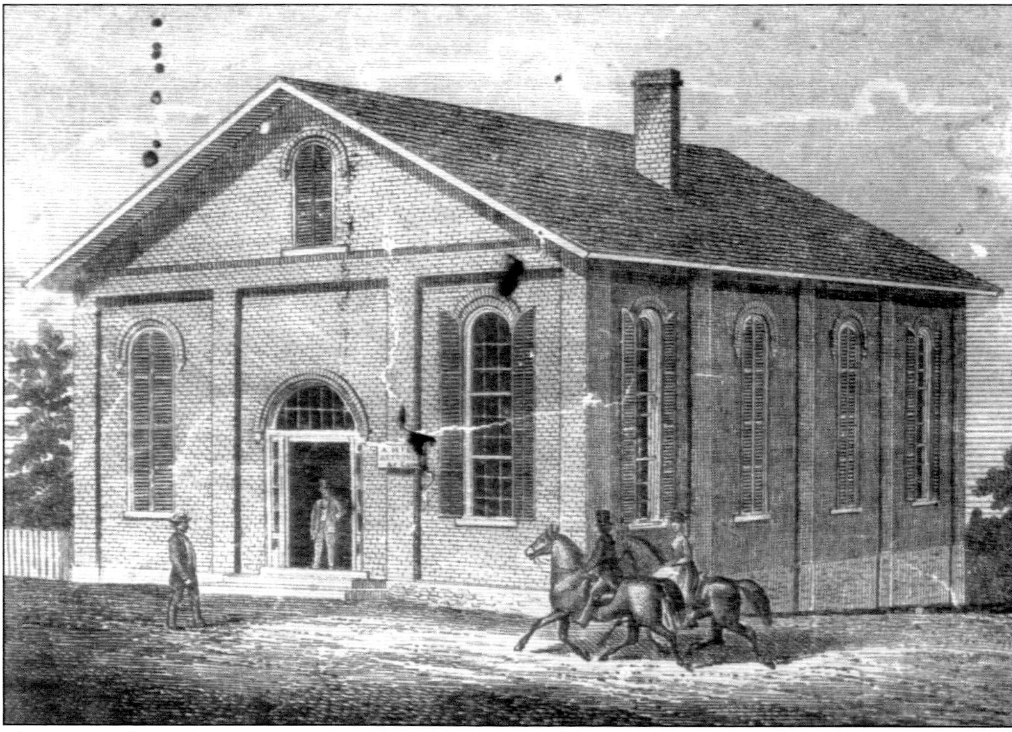

The newly formed county's political and commercial activities were conducted about four miles north of present-day Wauseon. When residents gathered on May 2, 1850, to stake out a site for the first county seat, Col. Dresden Howard was standing nearby. A county commissioner asked Howard to suggest a name for the town. Howard proposed Ottokee, after a local Indian chief. The community had two hotels, two newspapers, a bar, a blacksmith shop, a grocery, and clothing stores, as well as the first courthouse (above). The last court session in Ottokee was conducted in 1871. About that time, a fire destroyed the courthouse and all the county's records. With the construction of several sawmills, profitable lumbering operations sprang up. Felled trees were used for structural building material, siding, and roof shingles, as seen in the c. 1870 image below, which shows an early homestead.

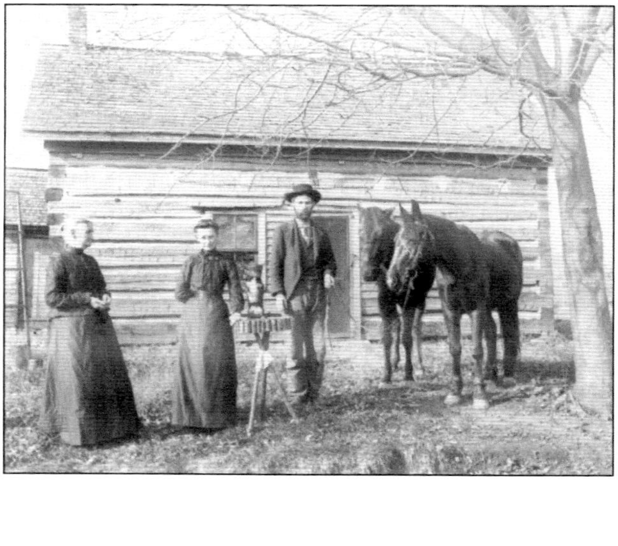

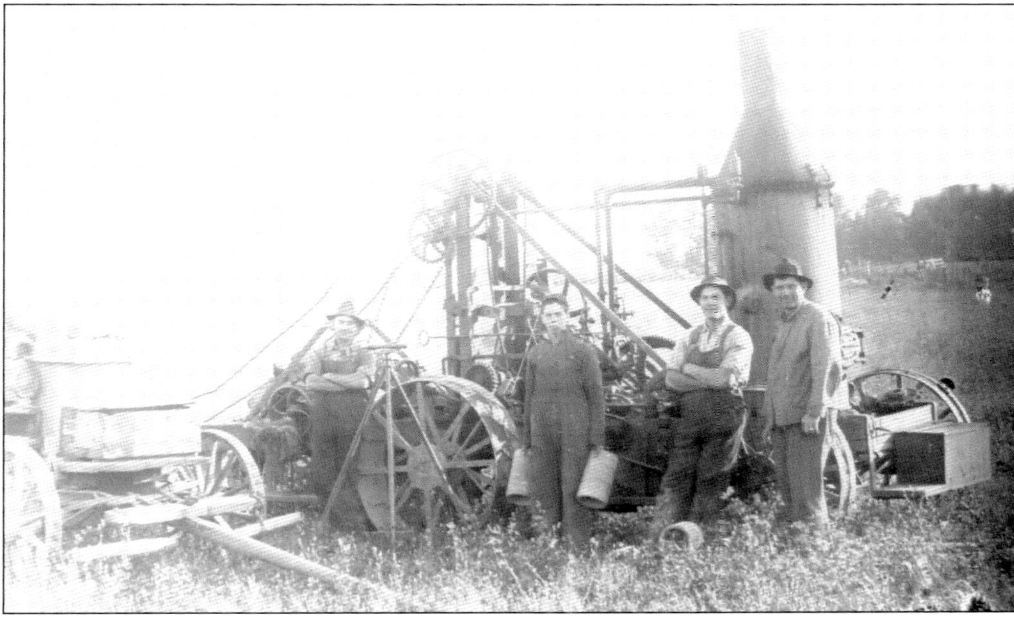

The geography of the Great Black Swamp retarded major settlement until the 1860s. In 1859, the Ohio Ditch Law was passed by the state legislature. It established a method for individuals and local entities to petition county governments to surface-drain the area. Shown here are crews, including Lloyd Mohrs and Abner Rupp in the photograph below, in the 1880s operating steam-powered trenchers for the placement of underground drainage tiles. The tiles drained into a system of ditches, located primarily along established roads. These ditches are still seen throughout the county. Slab wood from timber operations fueled clay tile and brick kilns, providing the material needed for the underground drainage of fields. Drainage of the county transformed this into one of Ohio's most fertile and productive farming areas.

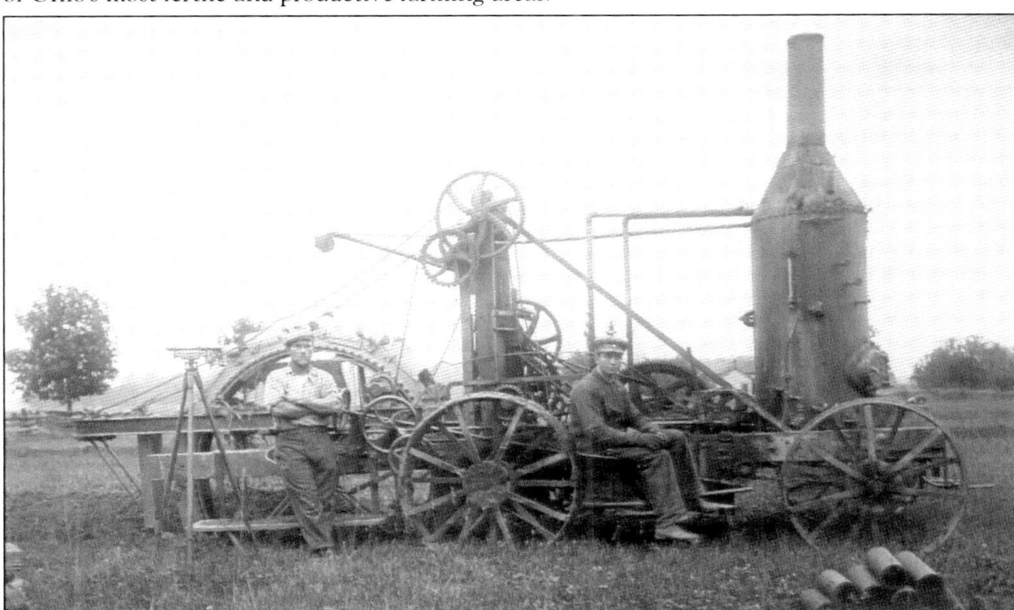

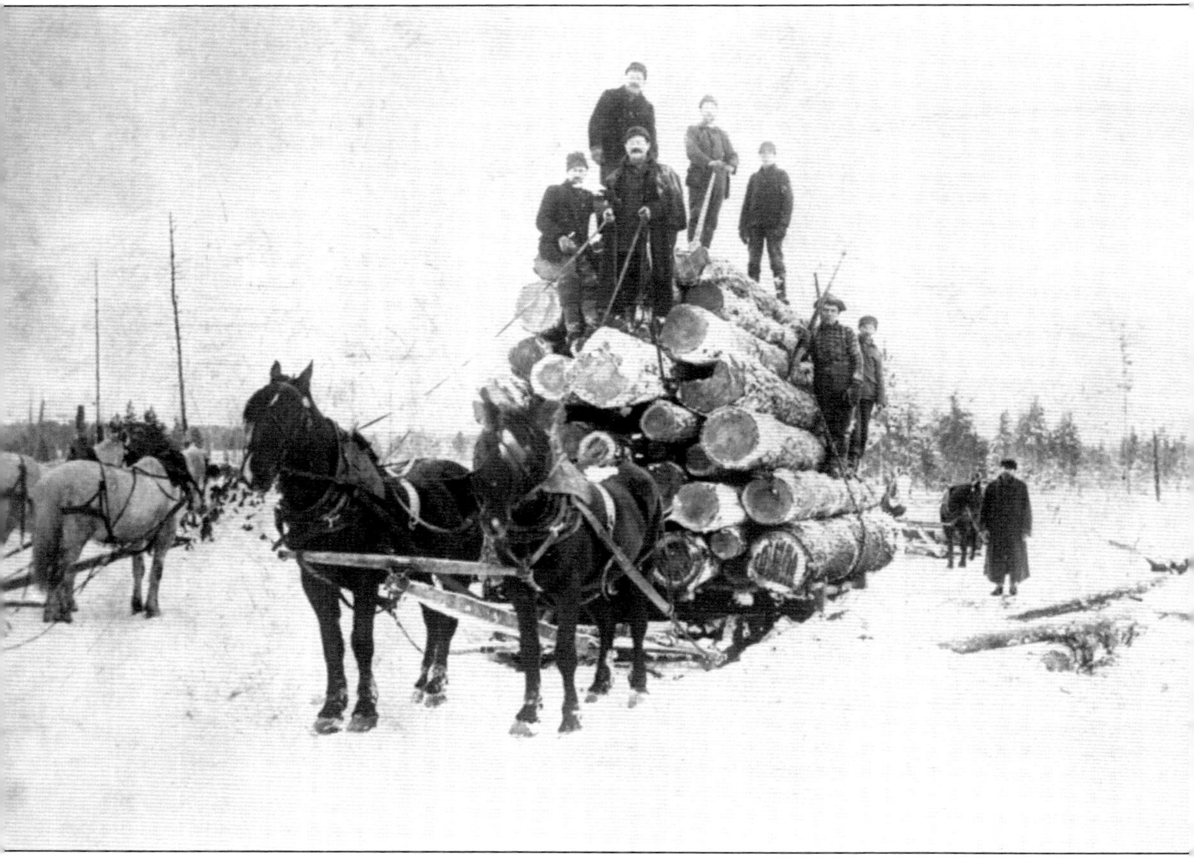

The availability of thousands of acres of trees, plus the need for lumber for construction and cordwood for heating, led to several profitable logging operations starting up. Early sawmills cut the wood, mostly oak and walnut, into dimensional lumber. Slab wood was used for heating, and cordwood was sold to the railroads to fuel their steam-powered locomotives.

Two

WAUSEON'S ROOTS

Just as the transcontinental railroad accelerated the pace at which the West was settled, construction of a railway line through Fulton County paved the way for settlement of Wauseon.

In 1850, rumors abounded that a railroad would be passing through the county. Many believed the county seat, Ottokee, would be on the line. This prospect turned sleepy Ottokee into a boomtown.

But, there was a problem: the railroad was asking the county to provide a $50,000 bond. Commissioners rejected this as out of hand.

A competing railroad, the Southern Michigan & Northern Indiana Railroad Company, ran a survey line through Swanton and Delta and about four miles south of Ottokee. The company was soon laying track through Fulton County toward Bryan and, ultimately, Elkhart, Indiana.

This offered an opportunity for visionaries to become wealthy by acquiring land along the route. Two such individuals were railroad engineers Epaphras Lord Barber and John H. Sargent. Knowing the route the line would take, they were undoubtedly encouraged by their employer to establish a new town. To expedite the project, they sought out Delta-area businessman Nathaniel Leggett and Fulton County treasurer William Hall.

The four agreed to become partners, contacting local settler Thomas Bayes, who had purchased his land from the federal government. The Bayes family lived in a log house standing nearly smack in the middle of the route, a few dozen yards west of the current county courthouse. The partners paid him $2,560 for 160 acres. This resulted in an impressive profit for Bayes, who had originally paid between $200 and $480 for the property.

Before the site could be platted, Hall died from cholera, so Leggett became an equal partner with Barber and Sargent in the project. Barber and an assistant surveyed and marked out the site. The main street would be named Fulton and intersected the railroad tracks at a 90-degree angle. The street would be wide, a symbol of the town's potential. North-south streets were named after prominent citizens, with east-west streets named after indigenous tree species.

Barber's plat for the new village was called Litchfield. There are two conflicting stories of who came up with the final name. Lesser known is H.L Hosmer, who assisted in recording the land deed and the new village's plat. The village was named after a local Indian chief whose brother, Ottokee, was the namesake of the original county seat. Hosmer, a Toledo attorney, was later appointed by President Lincoln as the first chief justice of the Montana Territory. The better-known story is that the daughter of storeowner E.L. Hayes proposed the name. The plat was recorded on April 11, 1854.

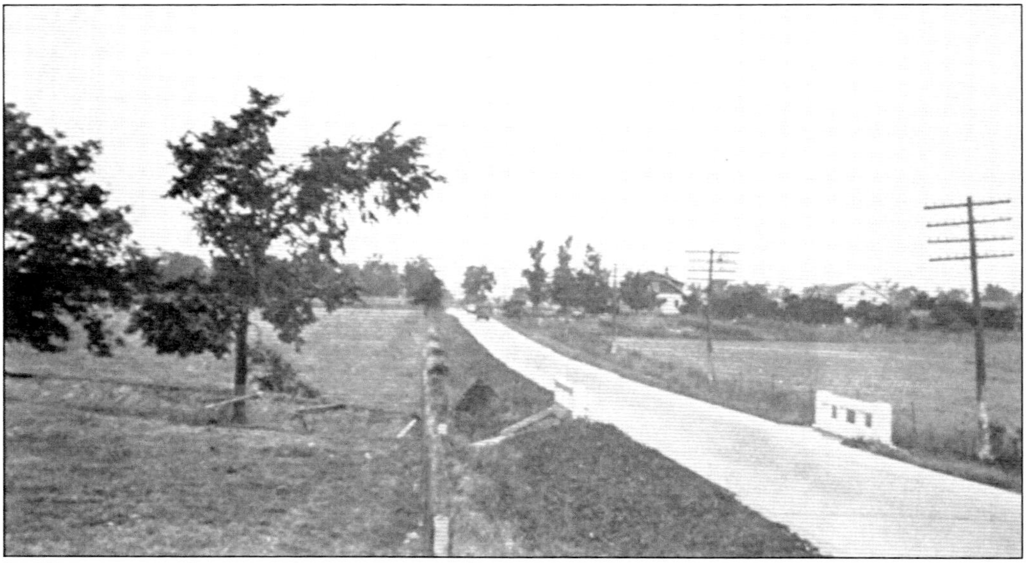

In Wauseon's early years, the primary north-south road became County Road 13, also known as the Adrian Highway. This was basically a single-lane track linking Napoleon to Wauseon to Adrian, Michigan. The main route between Napoleon and the Ohio Turnpike was eventually moved to State Route 108, also known as Shoop Avenue, where it passed through town. (Courtesy of the Sauder collection.)

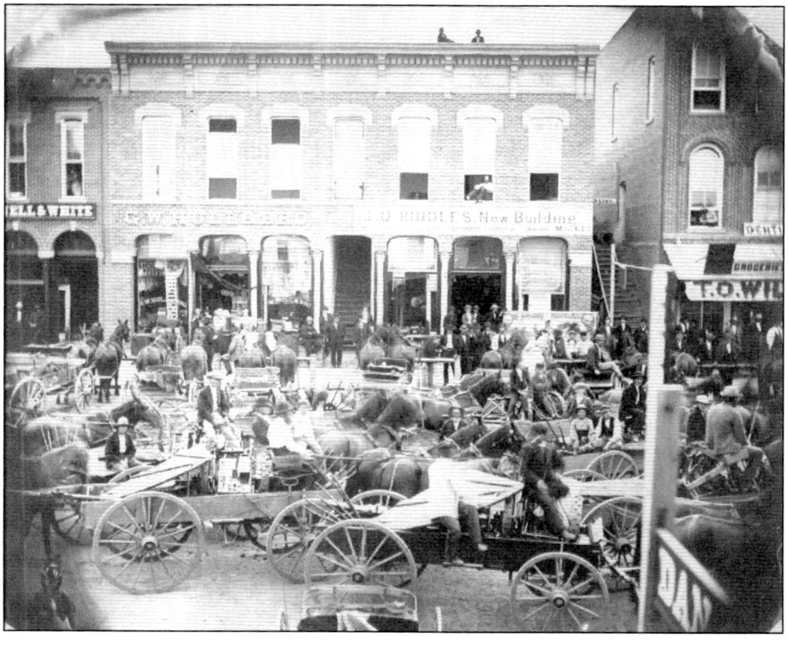

In 1872, families from outlying farms would travel to the village of Wauseon to collect their mail and packages, purchase supplies, and conduct business at the courthouse. Farmers often made the trip on Mondays to combine business with a little pleasure.

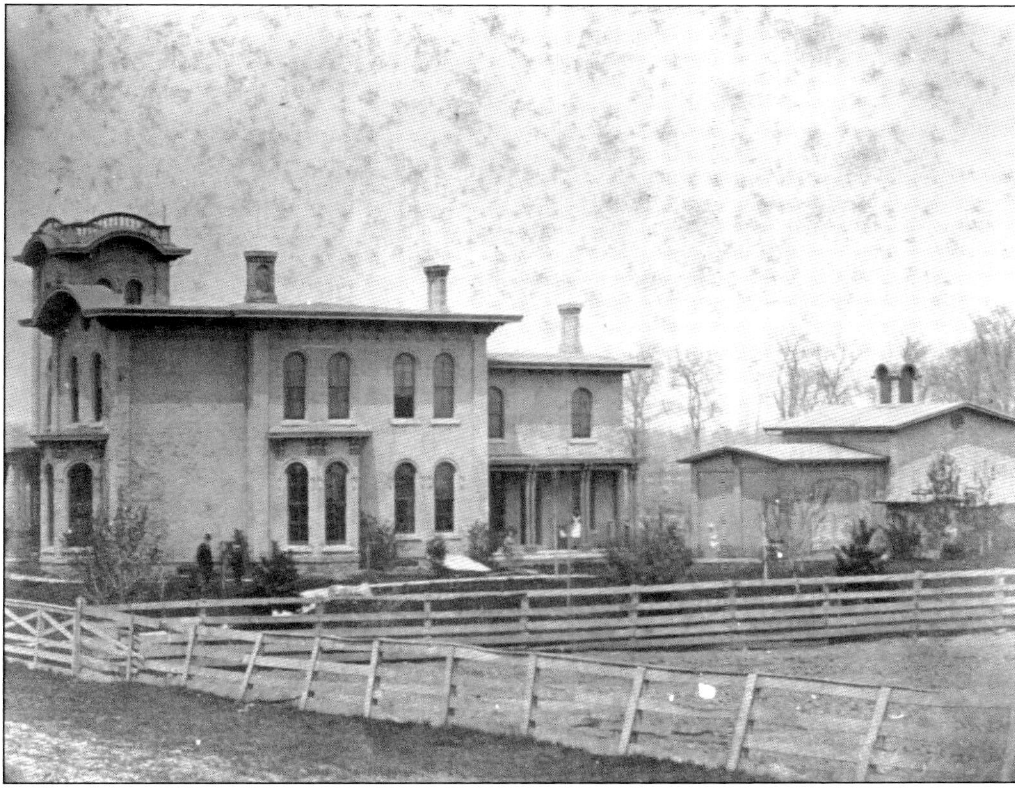

Built in 1865, Col. Dresden Howard's home (above) stood on North Prospect Street. The family often found arrowheads, as well as several tomahawks, on the property. The home was torn down in the 1930s. Colonel Howard helped the federal government negotiate a treaty with local Indians at the Council Oak, near Winameg. He later moved his family to Wauseon and was elected the first president of the Fulton County Historical Society. An early Wauseon businessman was Joel Brigham (pictured at right in 1888) who opened his store here in 1859. He sold general merchandise and then made the store a hardware store. Brigham, who died in 1908, was a leader in the village's affairs. Besides serving on the council, he was also a partner in the Brigham, Guilford & Co. department store.

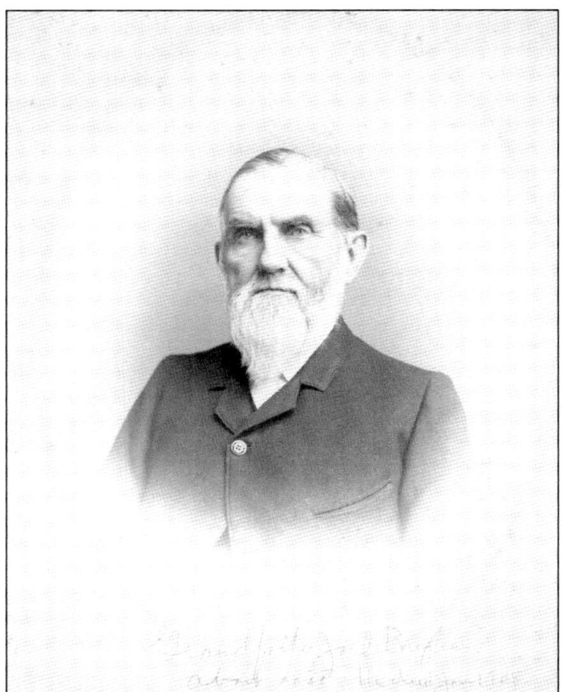

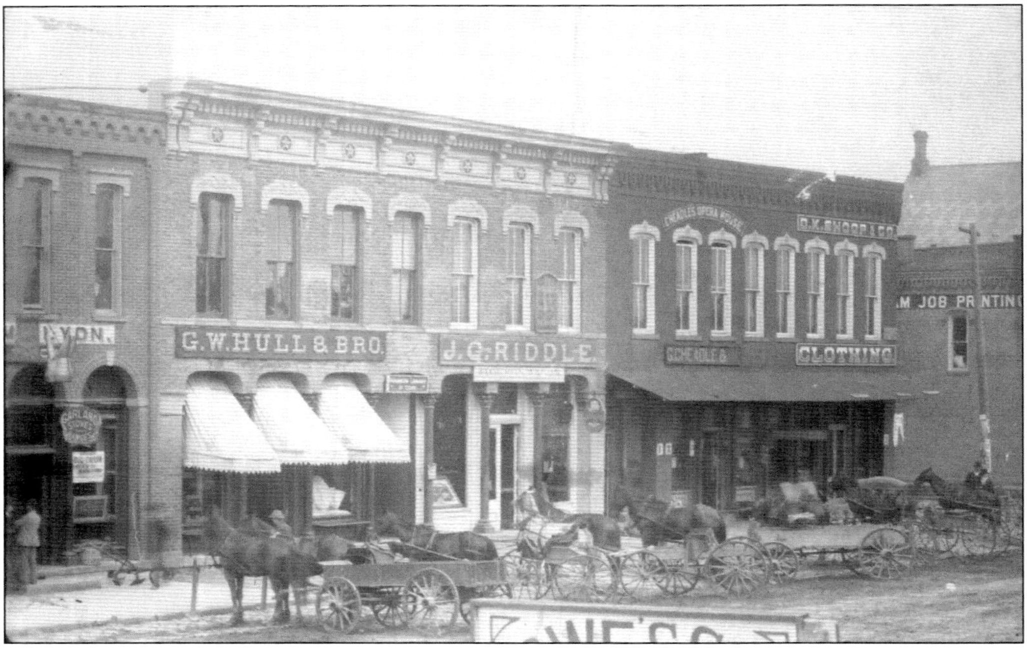

Seen above is the west side of North Fulton Street between Elm and Depot Streets. D.K. Shoop, who owned the popular clothing store seen on the corner, was also a prominent community leader and early banker. His stately home (below) was located on West Chestnut Street. Shoop invested in property around town. Shoop Avenue is named after him. The woods that comprise Reighard Park were known as Shoop's Woods. Like many prosperous early merchants, the Shoops' home was built to accommodate a live-in servant. In 1903, Shoop became president of the First National Bank, a position he held for 30 years.

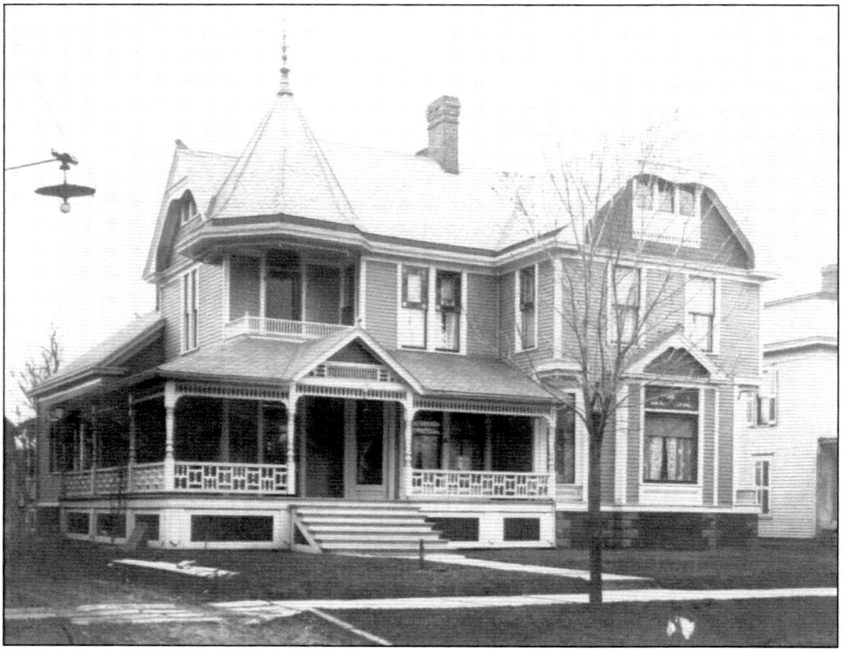

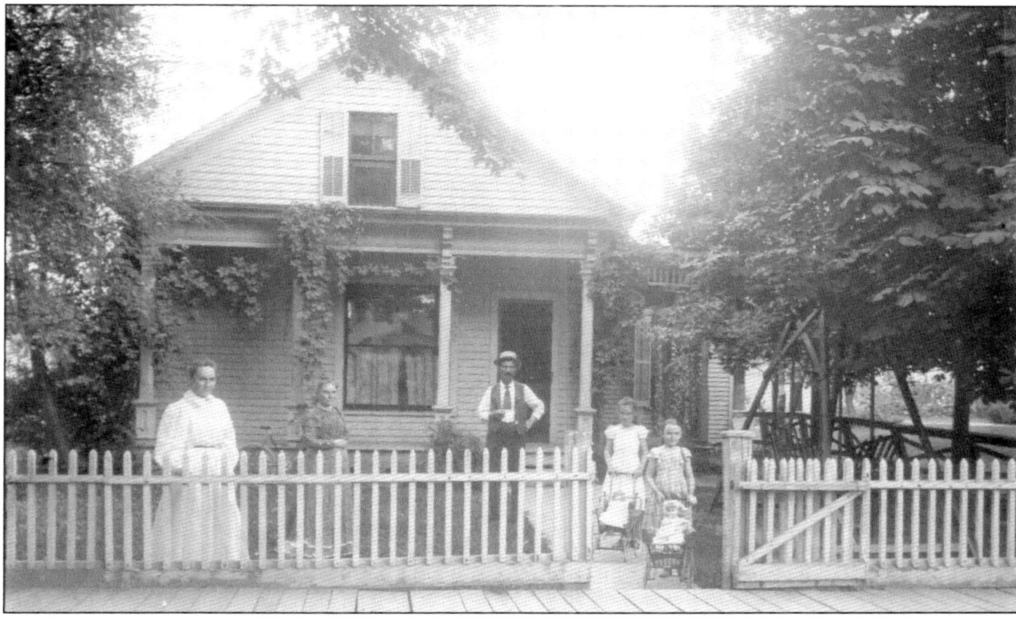

Charles Stotzer and his wife and daughters are shown in the front yard of their home on North Fulton Street in 1888. Stotzer was the area's leading dealer in carriages and harnesses, and his store once occupied the southeast corner of North Fulton and Elm Streets. Back then, every farm kid dreamed of owning a horse and buggy, and Stotzer helped make this happen. The foreground shows the wooden sidewalks mandated by the village council.

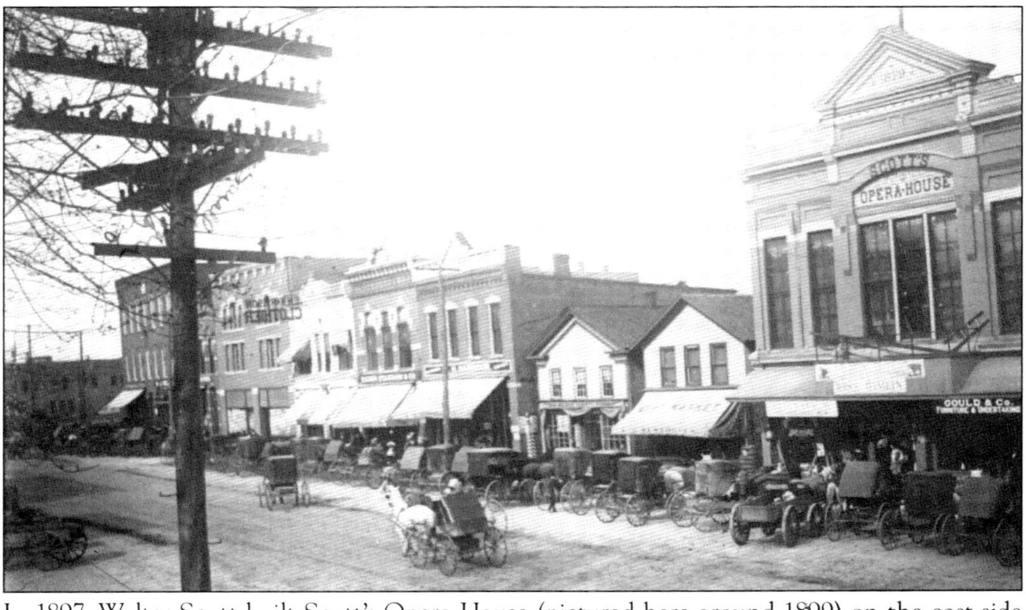

In 1897, Walter Scott built Scott's Opera House (pictured here around 1899) on the east side of South Fulton Street. The lower floor was used for stores, but the upper floor contained an auditorium, which could seat 600 people, where theatrical productions were performed. Playbills can still be found in hallways on that floor. The South Fulton Street structure has been remodeled many times, serving principally as a furniture store under various owners and names.

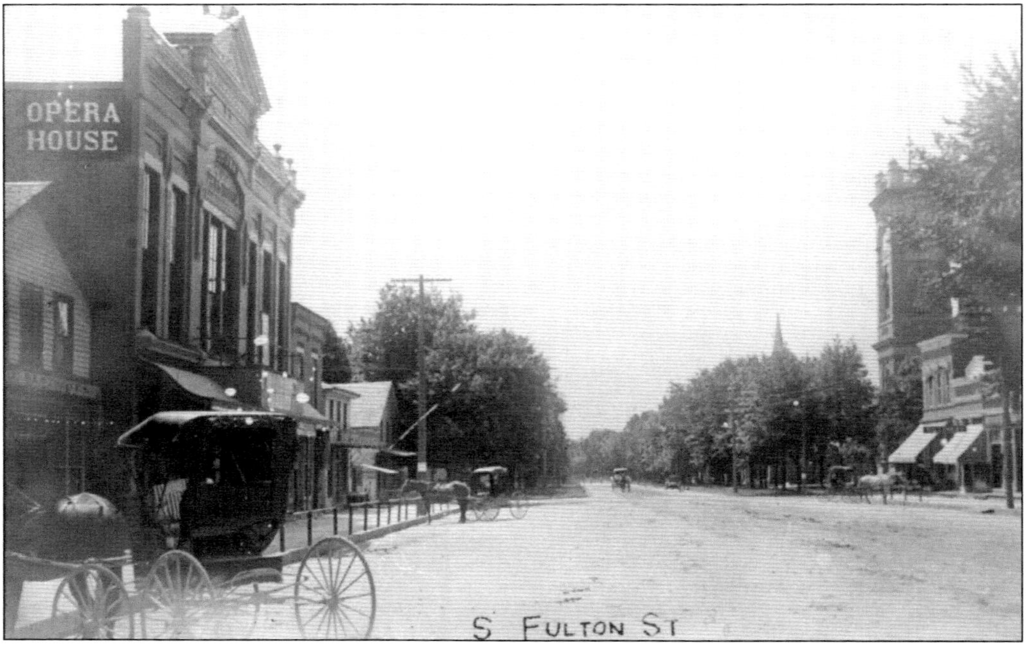

Above, doctor's carriages, the sports cars of their time, are tied up to hitching racks in front of Scott's Opera House. Used by doctors and many others, these lightweight vehicles were speedy and easy to handle. As seen in the winter view below, residents often had to fight their way through the snow. E.H. Harrison was a popular clothing store. It was an early practice of retailers to sometimes hang a store sign across all or part of the street for advertising.

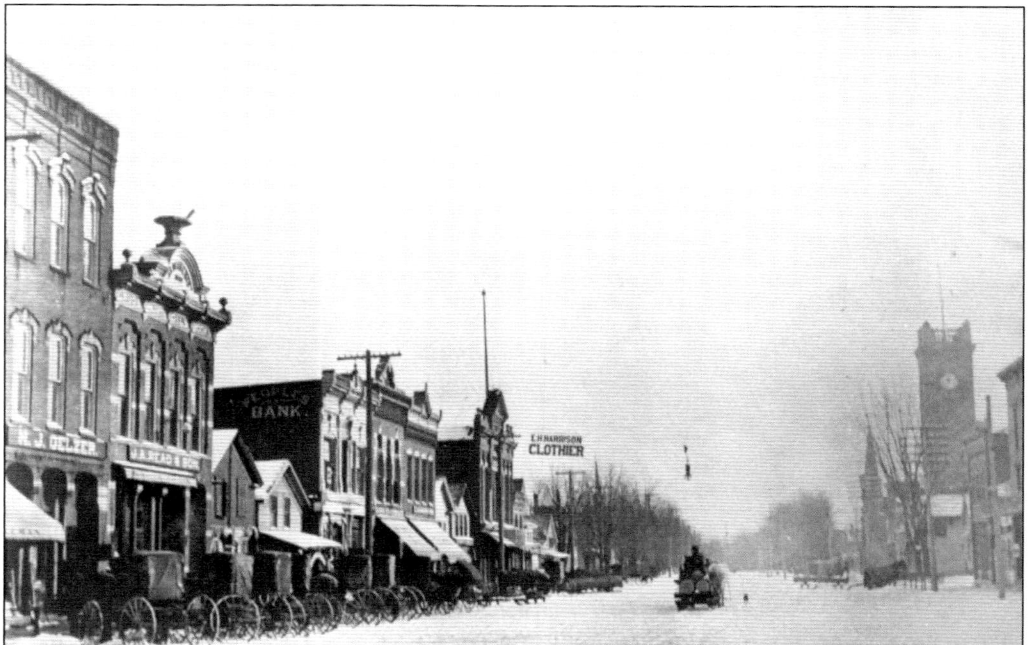

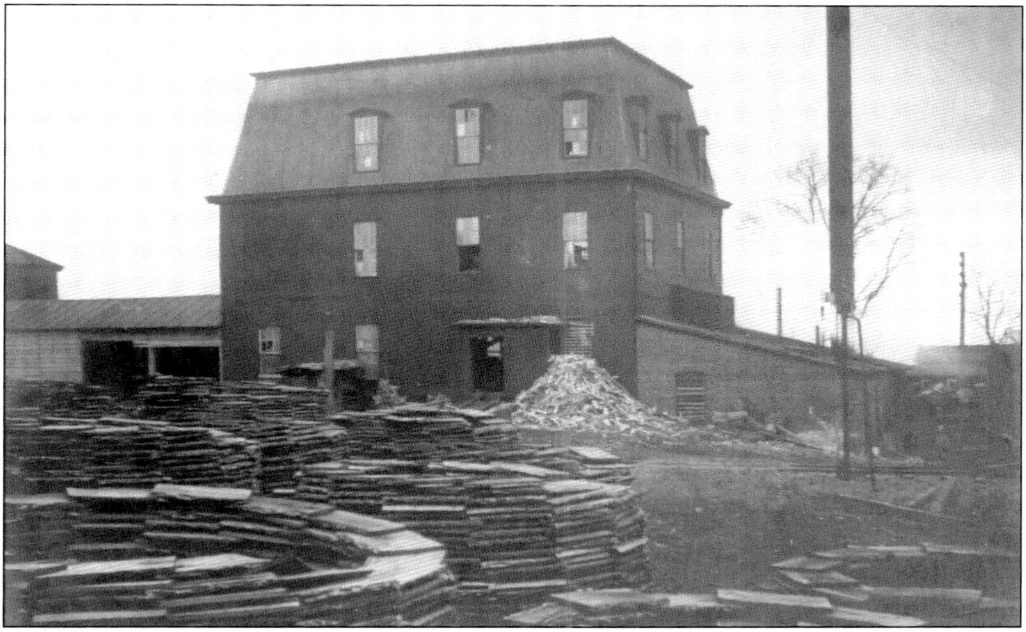

The railroad helped the community to become the retail center of the county, offering opportunities for businesses such as a farmers' cooperative, built along the tracks near Brunell Street. Besides supplying grain and other necessities to farmers, it also processed building materials. In the foreground are stacks of wood drying for use as roofing shingles, which were used locally and shipped by rail to other markets.

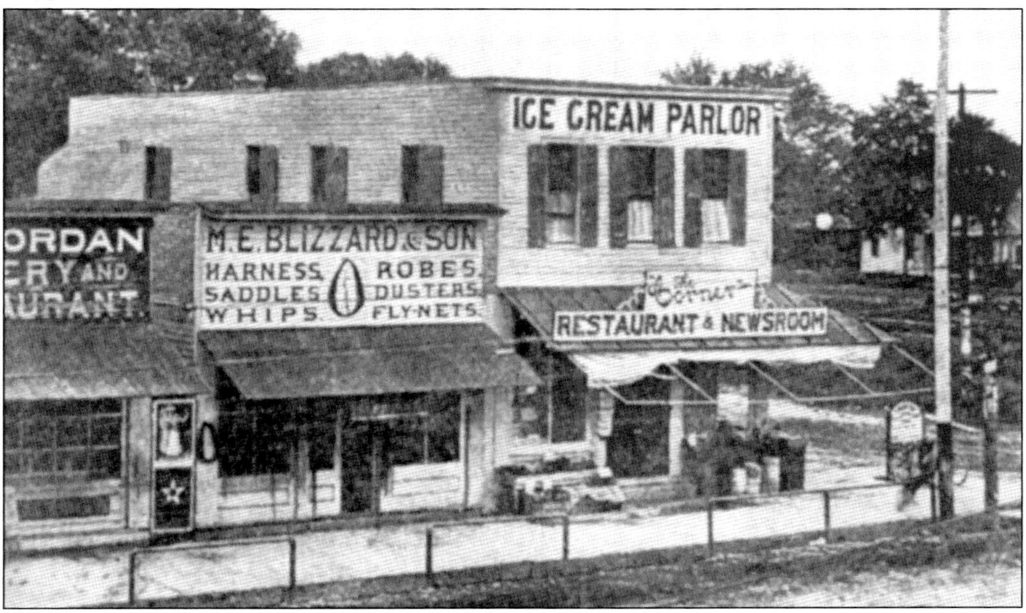

Prior to the construction of the Wauseon Arcade in 1901, these shops stood on the northeast corner of North Fulton and Beech Streets. M.E. Blizzard was a harness, saddle, and whip maker. He also sold robes that wagon and buggy riders would wrap around themselves to stay warm, as well as fly nets that were hung as curtains to keep pesky mosquitoes and flies at bay.

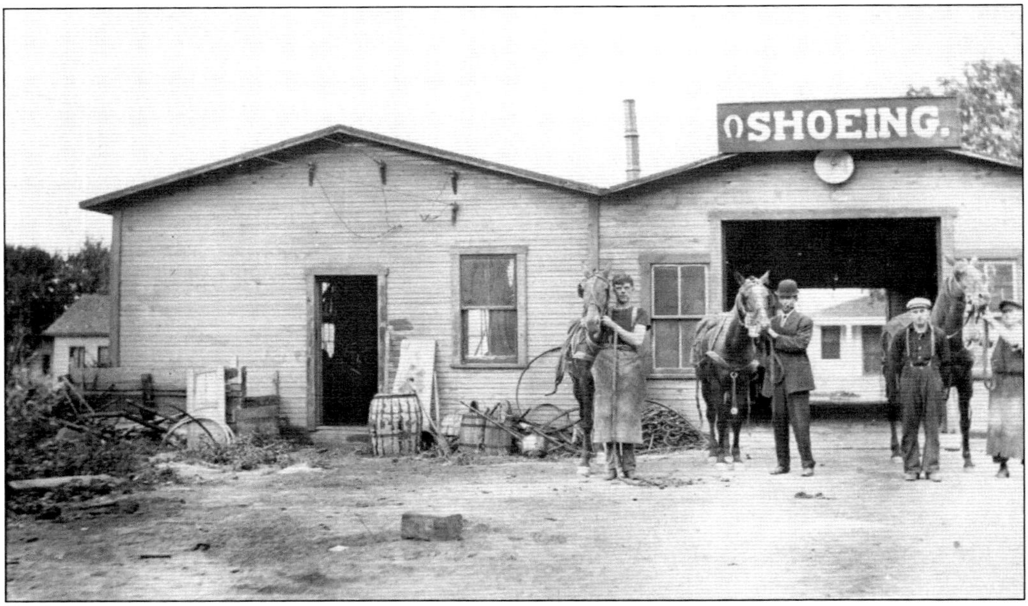

Farriers specialized in shoeing horses. This work was also done by blacksmiths, but farriers usually purchased the metal shoes from them. Some also hosted livery stables, where overnight visitors could keep and feed their horses. This shop was on an alley east of Fulton Street, behind the present-day post office. As motorized transportation grew in popularity in the early 20th century, farriers found themselves having to move into other professions.

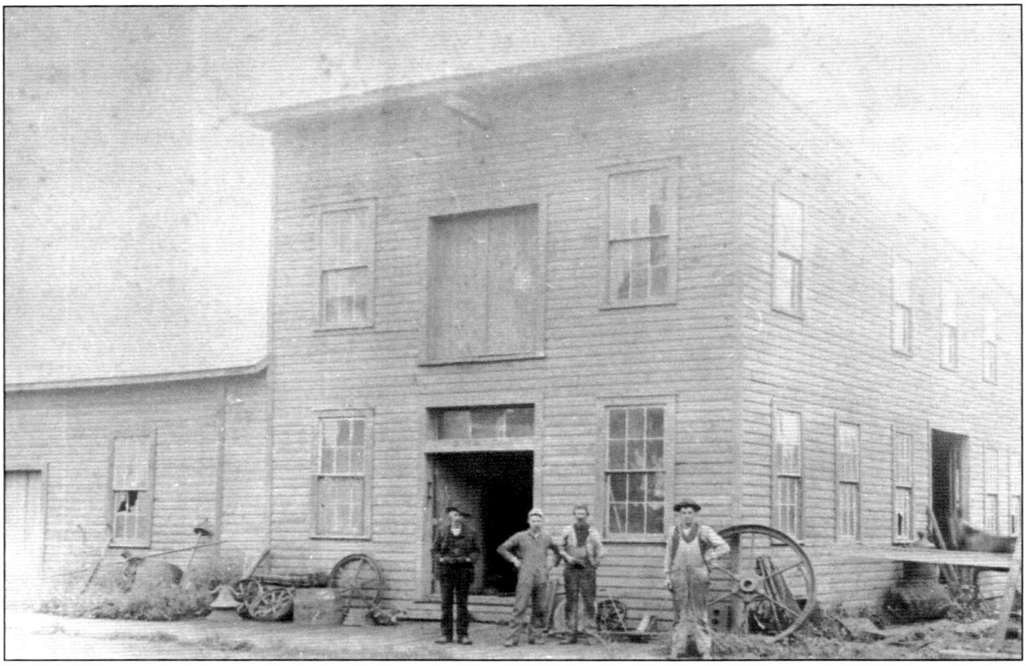

Phil Schletz (far left) moved with his parents to Wauseon in the early 1860s. He apprenticed with a local blacksmith to learn the art of welding and metalworking. He opened a machine shop on Brunell Street in the 1800s, specializing primarily in wagon wheels and equipment repair.

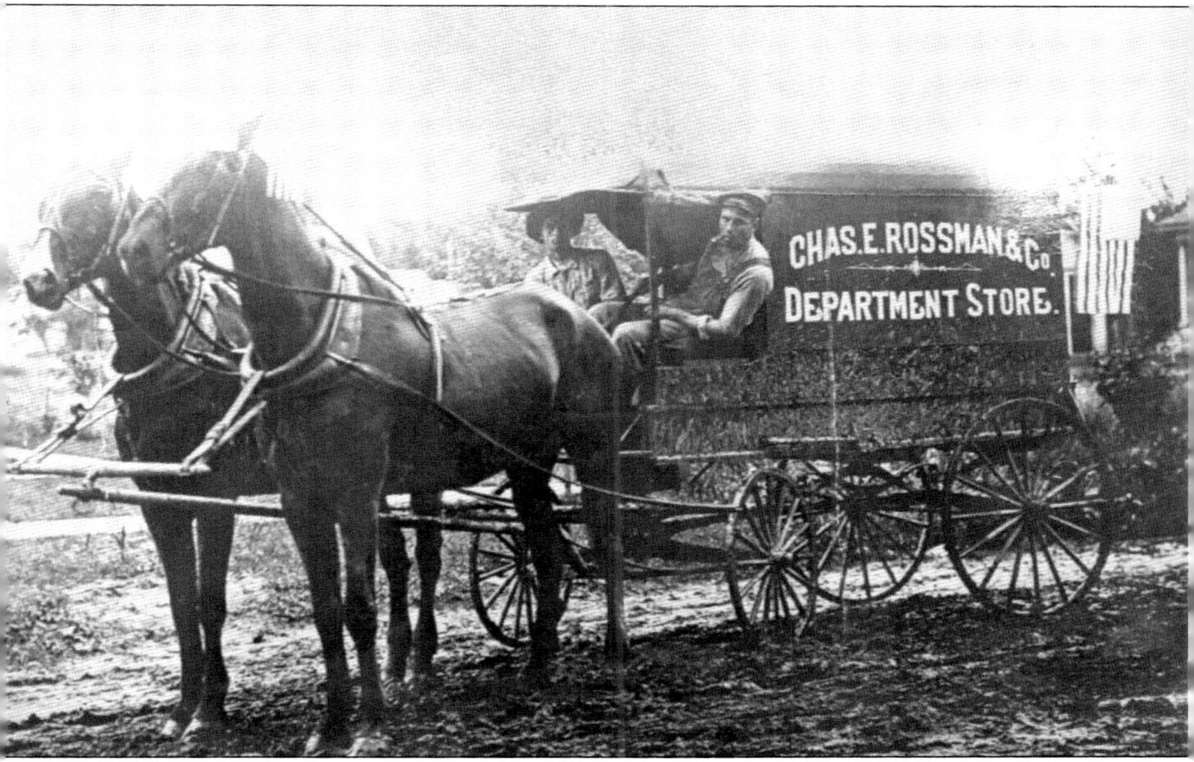

When farmers could not come to town to shop, the store came to them. Charles E. Rossman (next to sign), seen here with an unidentified assistant, sold myriad items, including food staples, cloth, and tools out of the back of a hardware store on wheels. The hardworking Rossman, well known and popular with rural residents, traveled a regular schedule of routes around rural Wauseon.

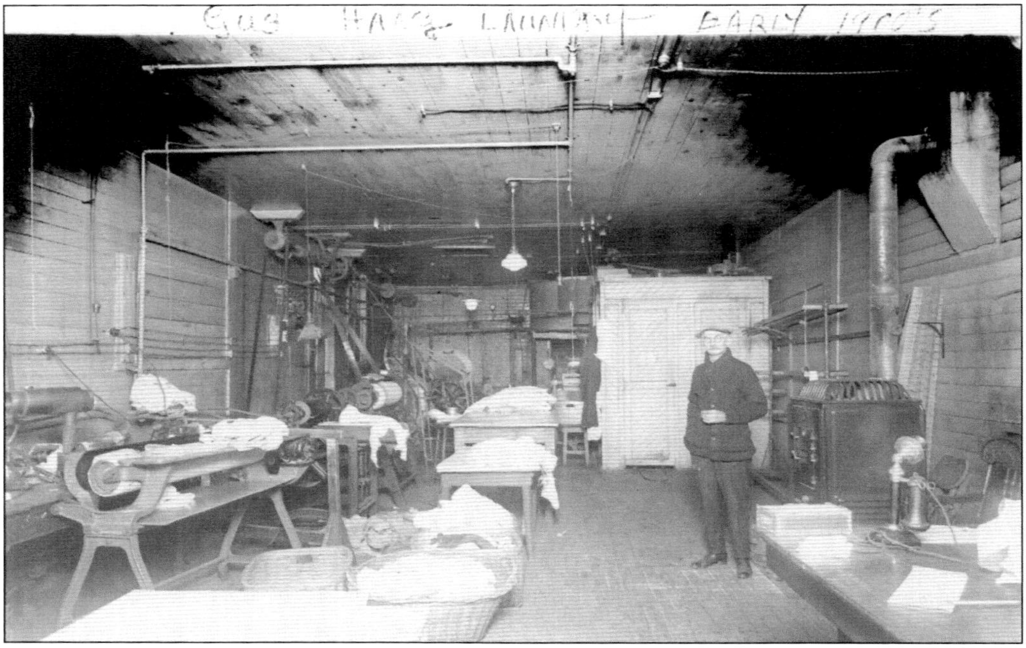

Gus Haag's laundry, seen here around 1886, was located on North Fulton Street, where Sterling Milk Company once stood and a production plant for Superior Dairy is today. Prior to the advent of washing machines, laundry was a two-day process. On Mondays, homemakers washed clothes and linens by hand and let them air-dry. On Tuesdays, they did the ironing. A laundry, such as Haag's, was a luxury usually used by a community's wealthier residents.

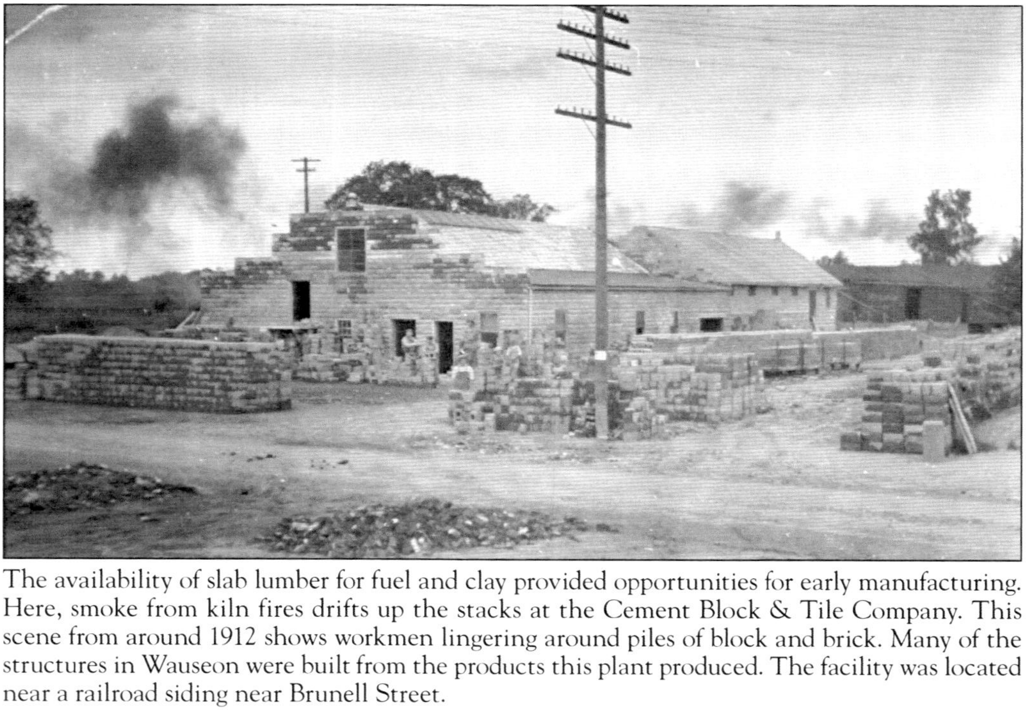

The availability of slab lumber for fuel and clay provided opportunities for early manufacturing. Here, smoke from kiln fires drifts up the stacks at the Cement Block & Tile Company. This scene from around 1912 shows workmen lingering around piles of block and brick. Many of the structures in Wauseon were built from the products this plant produced. The facility was located near a railroad siding near Brunell Street.

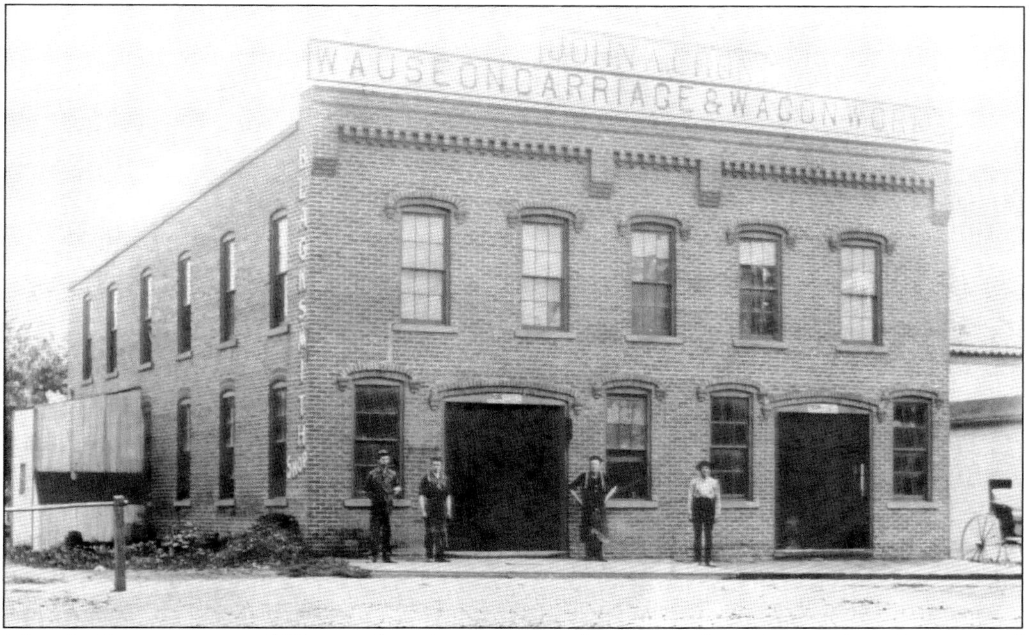

John A. Cron was one of Wauseon's early carriage and wagon makers. Located on Commercial Street, his reputation brought him business from throughout the region, including Toledo. Cron eventually sold the business to Ike Short. This photograph is from around 1900.

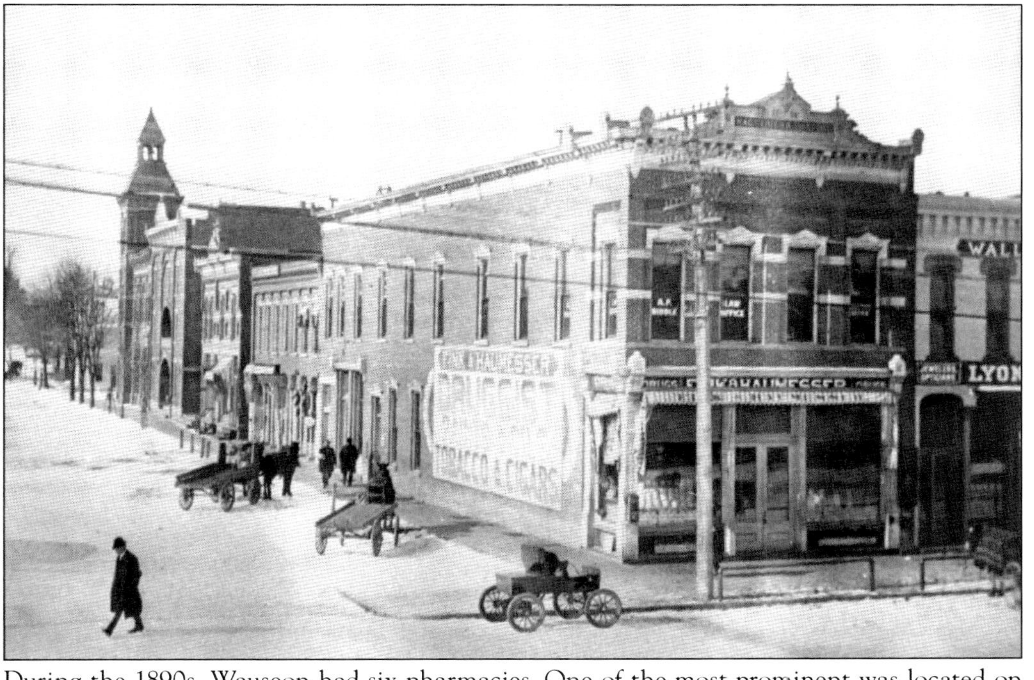

During the 1890s, Wauseon had six pharmacies. One of the most prominent was located on the corner of North Fulton and Depot Streets. It is currently the site for a branch of Farmers & Merchants State Bank. The building's second floor housed the offices of A.P. Biddle, a local attorney and justice of the peace who died in 1911.

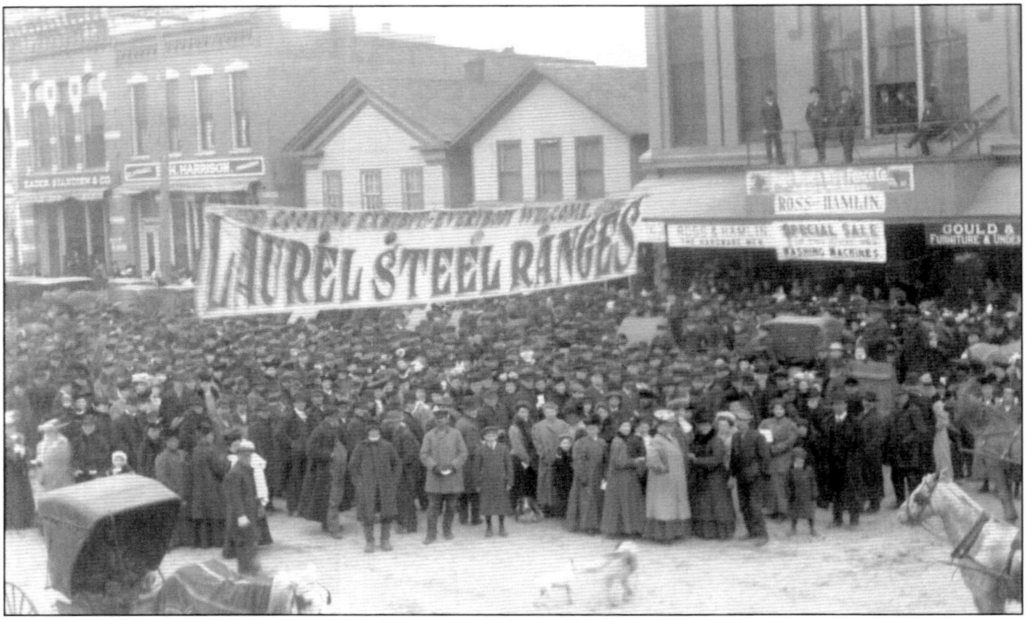

When the Ross & Hamlin Hardware Store offered a free cooking show and a sale on washing machines in 1899 to promote some of their products, hundreds turned out in their Sunday finest for the opportunity to enjoy some free entertainment and have their picture taken.

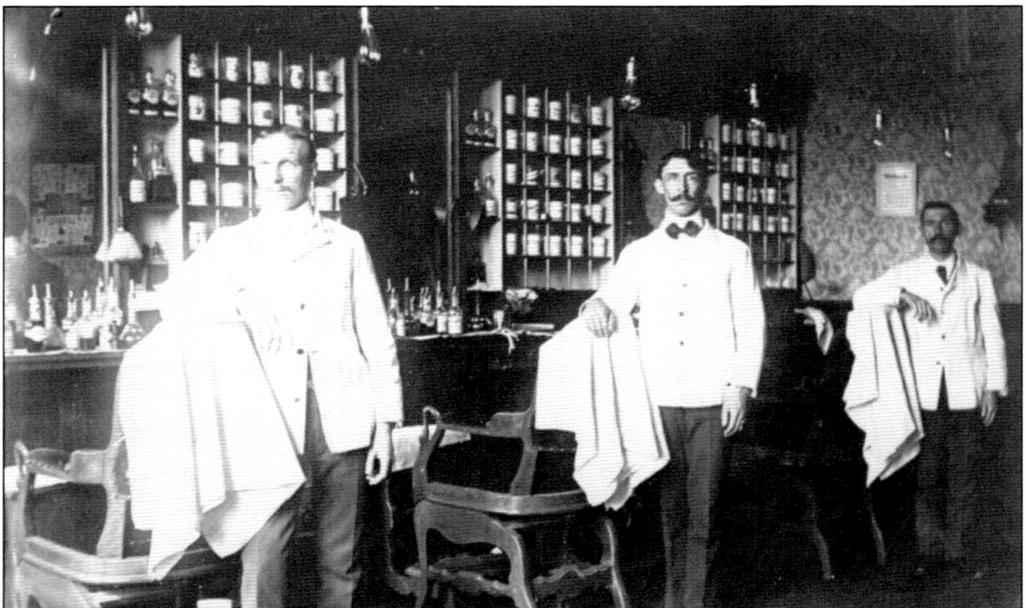

Lingle's Barbershop, located downtown, offered a fine shave and haircut in the 1890s. Patrons provided their own shaving mugs, which were used to eliminate shaving burn or shaving rash, which was caused by the cross-contamination of the razor, the shaving soap, or the brush used to apply the soap. From left to right, Ed Lingle, Ward Mercer, and Gordon Trumprew stand by for their customers. On the wall are the cabinets that held their customers' shaving mugs.

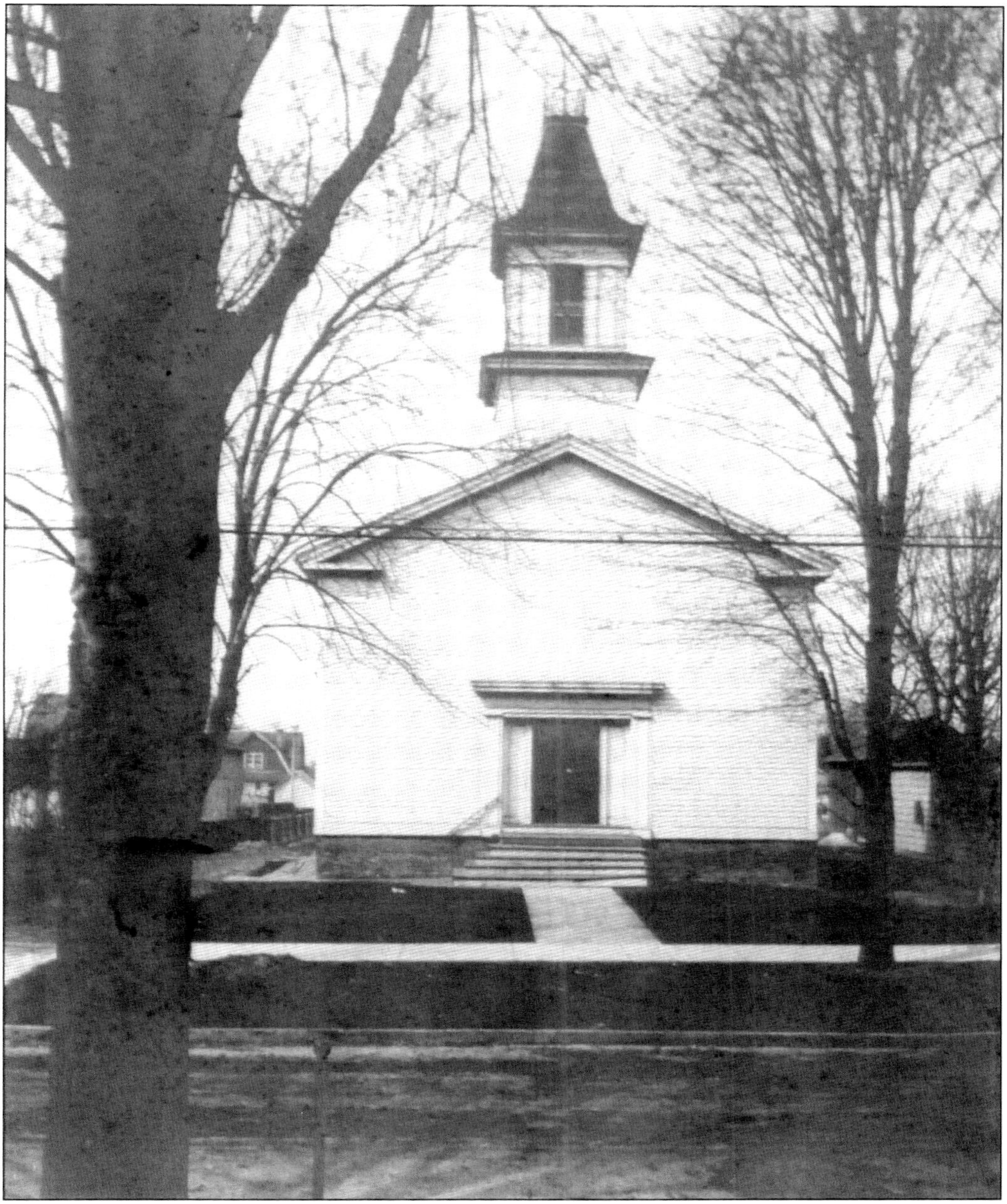

Wauseon newcomers brought their religious beliefs with them. The first church was built by the Methodist Episcopal Church (now Christ United Methodist Church) in 1855 on the northwest corner of Fulton and Elm Streets. It was quickly followed by the First Christian Church, shown here, which was built in 1864, the First Baptist Church (1868), St. Caspar's Church (1875), Trinity Church (1895), the Church of God (1911), and many others.

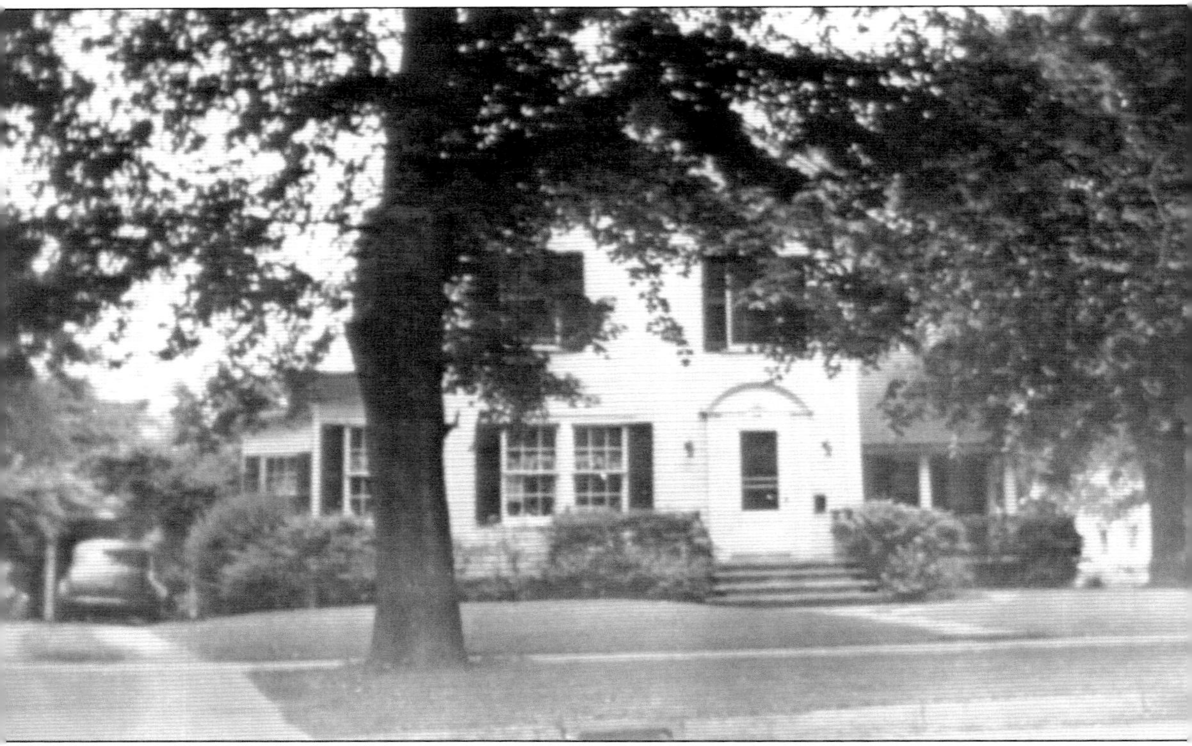

This home across from South Park is one of Wauseon's oldest. It was built in the 1860s by E.L. Hayes and was moved to its present location to make room for the new courthouse. Hayes constructed the first store in the village, on the corner of South Fulton and Birch Streets. He served as a brigadier general during the Civil War, returned from service in poor health and financial ruin, sold everything he had, and moved to New Jersey to start a new life.

Three

Role of the Railroads

Three railroads once passed through Wauseon. In 1853, the first tracks were extended from Delta. Wauseon's depot was built before the tracks reached town. The wooden structure was located a few yards to the west of the present depot on Depot Street.

In 1854, the tracks reached Wauseon and then extended to Pettisville and Archbold, eventually linking up with the Indiana Northern Railroad.

By 1855, there was one train stopping daily. One day, it was westbound, and the following day, it stopped for fuel and water on its eastern leg. Eventually, a second line was built, allowing transit between the East Coast and Chicago without any delays.

The arrival of the steam-driven locomotive was a big event. Residents would visit the depot to await its arrival. The noisy, smoke-belching, fire-eating engines pulled five to eight passenger and freight cars, plus a caboose, all at the remarkable speed of 15 to 20 miles per hour.

The railroad became Wauseon's pathway to prosperity and connected it with the rest of the country, bringing new settlers, cargo, and mail. From 1854 to 1861, the depot served as a combination passenger and freight station. With increased activity, a freight building was constructed across the tracks and to the west of the depot in 1861. That original structure still exists, remodeled to serve, most recently, as a warehouse for a former concrete business.

The first depot was converted into a freight office when the present passenger depot was built in 1896. The first depot also still exists and is now part of a house on West Chestnut Court.

Steel mail cranes were built next to the tracks in 1907 and 1910. Outgoing mailbags were hung from these cranes, to be picked up with hooked poles from the moving mail cars. This eliminated the need for trains to come to a complete stop.

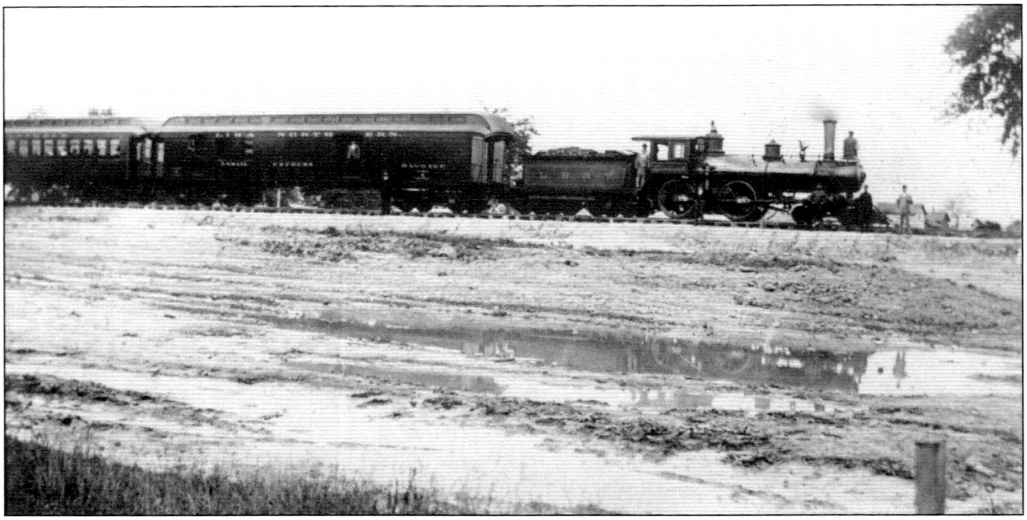

The first trains hauled passenger cars near the engine and freight cars in the rear. There were usually less than 10 cars total. In 1898, the Lake Shore & Michigan Southern Railroad purchased property near Brunell Street and built a livestock yard. Pens and loading shoots ran diagonally for almost 1,500 feet south of the tracks. The complex served to water and feed cattle being shipped over the rails, primarily back east.

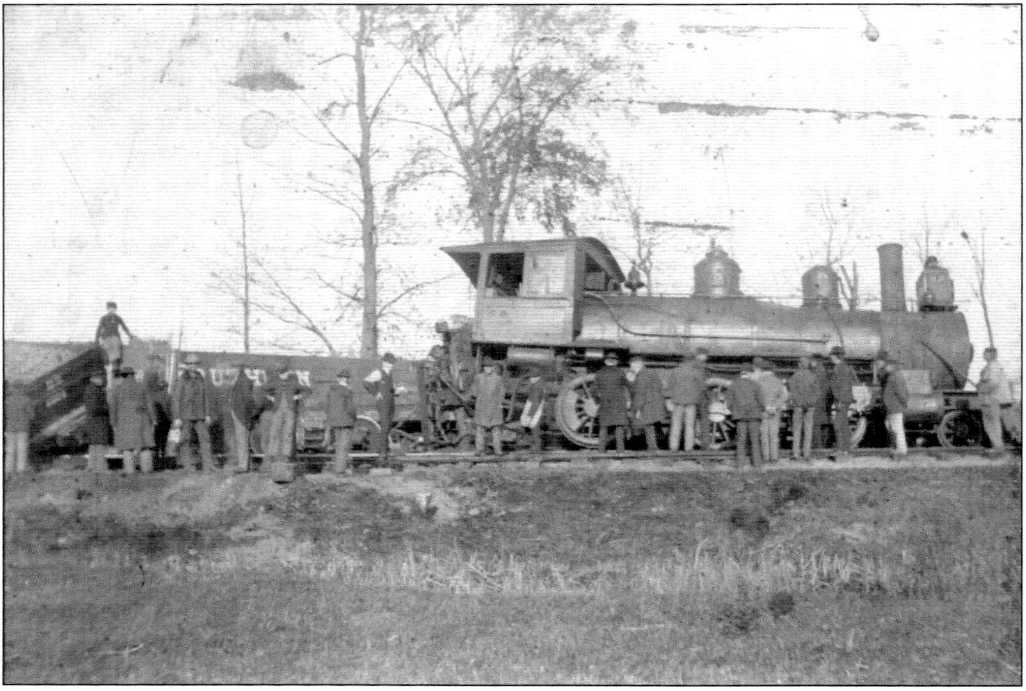

Accidents were commonplace in the early decades of railroading. This one occurred east of Wauseon about 1900. Train wrecks were most commonly caused by human error, but vehicles blocking crossings, debris, floods causing washouts, and mechanical or track defects were also common causes. While rail accidents still occur today, they are much rarer in frequency. (Courtesy of John Kessler.)

The New York Central water tank stood on the corner of Commercial Street, on the south side of Brunell Street. Most railroad stations were spaced about nine miles apart, in order to supply fresh boiler water and fuel for the early steam-powered locomotives. This water tank was torn down in the late 1950s.

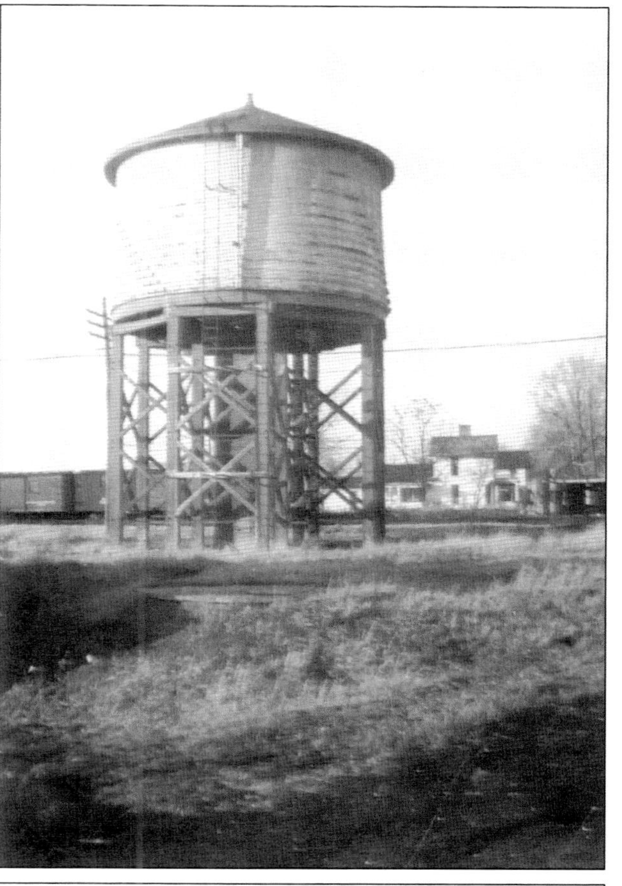

The Lake Shore & Michigan Southern Railroad was also known as the Airline Railroad. Crashes such as this one in Wauseon could cause property damage and loss of life. Accidents were often scenes of community interest. The cause of this wreck is unknown, but it was significant enough that the caboose, the last car on the train, ended up on top of other cars.

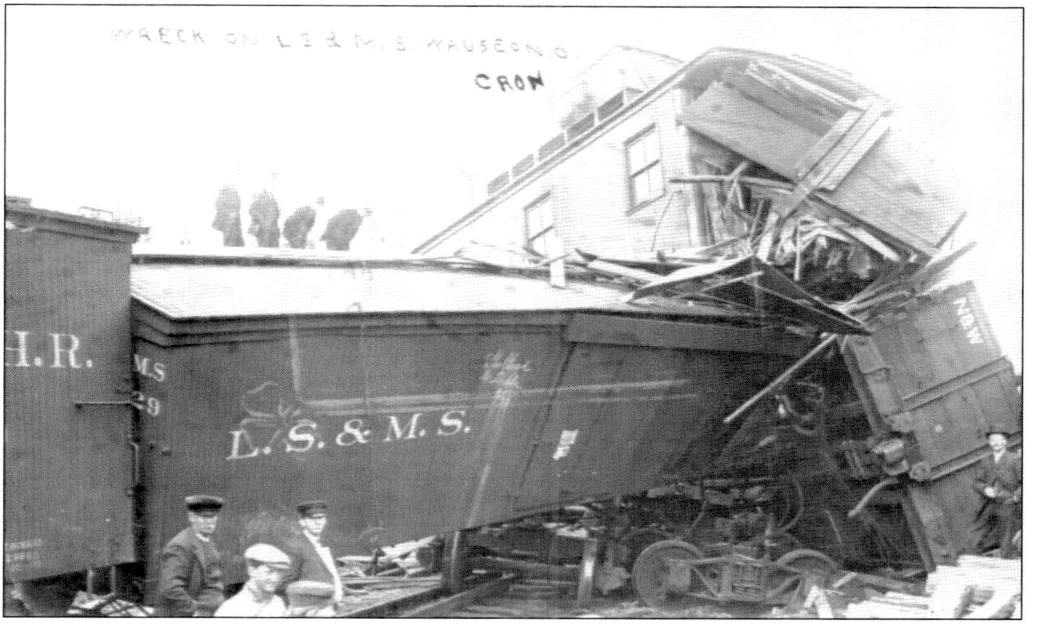

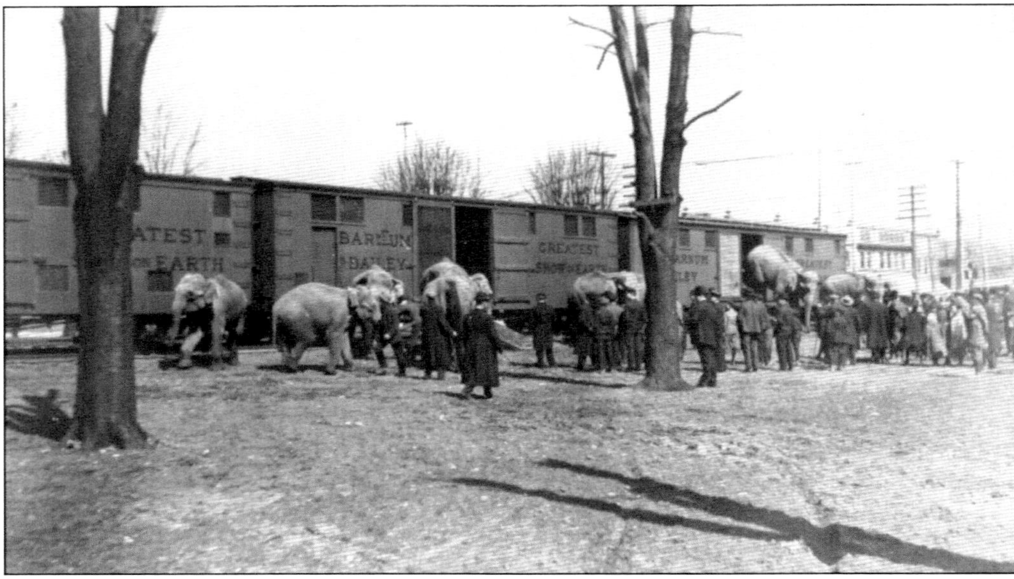

P.T. Barnum got into the circus business at age 61 with P.T Barnum's Grand Traveling Museum, Menagerie, Caravan & Hippodrome. In 1881, it became known as P.T. Barnum's Greatest Show on Earth. In 1888, Barnum & Bailey began to tour the country. It was the first circus to travel by railroad, via Barnum's personal train. Consequently, they could cover more ground and make more money than any other circus before them. The circus made $400,000 in its first year. The trains often passed through Wauseon, occasionally stopping overnight to water and rest the animals. In 1905, with the encouragement of his business associate and Wauseon native, the circus put on a show at the county fairgrounds.

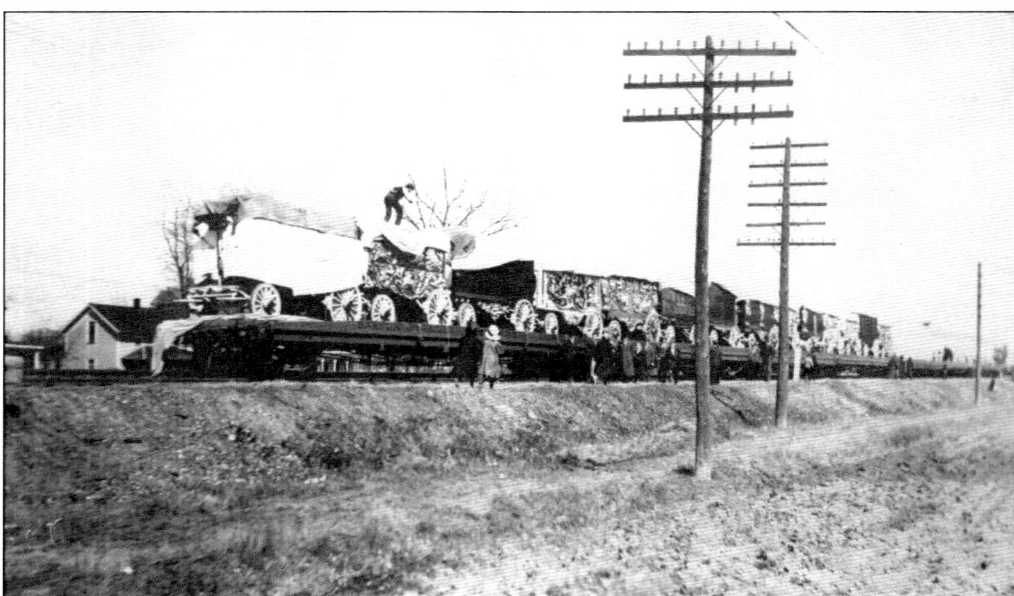

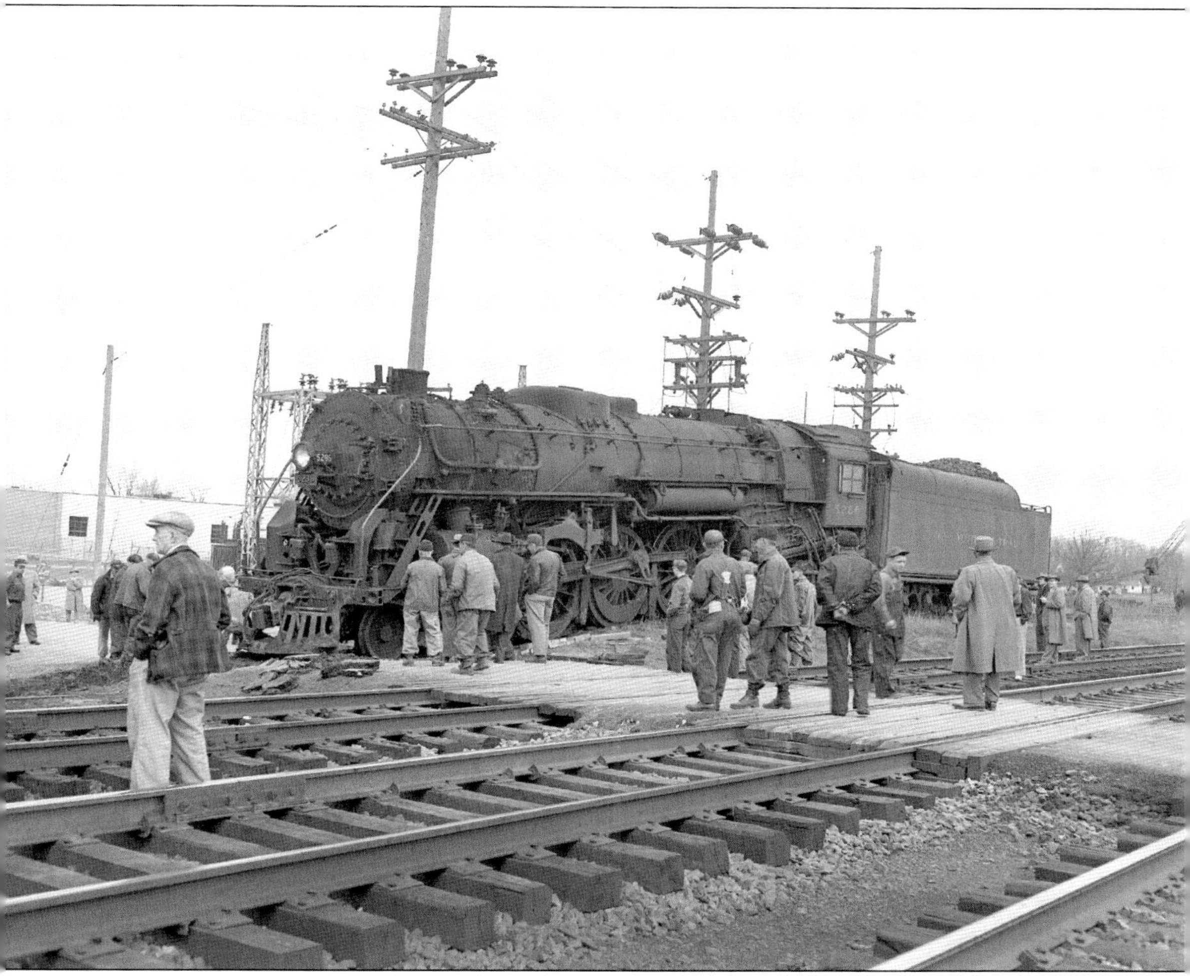

During World War II, the country's network of rails became vital to hauling material needed for the war effort. Railroad traffic reached a new high. Steam locomotives grew in size and sophistication, using coal instead of wood for fuel. Accidents still happened, such as this one near the Lawrence Avenue crossing in the 1940s. Note the three sets of tracks that were used during that period.

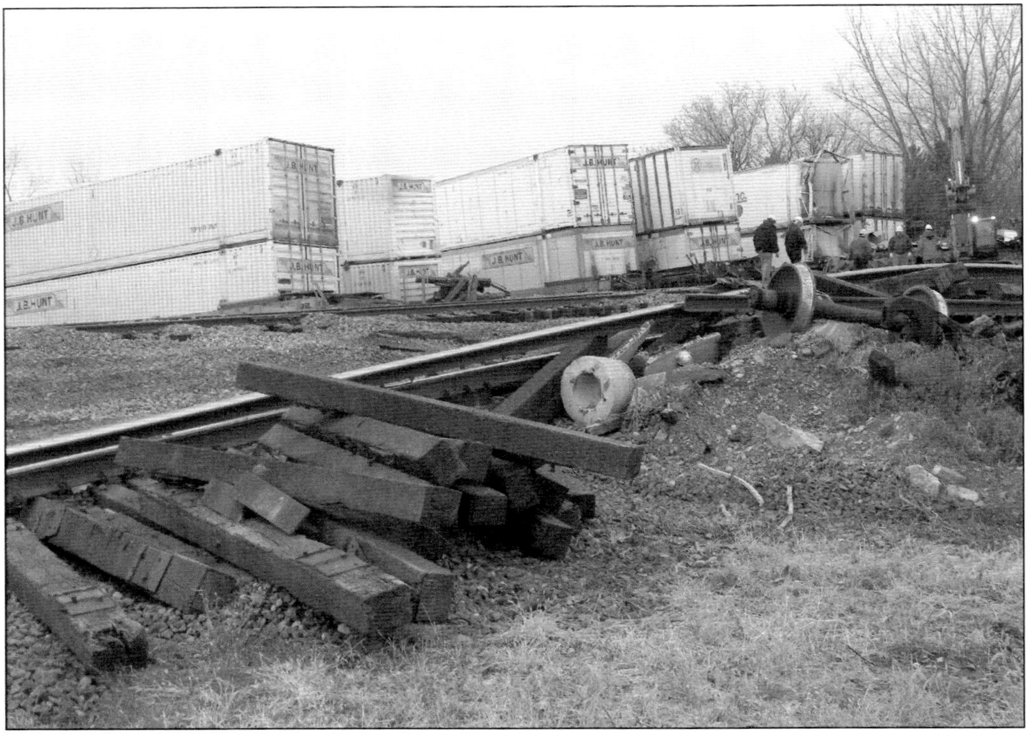

Albeit less frequently, crashes continue to plague railroads today, including this one near downtown Wauseon in 2011. The accident, involving a single train with several derailed cars, held up traffic on the lines for nearly a day, until crews could remove the wreckage and repair the tracks. (Photograph by the author.)

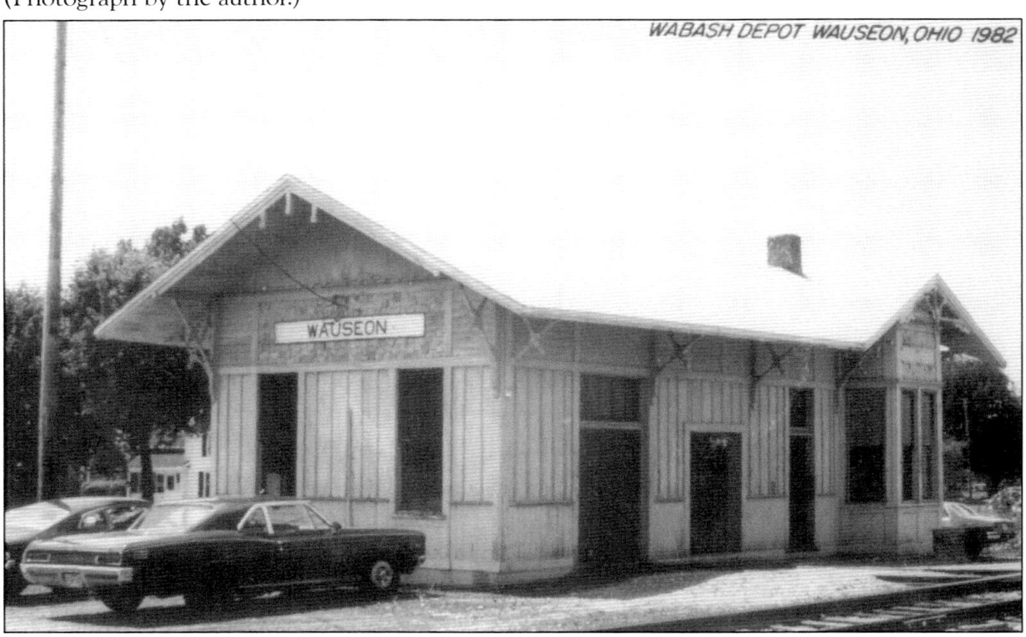

This is an early-1980s view of Wauseon's Wabash depot, located near North Ottokee Street.

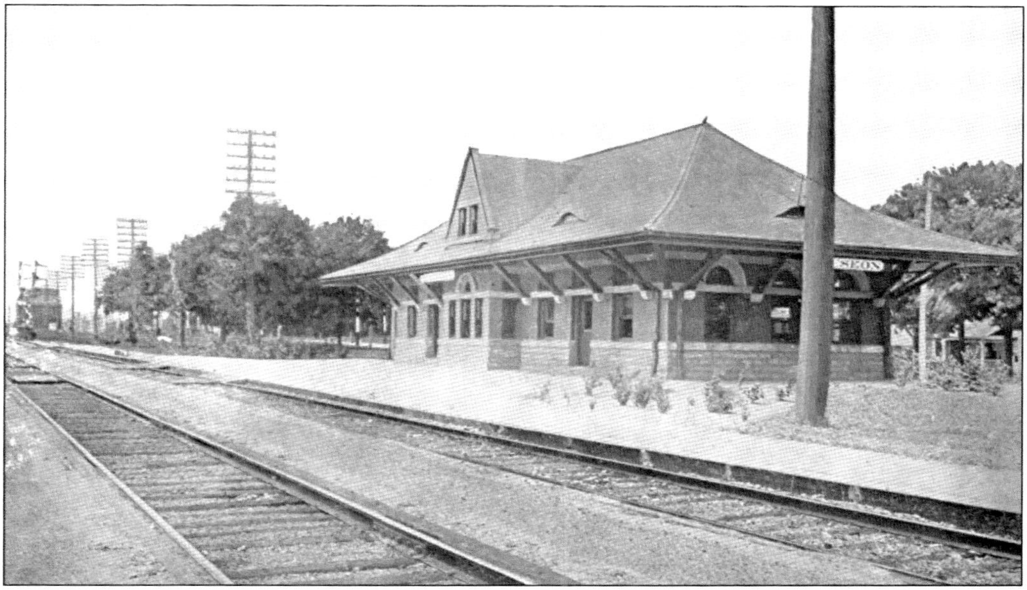

The New York & Central depot, built in 1896, is now owned by the City of Wauseon and leased to the Fulton County Historical Society. Through the efforts of Wauseon native Bob Cohen, it was added to the National Register of Historic Places on March 11, 1993. (Courtesy of Hal and Jayne Bailey.)

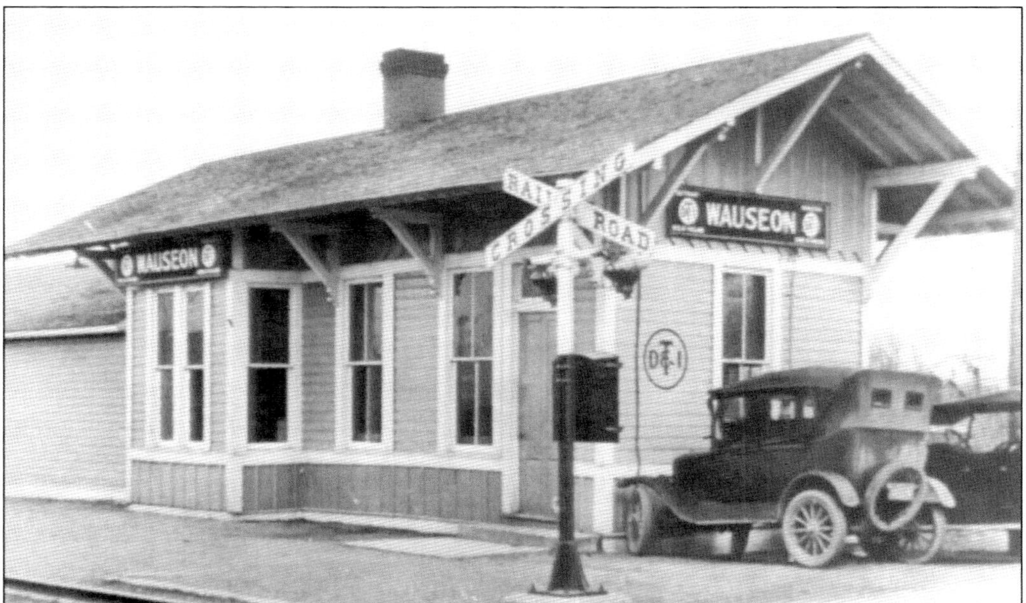

The Detroit, Toledo & Ironton (DT&I) depot was located on Elm Street. Henry Ford purchased the railroad in 1920 and undertook a massive capital improvement program. A successful Ford-era project was a new 55-mile line through Wauseon, constructed between 1925 and 1929. It ran along the village's western edge, then south to Napoleon. Deteriorating track and insufficient business eventually brought about the abandonment of the Wauseon-to-Napoleon portion of the line in May 1978.

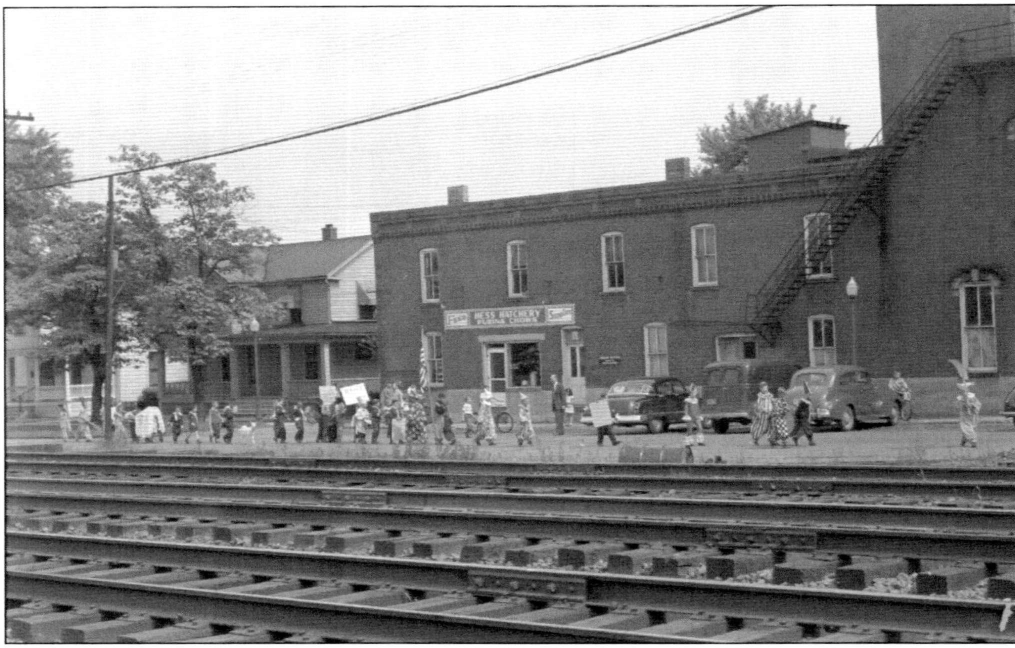

Frequent trains passing through Wauseon have always presented delays during the town's parades. For safety, the 1954 Wauseon homecoming kids' parade was held on Birch Street, passing by the Hess Hatchery, relieving participants from having to cross the tracks.

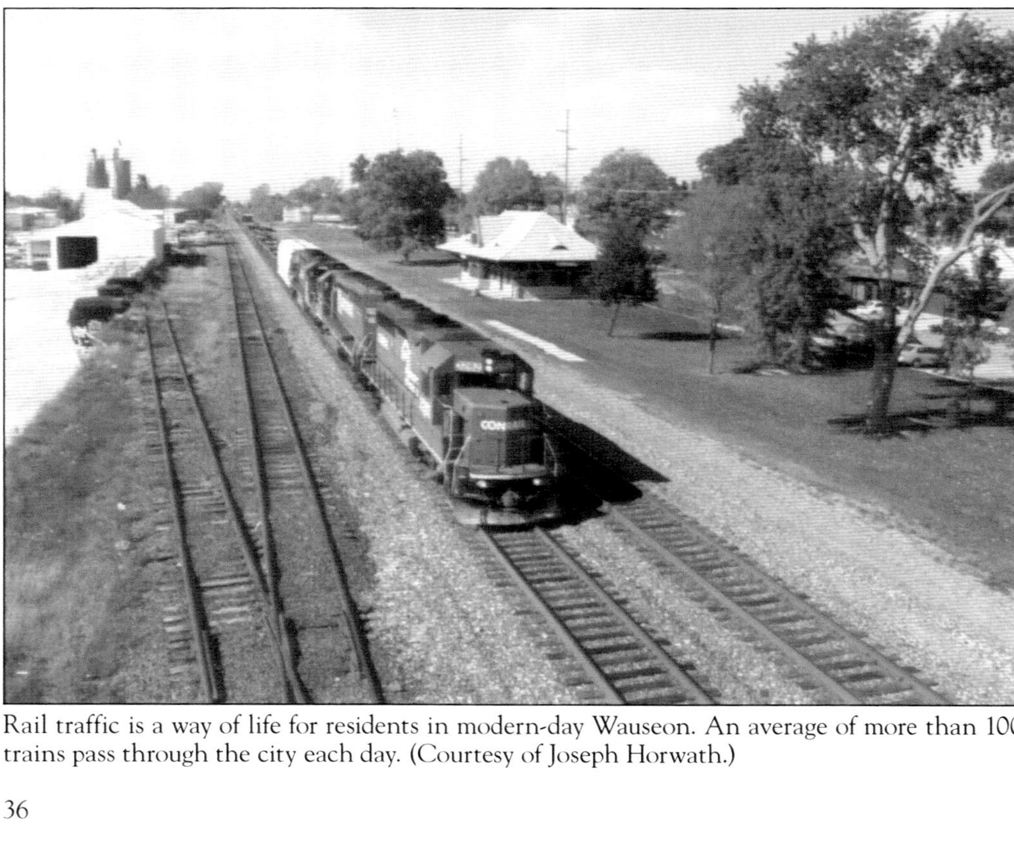

Rail traffic is a way of life for residents in modern-day Wauseon. An average of more than 100 trains pass through the city each day. (Courtesy of Joseph Horwath.)

Four

Wauseon Comes of Age

When the first train passed through Wauseon in 1854, the village's population consisted of a mere 15 individuals. Fresh arrivals purchased lots to build homes and businesses. They were also spurred by the desire to establish schools for their children.

The first school, a stately two-story structure with clapboard siding and a picturesque bell tower, stood near the corner of East Elm and Clinton Streets. In 1856, for the whopping cost of $1,100, what was known as the Little White Schoolhouse was constructed from trees taken from the lot.

Near the tracks, Thomas Bayes built a sawmill from a portion of the profits he earned from the sale of his land. His mill quickly went to work to cut the boards for the school. For nearly half a century, the youngsters of the community learned to read and write in that building, which remains standing today, 158 years later. In the early 1900s, it was moved to an empty lot on Elm Street, just west of Monroe Street, where it was converted into a home.

By the end of its first decade, there was rapid progress in Wauseon, as it leapt 100-fold in population to nearly 1,500 residents.

In April 1857, Wauseon became an incorporated village. In 1858, the first council meeting was held, with Nathaniel Leggett as mayor. In 1862, following Leggett's death, Wauseon Union Cemetery was established. In 1863, a firefighting brigade formed, and then borrowed $600 to purchase a "hose and fixtures" for a fire engine. In 1869, Wauseon became the county seat, after a close countywide vote pitting it against Ottokee and Delta.

By the end of its first 15 years, Wauseon had a taxable valuation of nearly $170,000, five churches, a large, brick school building, several blocks of brick-constructed businesses, two newspapers, a Masonic hall, ten grocery stores, six dry good stores, two hotels, three furniture dealers, two shoe stores, two hardware stores, several meat vendors, three drugstores, and numerous tailoring and millinery shops. Industrial Wauseon included a flouring mill, a foundry, four saw- or planing mills, a shingles mill, a door and blind factory, several blacksmith shops, a tannery, a brewery, wagon and harness makers, and livery stables.

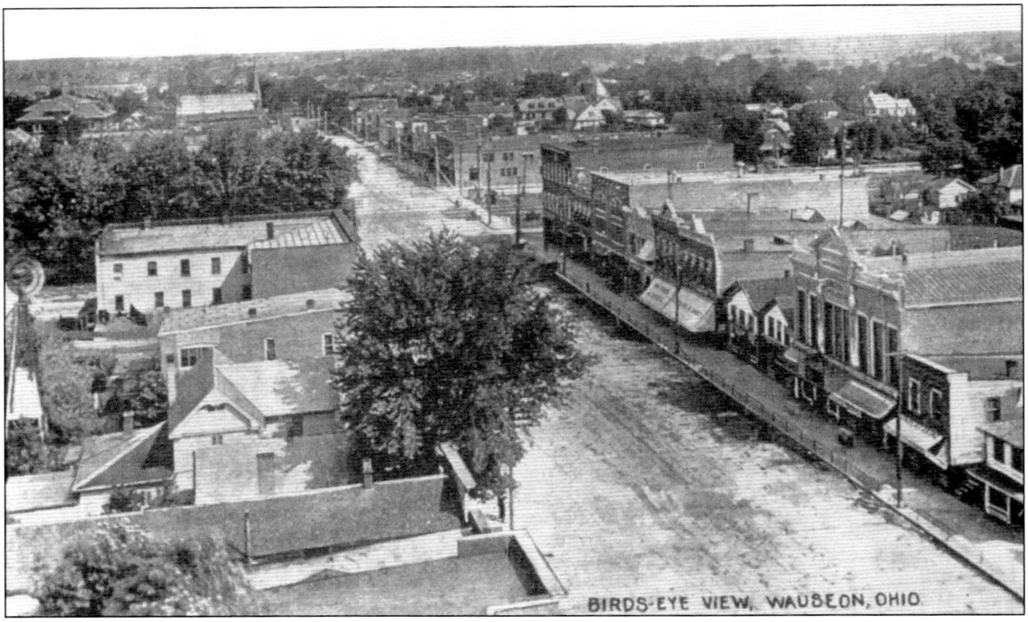

This is a bird's-eye view of South Fulton Street taken from the courthouse clock tower around 1870. Note the dirt street, wooden sidewalks, and hitching rails for tying up horses.

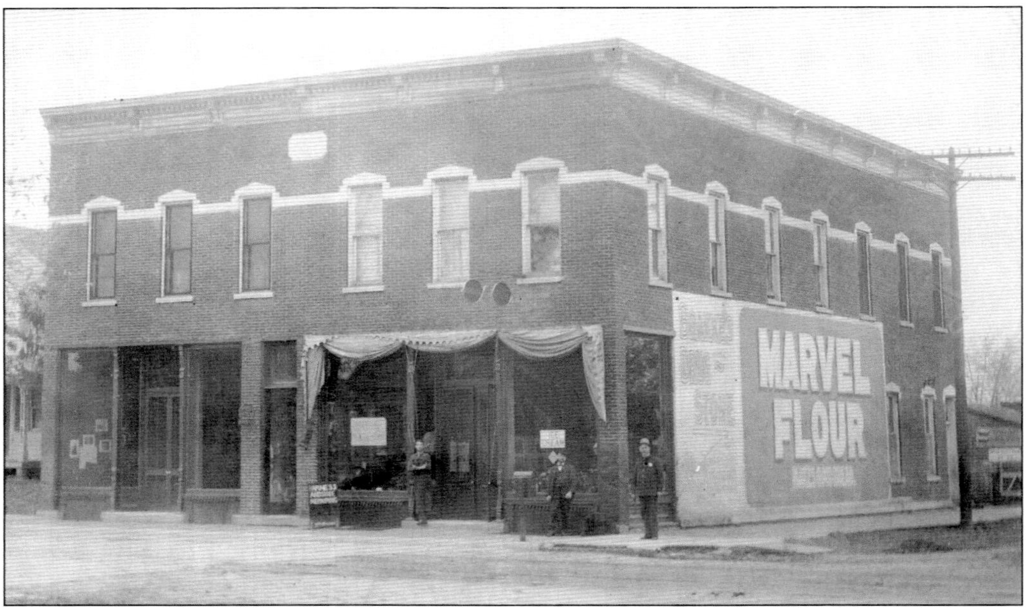

For many years, J.A. Read was the "south side" druggist, starting in the 1870s. Brake's Drug-Store took over from Read, standing on the corner of North Fulton and Elm Streets. There were several stores in the building, offering shoe and harness repairs, ice cream, and eye exams. Note the police officer standing on the corner in this image from around 1905.

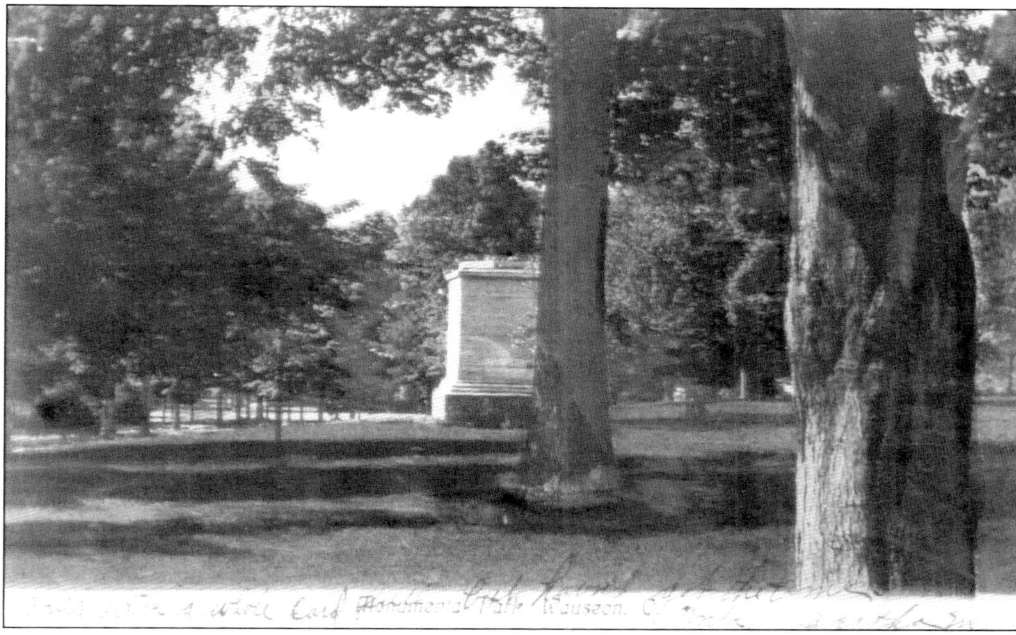

In the original plat of Wauseon, the surveyors set aside land for a park. This was at times called Monumental Park, where a Civil War statue was constructed, and later, North Park. As the community expanded, another area at the end of South Fulton Street was set aside for the village's second park. This time, following naming nomenclature, it was called South Park. A Victorian-era gazebo, shown below in 1910, stood near the center of the park. It was replaced in the 1980s.

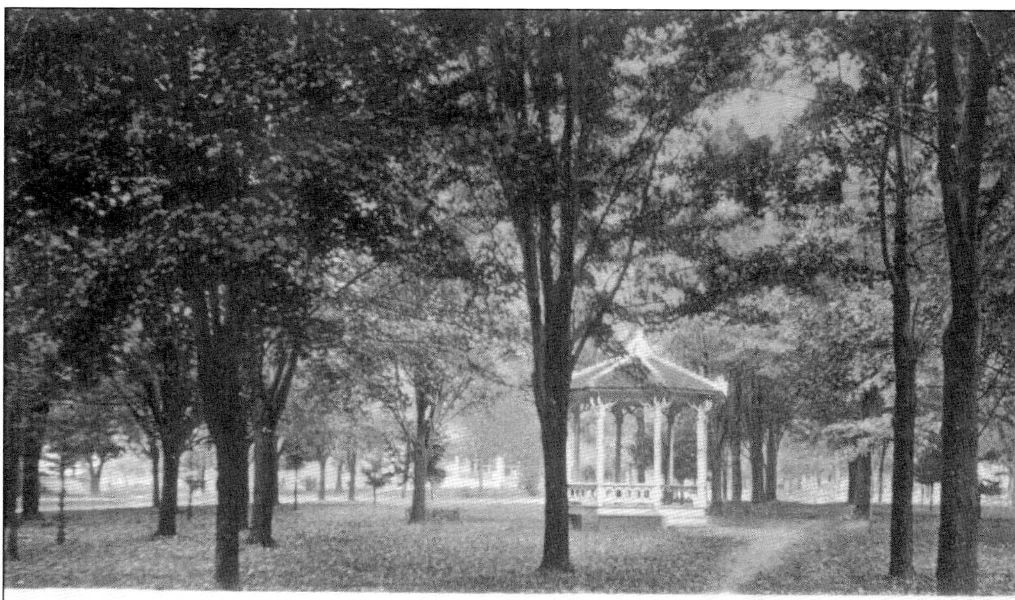

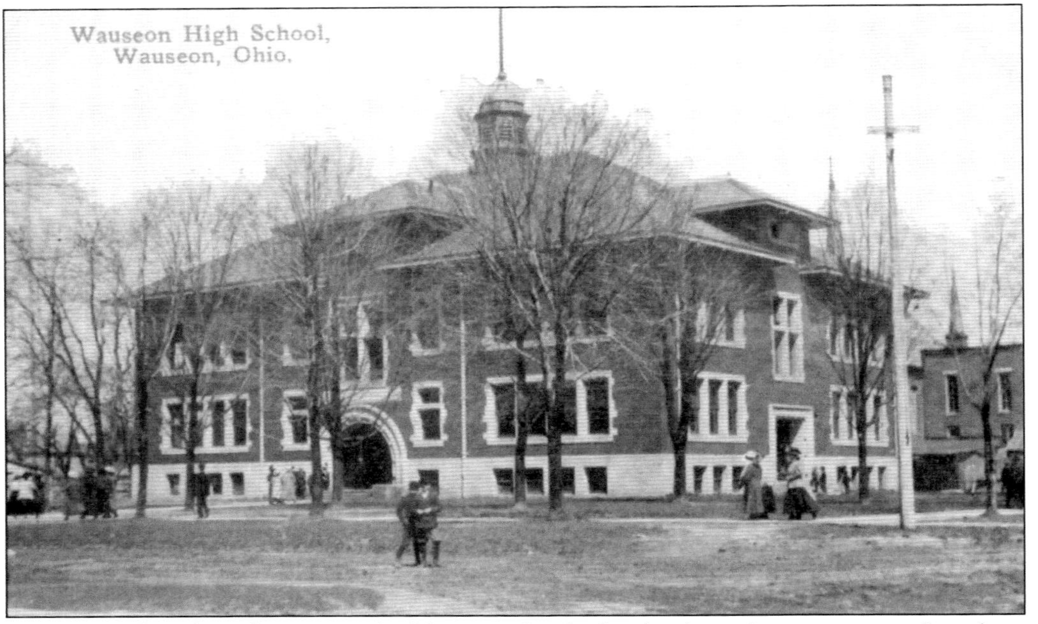

Over time, there have been many buildings used as high schools in the community. Seen here around 1914 is the second of four buildings to serve as Wauseon High School and the second at this location, on the northeast corner of Clinton and Elm Streets. It was destroyed in a fire in 1941.

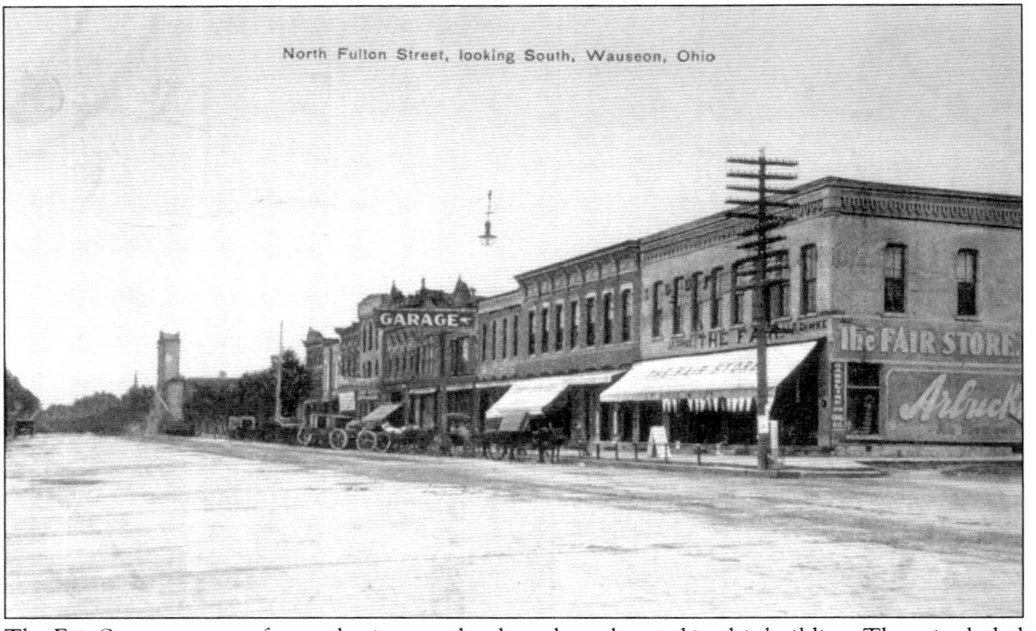

The Fair Store was one of many businesses that have been located in this building. These included one of the first department stores in the region, Waldeck's, and several others over the years.

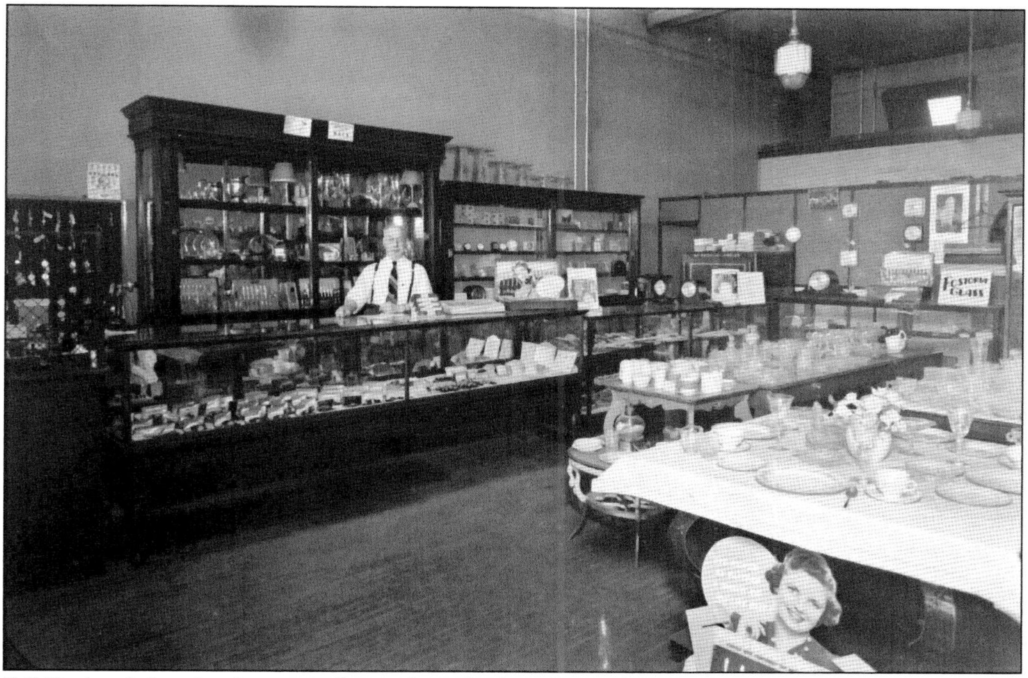

Bill Brokaw's Jewelry Store was located on the first floor of the Ohio Citizens Bank building. He allegedly got tired of fighting the northern winters, which resulted in his closing his store in 1943, leaving all of his property to the Methodist church, and moving to Florida.

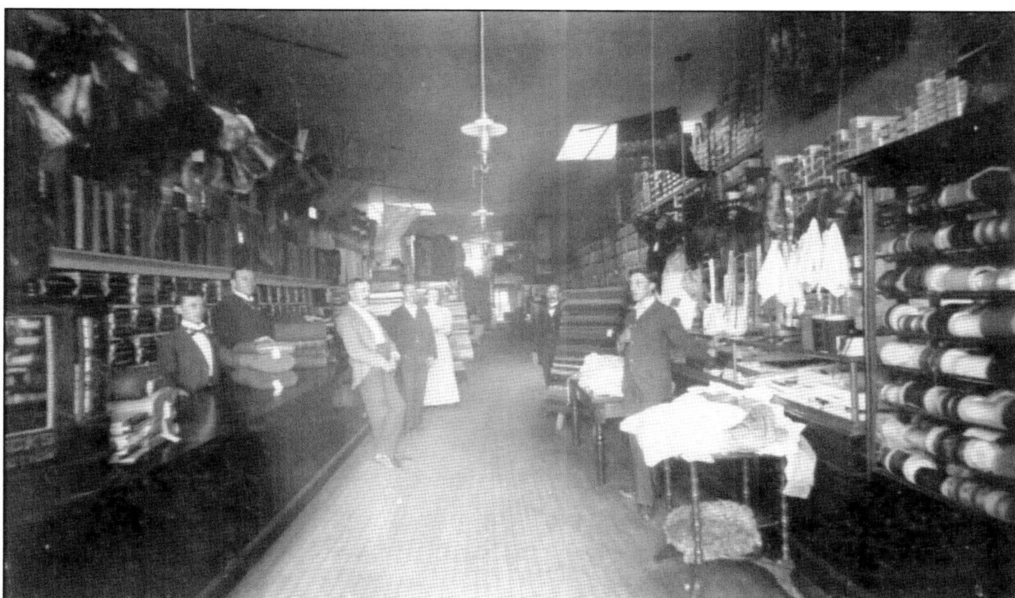

This is the interior of what is believed to be E.H. Harrison's Clothing & Home Furnishings Store in about 1880. Harrison opened his business early in the village's history, operating a very profitable enterprise, which allowed him to build a home on South Fulton Street that included quarters for a live-in maid.

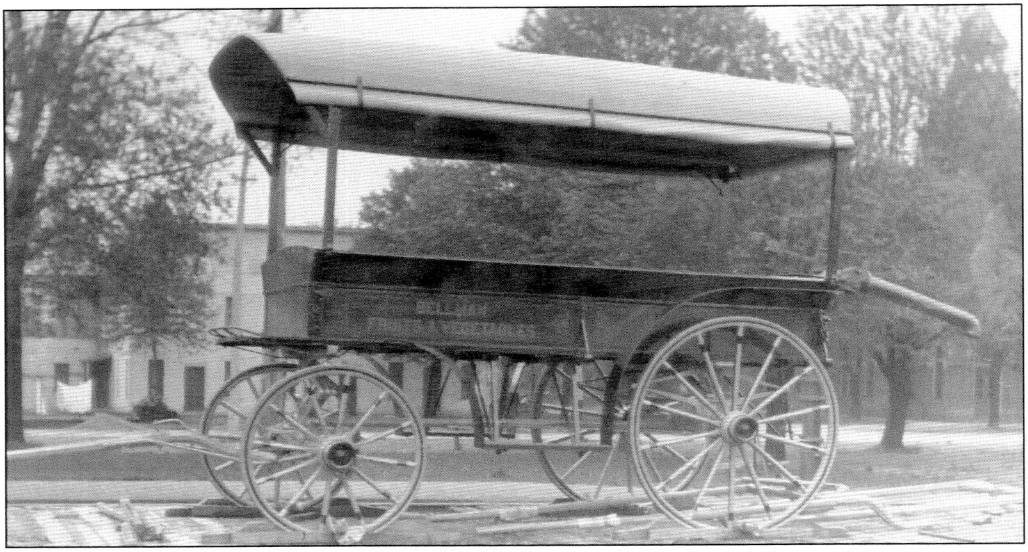

A fully restored delivery wagon, used by George Bellman to deliver fruit and vegetable to area homes in the early 1900s, sits on a trailer prior to serving as a float in the 1954 Wauseon homecoming parade. Bellman was a farmer who grew fruit trees and vegetables.

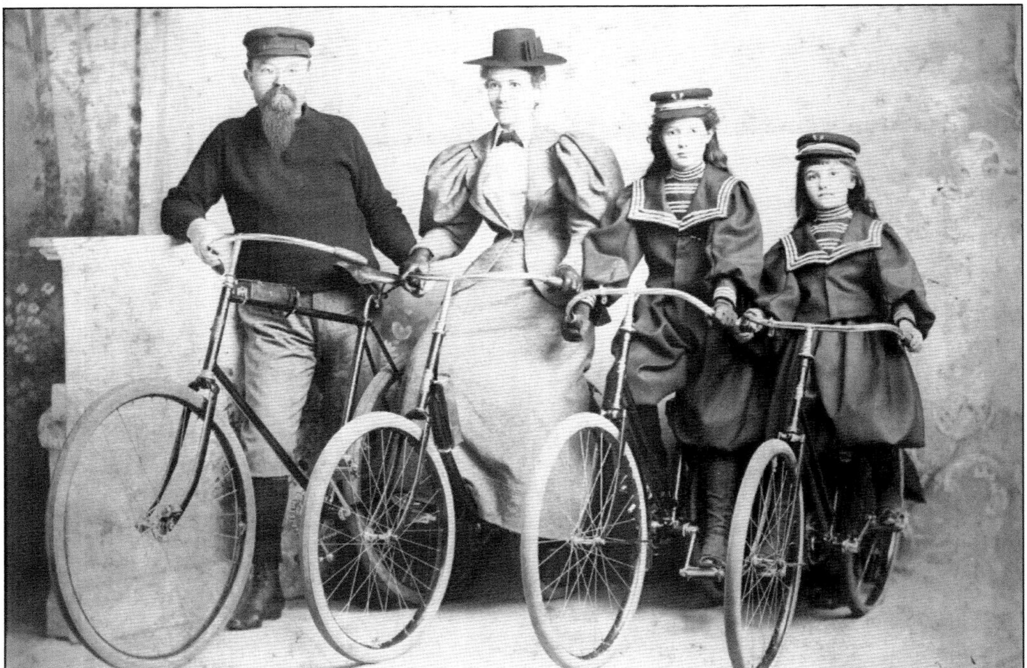

This c. 1895 image shows an unidentified Wauseon family with their bicycles. While many early residents owned horses, bicycles became a popular mode of transportation for youngsters and adults—both men and women. Horses were expensive to purchase and feed, requiring resources that some residents could not afford. There are an estimated 45 horse-related barns and stables still standing in the Wauseon city limits.

This unidentified Wauseon couple is shown riding an Excelsior Auto Cycle in about 1914. Soon after internal combustion engines gained popularity, they were put on bicycles. In 1912, an Excelsior was the first motorcycle to be officially timed at a speed of 100 miles per hour. By 1928, Excelsior was in third place in the American motorcycle market behind Indian and Harley-Davidson. The Great Depression ended Excelsior's operations in 1931.

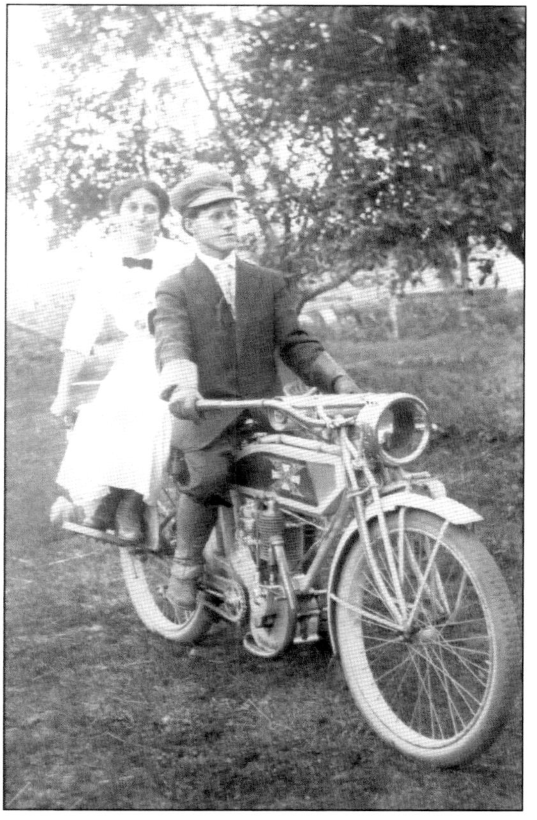

Early land transaction agents Tom Miley (left) and Lucas Guilford pose in front of their office on Beech Street, in one of the village's early wooden buildings. As seen here, bicycles were common, providing much more convenient transportation than horses for short distances. While the community's early founders made their fortunes selling lots to settlers, competition soon sprang up when property owners began selling off homes or businesses.

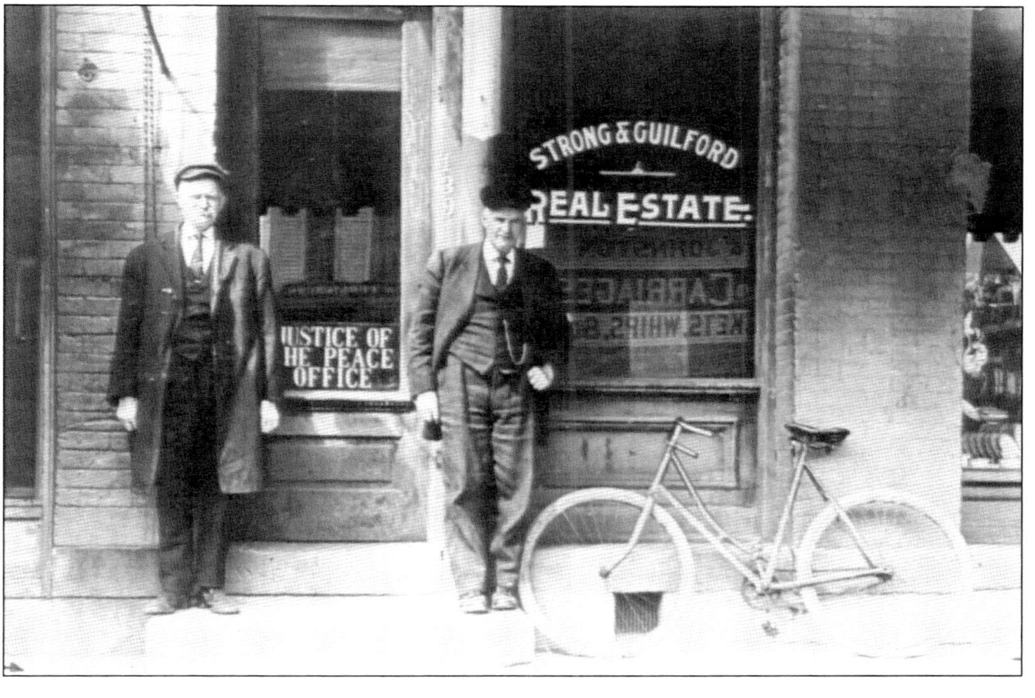

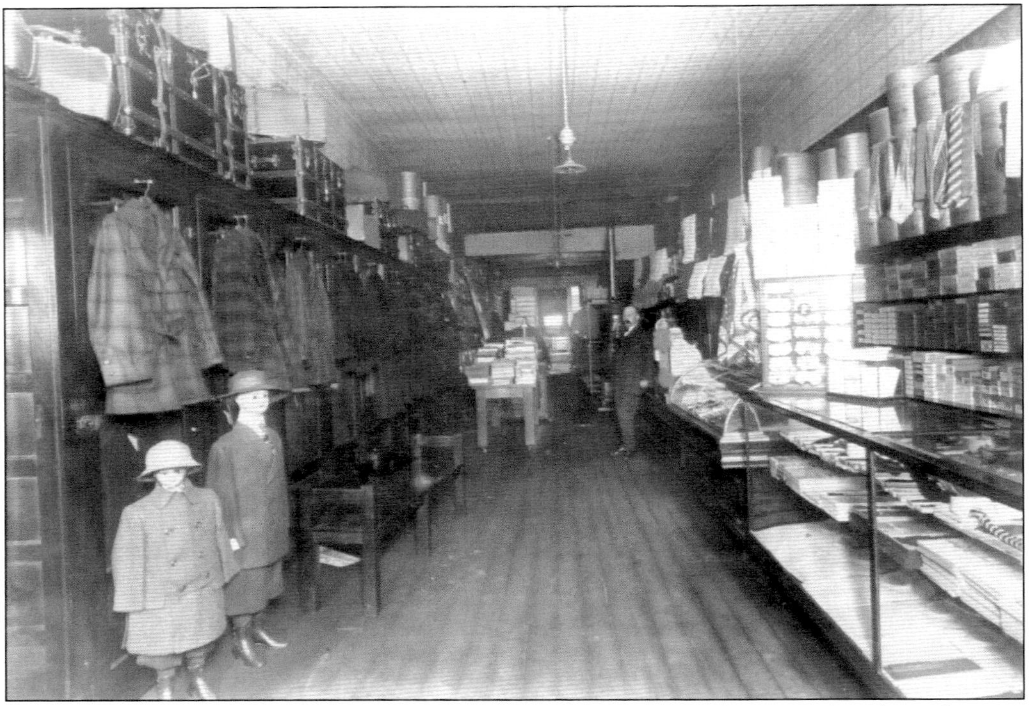

Christ Domito was a longtime merchant and tailor who offered hand-sewn and ready-made men's clothing. His long, narrow store was on the east side of North Fulton Street near Elm Street. It later became the site of a popular local hangout, Edna's Restaurant.

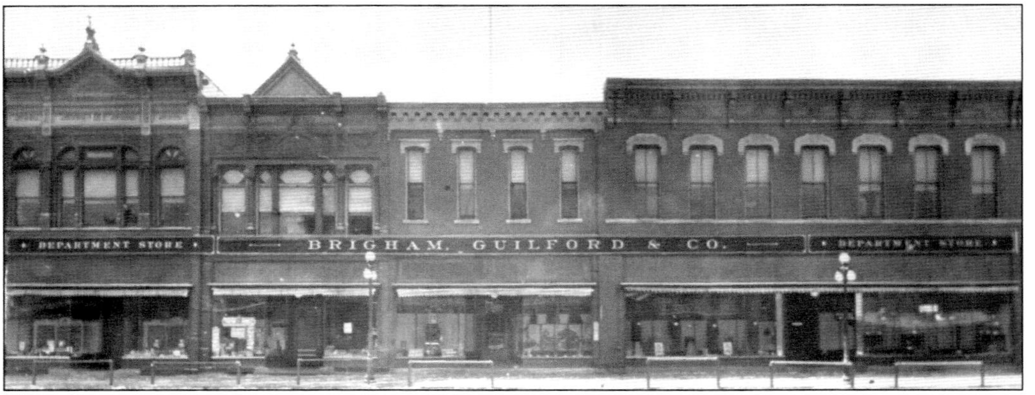

The Brigham, Guilford & Co. department store was a complex of shops that offered clothing, home furnishings, and hardware supplies. It operated in Wauseon from 1909 to 1930. Various departments were connected by interior doorways between the buildings and one of the country's first electric intercom systems. The Great Depression put the operation, once considered one of the finest department stores in northwest Ohio, out of business.

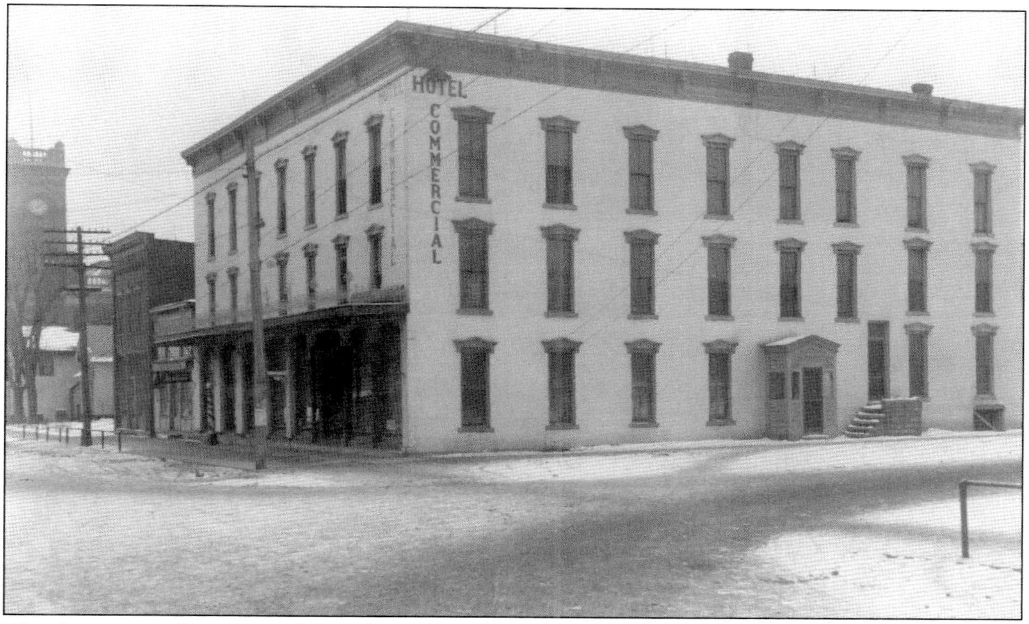

The three-story Commercial Hotel stood on the corner of South Fulton and Commercial Streets. It was built in the 1870s by Zion Eager and was first called the Eager House. The building offered rooms for weary travelers and was a favorite place for local dining. The hotel was torn down in 1913 to make way for the erection of the People's State Bank building.

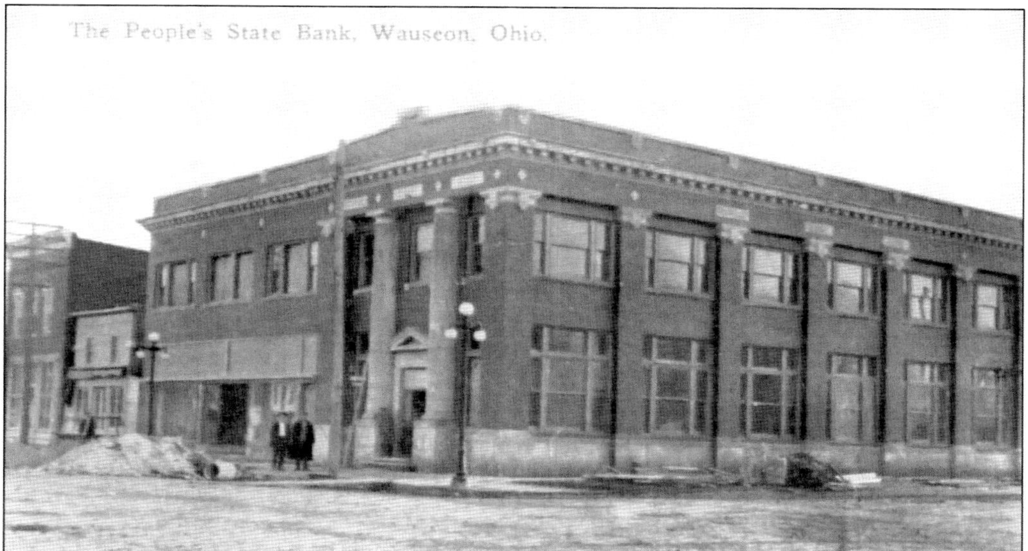

The former People's State Bank dates back to 1889, when it was founded by local businessmen. In 1913, its board approved construction of a larger building across from its original wooden structure. The Commercial Hotel was purchased and demolished, and the facility pictured here was built. It had the first elevator in Fulton County. Today, the building is used by several entities, including as administrative offices for the Wauseon schools.

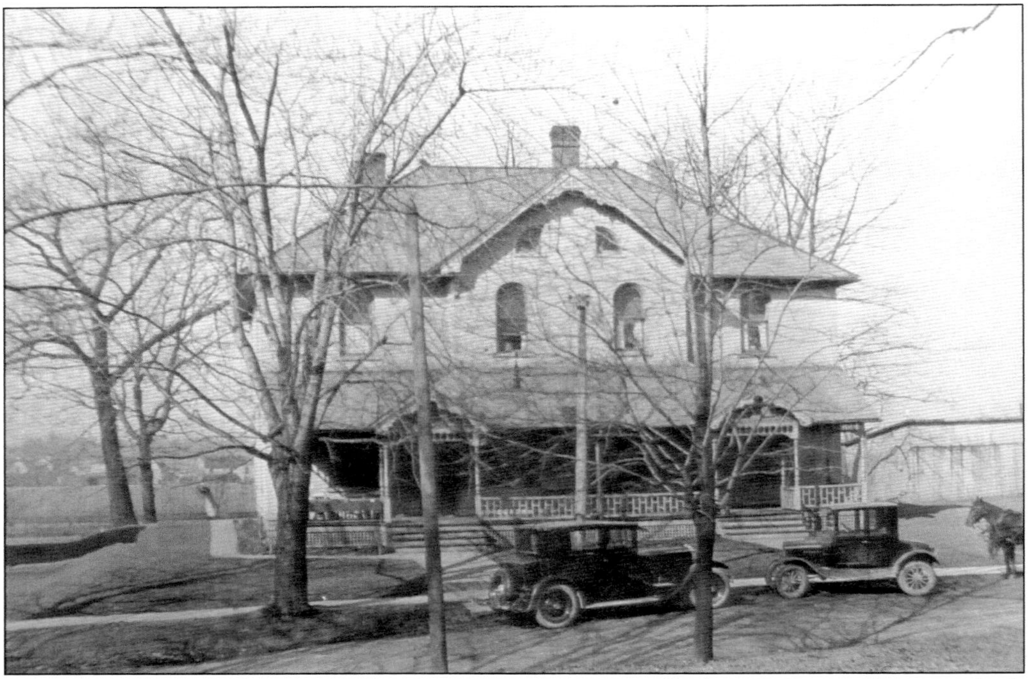

Wauseon's first hospital was located on Monroe Street. Originally, from 1868 to 1897, it was a high school. During the 1896–1897 school year, the building was condemned when the foundation began sinking. In 1903, local doctors bought the building, operating it from 1905 until 1930 as the county's first hospital. In 1945, it was converted into apartments. The building was donated to the Fulton County Historical Society in 1969.

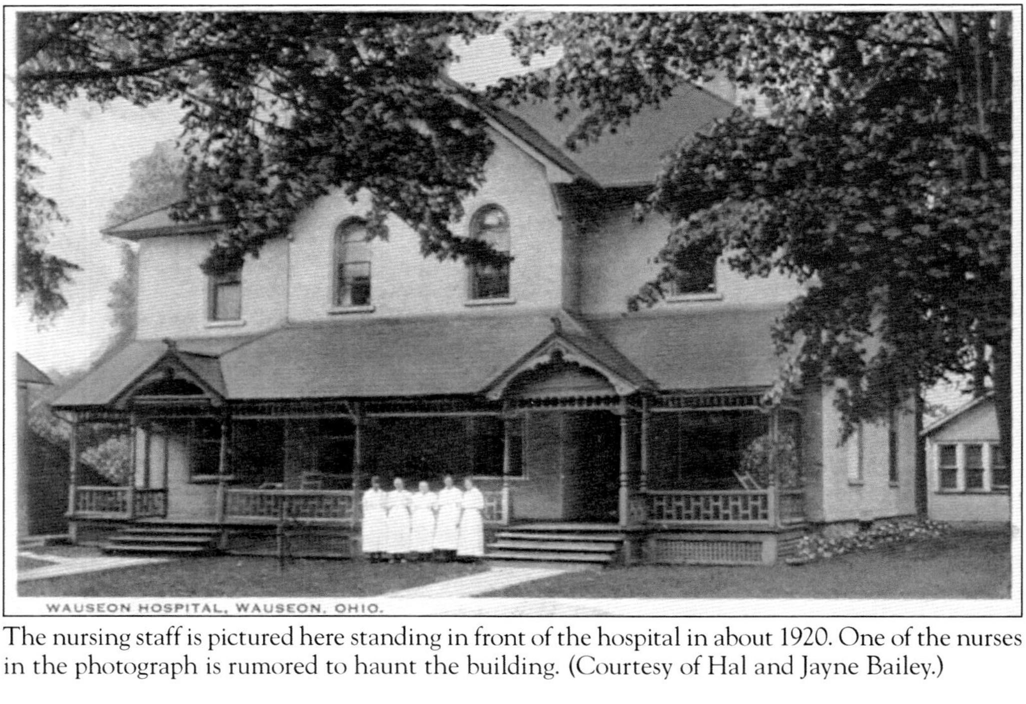

The nursing staff is pictured here standing in front of the hospital in about 1920. One of the nurses in the photograph is rumored to haunt the building. (Courtesy of Hal and Jayne Bailey.)

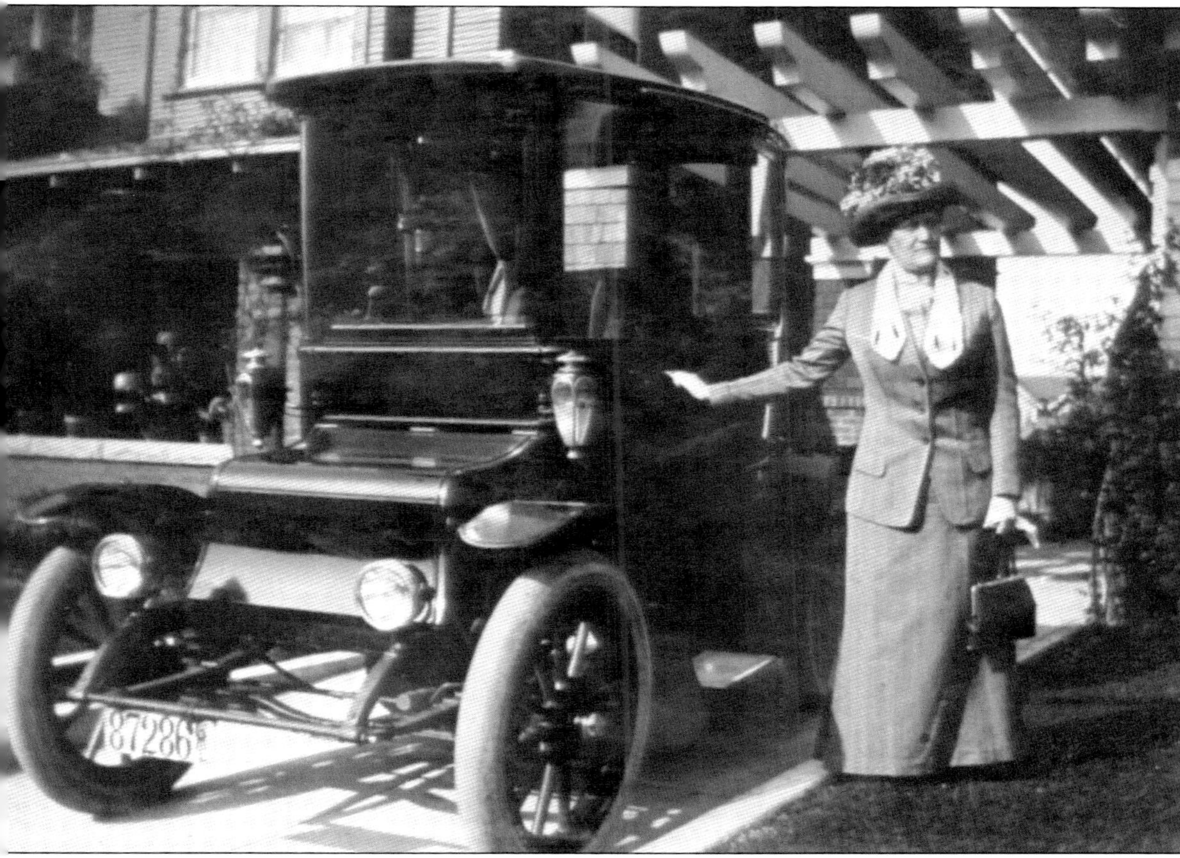

When Wauseon native and Cleveland socialite Deeta (Harrison) Detwiler passed away, her grieving husband, a successful businessman and former partner of John D. Rockefeller, donated $75,000 to build Detwiler Memorial Hospital. Deeta Detwiler is seen here beside her electric car during a visit to Wauseon. The hospital operated from 1930 to 1973, when the new Fulton County Health Center was opened. The building continued to function until 1997 as the county nursing home.

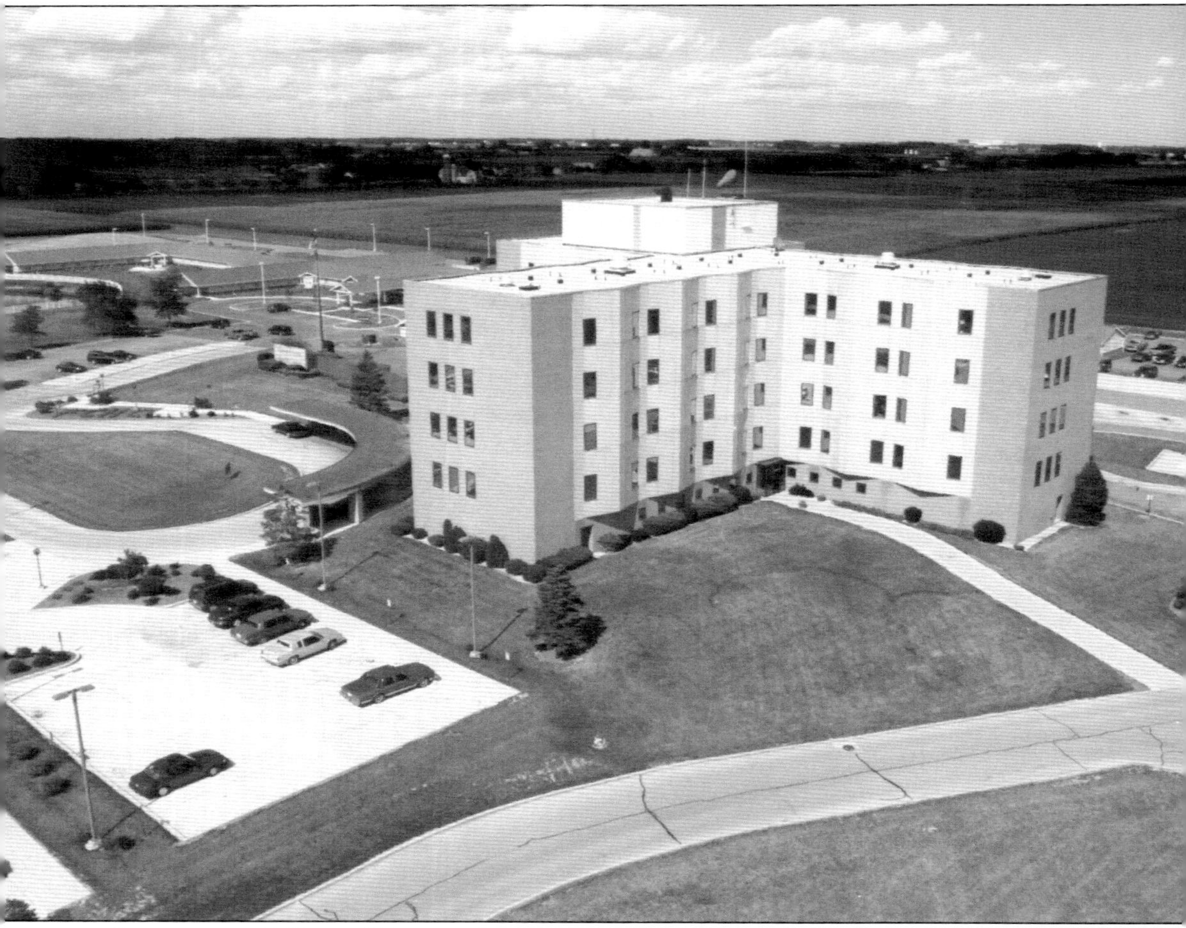

Beginning in 1973 as a full-service hospital, the Fulton County Health Center has grown through the years to include a wide variety of programs and services, many of which were requested by the health center's patients. They include a stress unit, oncology treatment, an expanded emergency room, outpatient surgery, radiology and laboratory departments, a physical rehabilitation facility, a nursing home, a sleep disorder center, and a diabetic education program. The facility has undergone three major expansions to meet patient needs. (Courtesy of Joseph Horwath.)

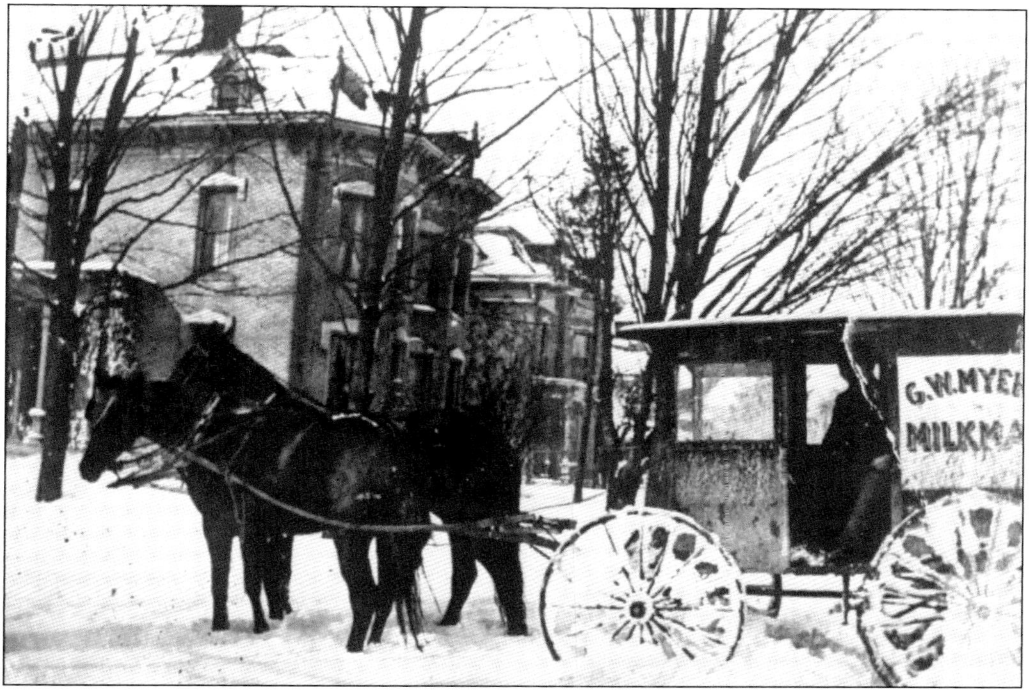

G.W. Myer delivered fresh milk to area homes for many years. His horse-drawn wagon is seen above in about 1902, struggling to make it through the snow. Before Pete Goldsmith started the Sterling Creamery in the late 1920s, which later became the Sterling Milk Company, with his son Marvin as company president, the Franklin Creamery delivered fresh milk to area homes. Below, the staff assembles in front of delivery vehicles for a company photograph in about 1925. The dairy was located on South Fulton Street's east side, where Sterling Dairy eventually built a bottling and processing plant.

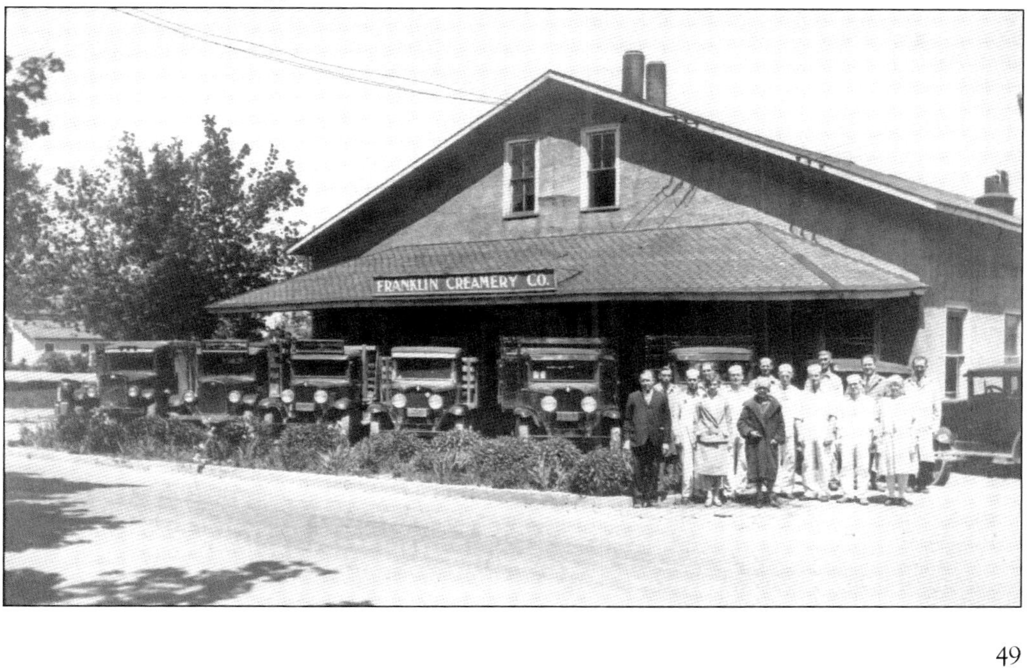

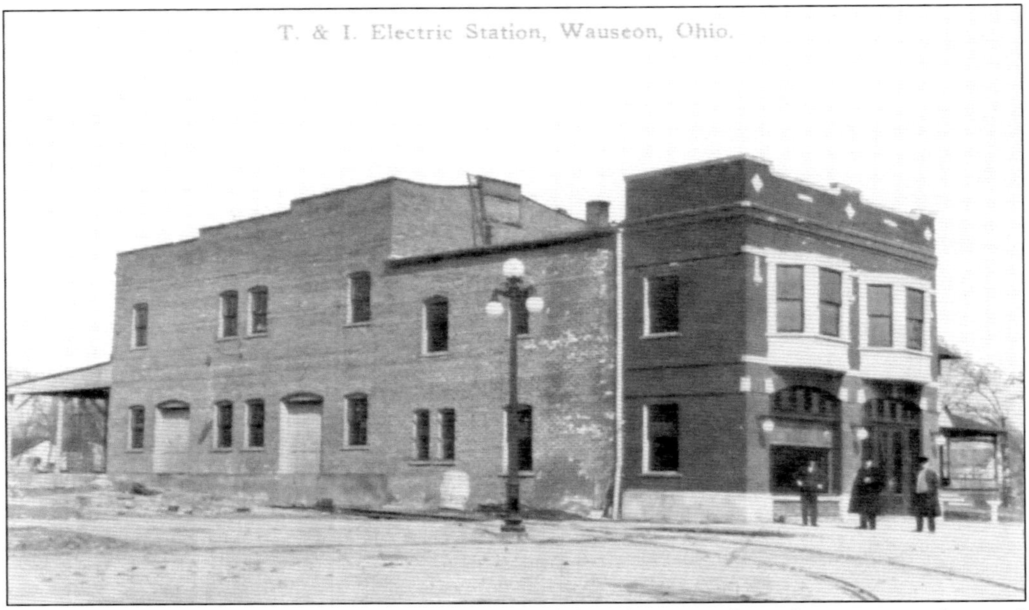

From 1905 to 1939, the Toledo & Indiana Railroad (T&I) operated an electric interurban rail service between Wauseon and Bryan, with stops in Wauseon and other communities. Competition from automobiles and the bus service eventually forced the T&I out of business. Pictured is the Wauseon station, located on Beech Street.

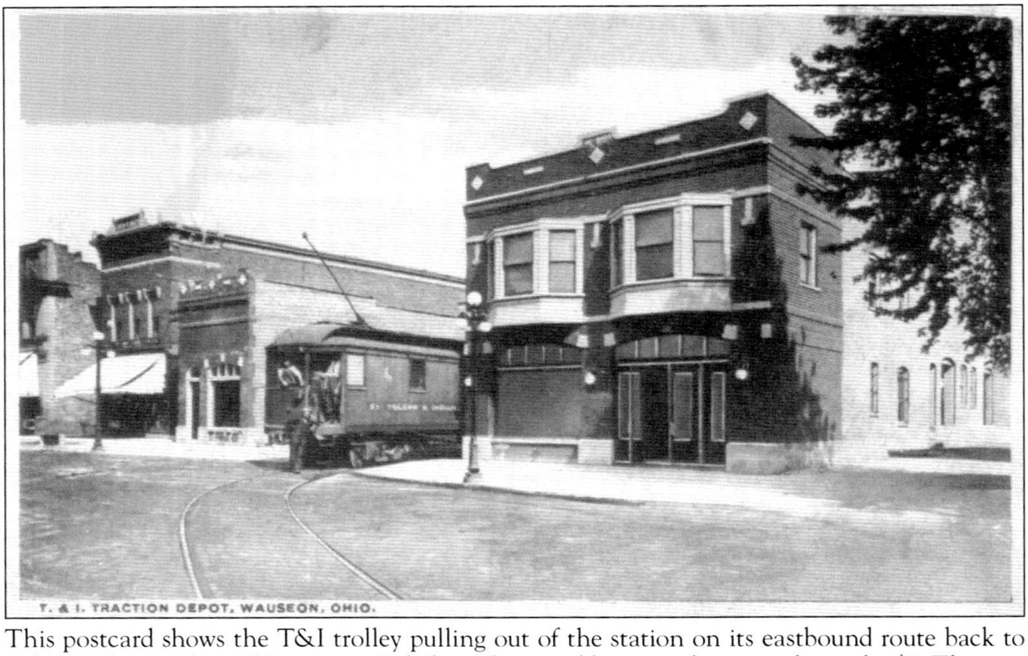

This postcard shows the T&I trolley pulling out of the station on its eastbound route back to Toledo. The trip from Wauseon to Toledo took several hours and cost a rider under $1. The cars were built by the Pullman Company, which also manufactured railroad passenger cars.

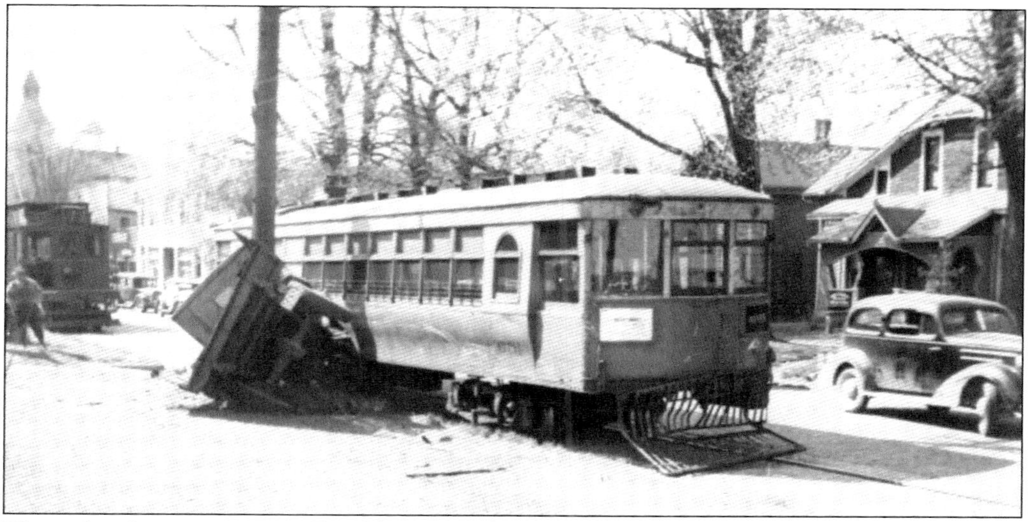

The railroad intersection on Franklin Street, between Beech and Birch Streets, was dangerous, and an accident between the trolley and a car in the 1930s gave cause for the village council to close the intersection.

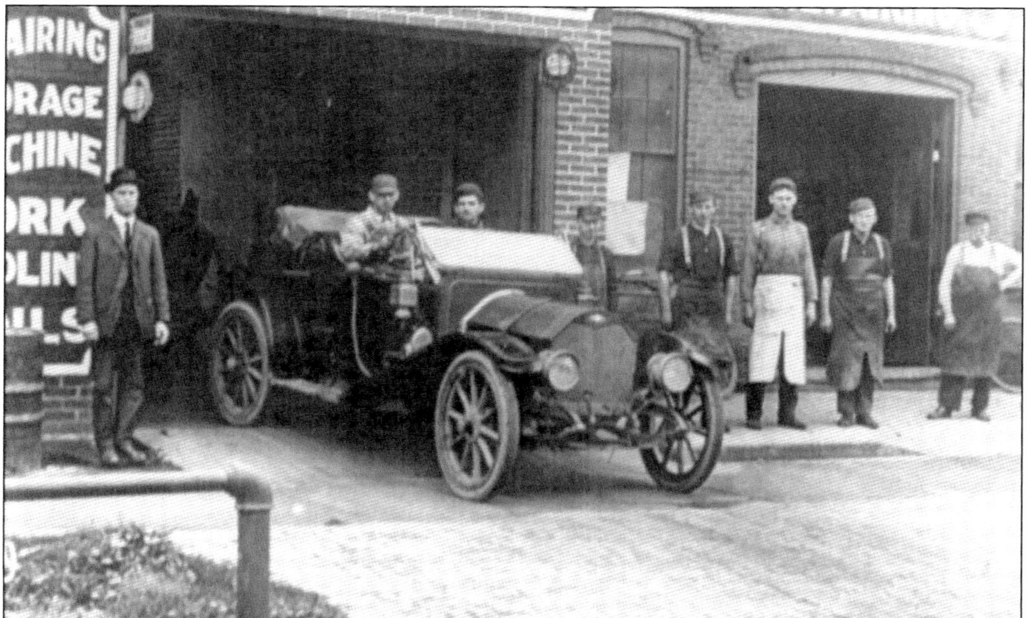

Another building with longevity is John Crone's shop on Commercial Street. Crone was one of the village's early wagon makers, selling many of his wagons to distributors in Toledo. The building eventually became Ike Short's Garage. Short assembled Ford Model Ts there, after the cars had been packed into wooden crates and sent to him for final assembly. The first locally owned vehicle to appear in Wauseon was owned by merchant and tailor Henry Yeager in 1899. The building is currently owned by Short's grandson.

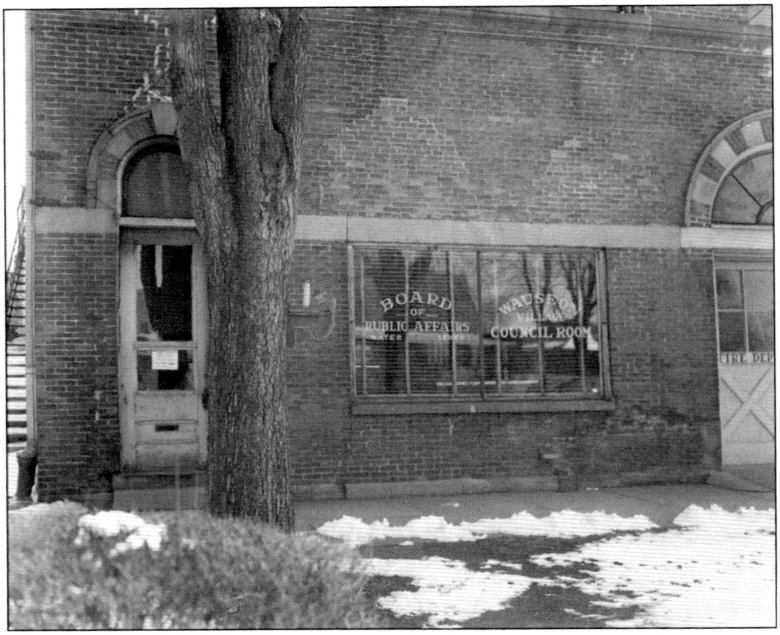

After years of meeting in the backs of businesses, in the 1880s, village council constructed a municipal building on the corner of Depot and Clinton Streets. The council shared the building with the volunteer fire department. On the first floor were village offices and the fire station. The main entrance to the offices faced Clinton Street.

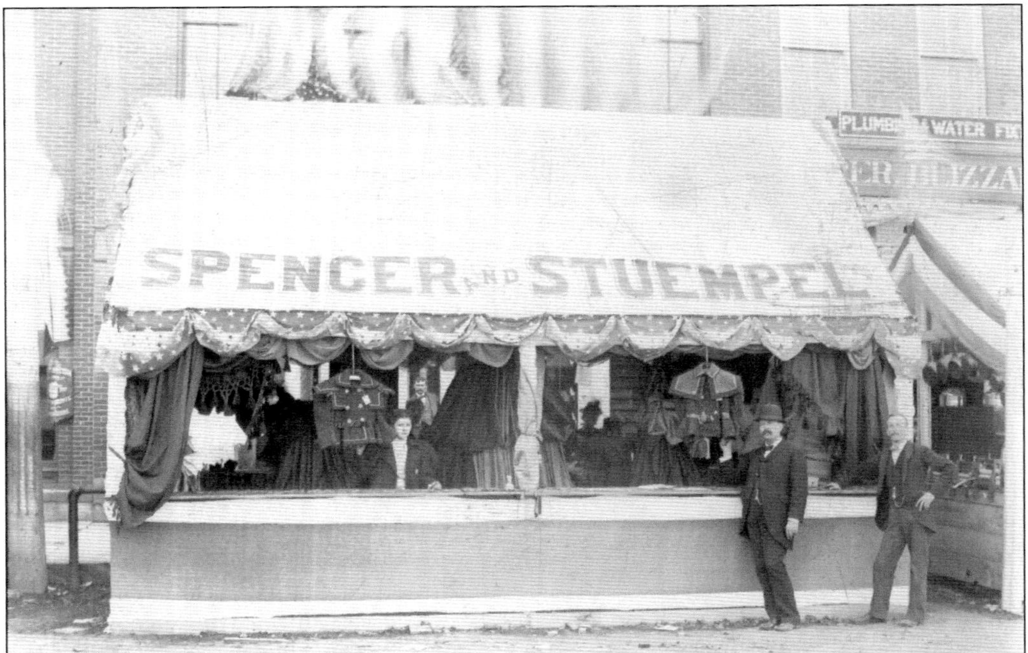

Merchants often set up booths outside their stores on Fulton Street during fair weather. Spencer & Stuemple was a men's and women's clothing and dry goods store located on the west side of the street. It was later the site of Shaw's Clothing until a major downtown fire destroyed the building in April 2007. Premade clothing became readily available in several Wauseon stores by the end of the 1890s.

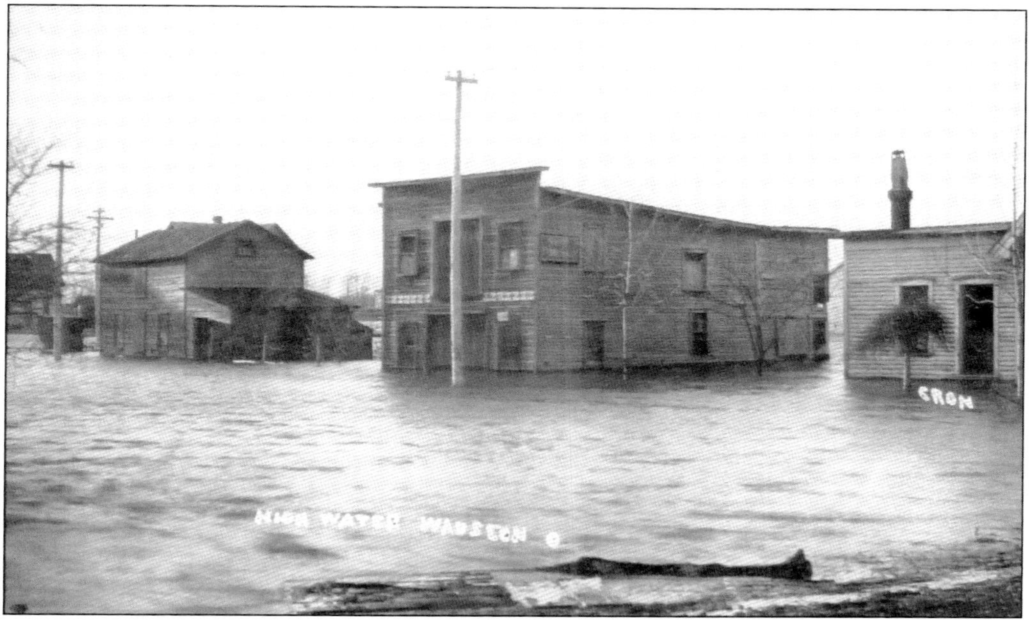

In 1913, massive floods engulfed Illinois, Indiana, and Ohio. In northwest Ohio, just about every river overflowed its banks. On March 24–25, some areas received six inches of rain in 24 hours. Even areas not immediately near waterways received so much water the ground could not soak it up. At the time, there was no Federal Emergency Management Agency, and the American Red Cross was not set up for such an emergency. What was then known as the National Weather Bureau did not have the technology available today and was hampered when its basic communications systems failed. These two images show the results of the flooding along North Fulton Street in the vicinity of the Assembly of God Church.

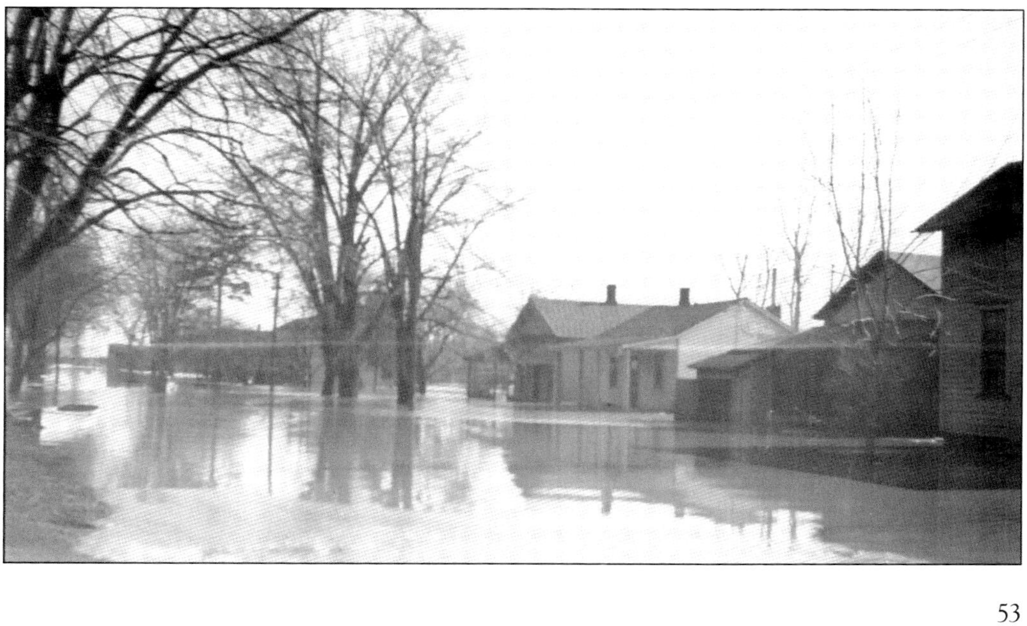

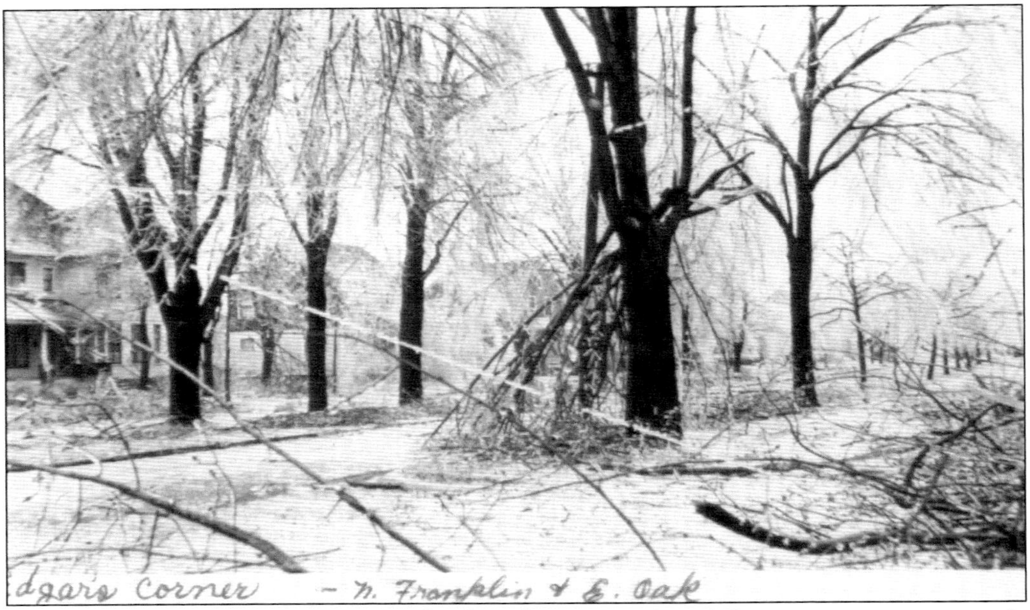

Just a few weeks prior to the infamous flooding that occurred in 1913, a major ice storm in early March acted as a precursor. This postcard shows the results of that storm at the intersection of North Franklin and East Oak Streets. At that time, the intersection was referred to by locals as Edger's Corner.

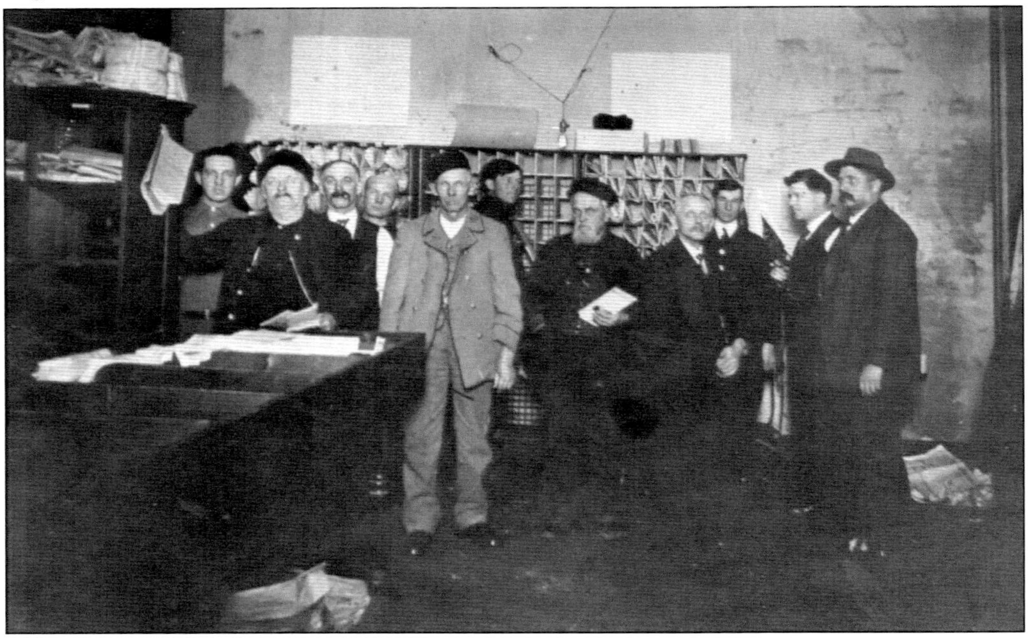

This photograph shows the sorting room at the Wauseon post office around 1900. The post office was inside the Arcade Building, facing Beech Street, allowing easy access to passing trains, which delivered out-of-area mail and packages. Levi Hoy, the town's first rural delivery carrier, is seventh from the left. Hoy used his own horse and wagon to deliver the mail. Postmaster Frank Outcalt (second from right) was appointed to the position by Pres. William McKinley.

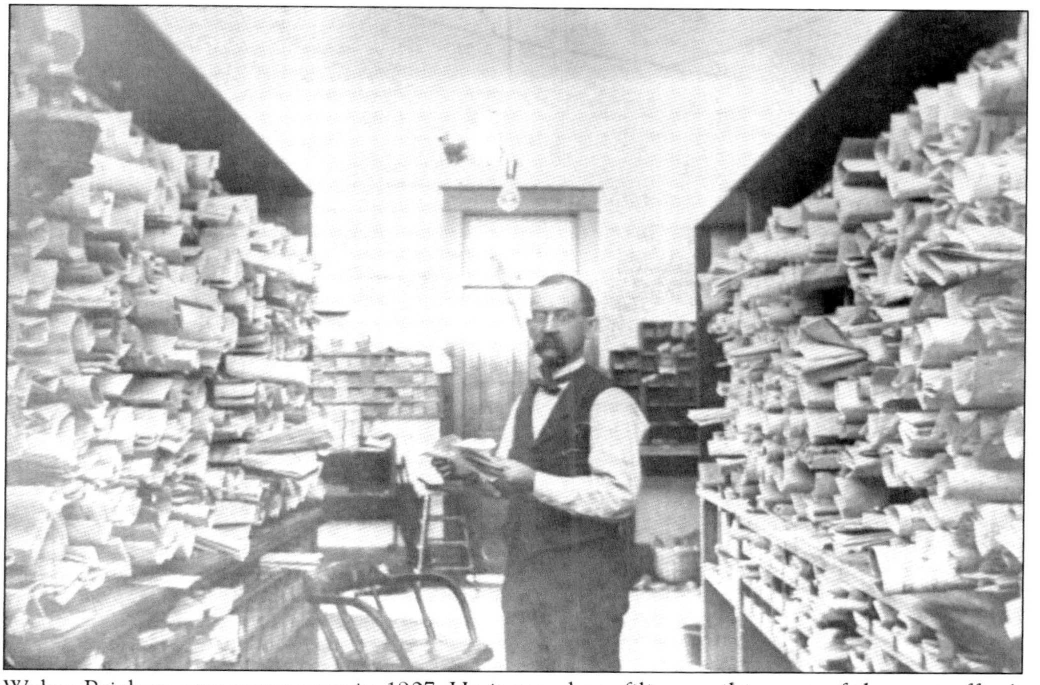

Walter Brigham was postmaster in 1907. He is seen here filing mail in part of the post office's sorting room. Until the 1950s, the post office delivered all newspapers postage-free as a way to ensure that the general public could keep up with the local and national news. Rising costs ended this century-old practice.

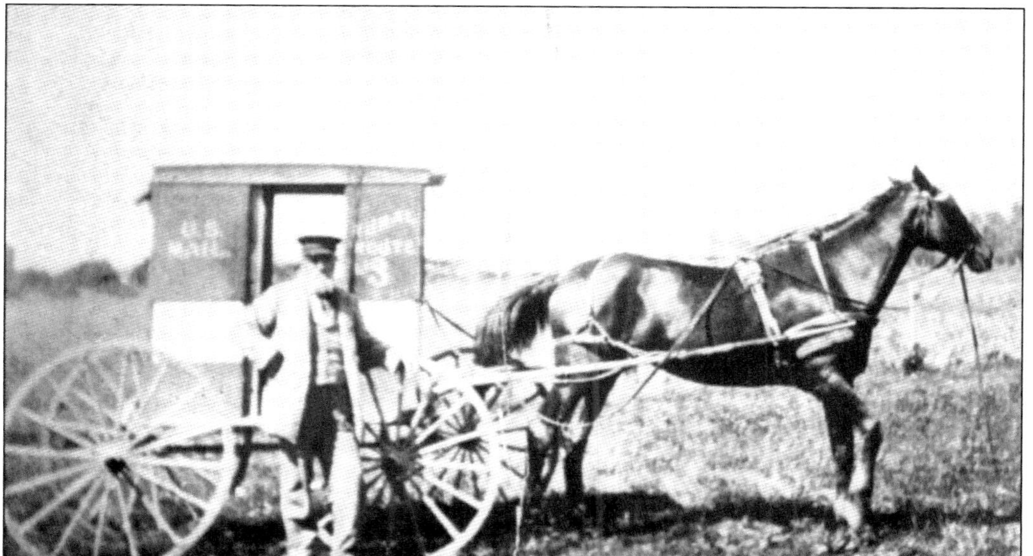

Until the opening of a new, standalone postal center in 1936, in-town and rural mail operations were conducted in the Arcade Building. In 1936, a more extensive facility with rear loading docks was constructed on Elm Street. Until recently, outgoing letters were sorted and postmarked at the local post office.

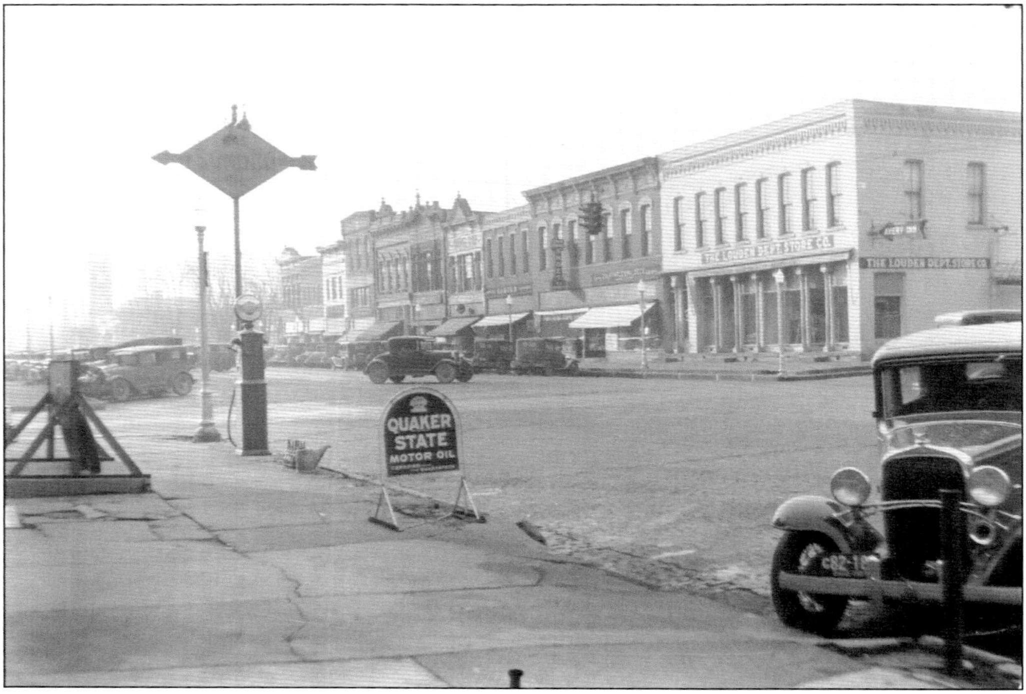

In the 1930s, one of Wauseon's busiest gas stations was located on the east side of North Fulton Street. Tall, glass-topped pumps stood on the sidewalk adjacent to the curb, allowing drivers to pull up for a fill-up. Back then, gas stations were full-service, and attendants pumped gas, checked oil levels, and washed windshields. A gallon of gas in 1933 cost 10¢. The average annual household income was $1,550.

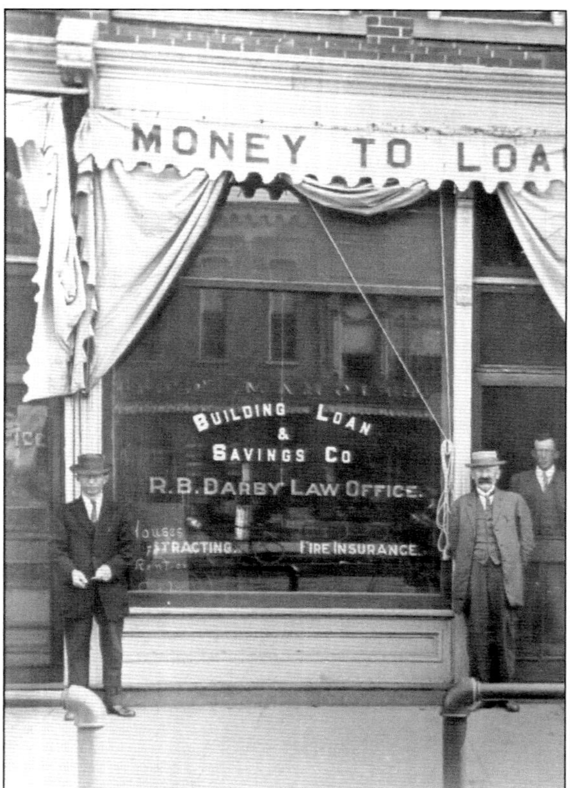

In 1910, the Building & Loan Company shared space with local attorney R.B. Darby on North Fulton Street. Darby's son John followed in his footsteps as a popular Wauseon attorney. For years, the intersection of West Elm and Franklin Streets was known as "Darby's Corner" because John Darby's house was located there.

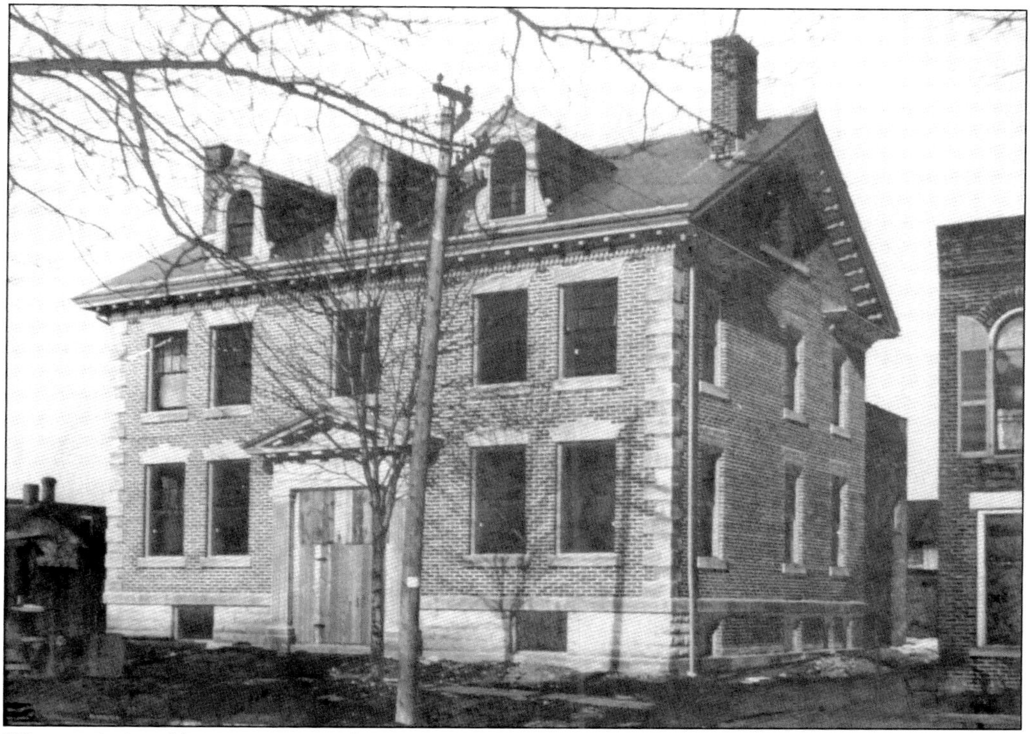

Wauseon's first library was a small room in the municipal building, on the corner of Clinton and Depot Streets. It was organized by a group of residents who borrowed books on a subscription basis. This preceded the Wauseon Public Library (shown here under construction), which opened in 1906 through a grant from Andrew Carnegie. (Both, courtesy of Hal and Jayne Bailey.)

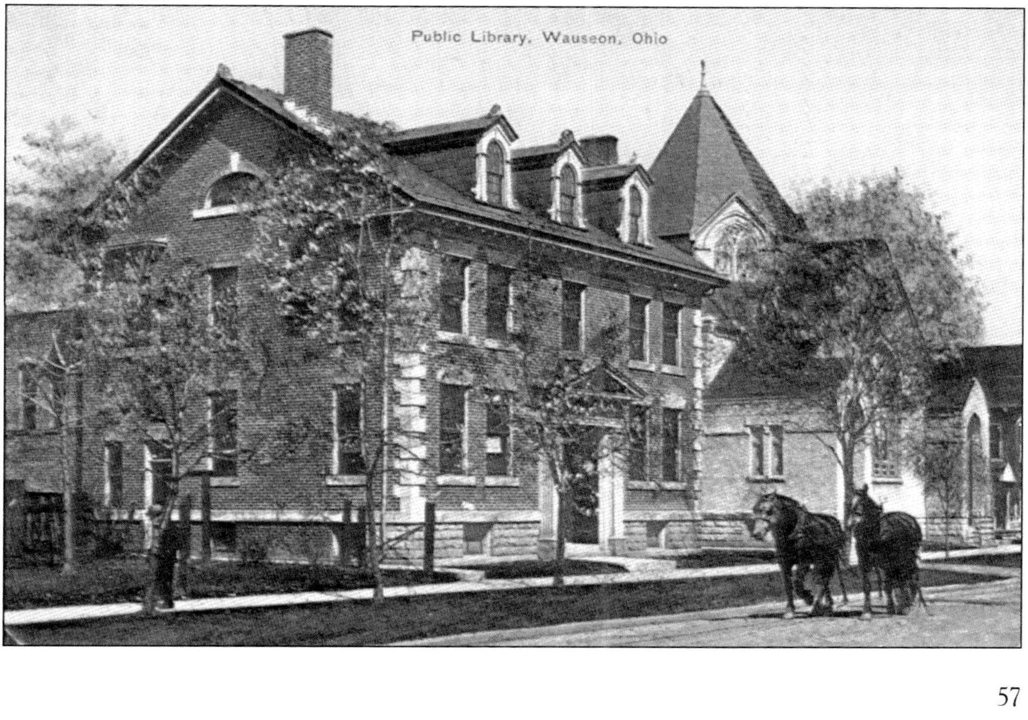

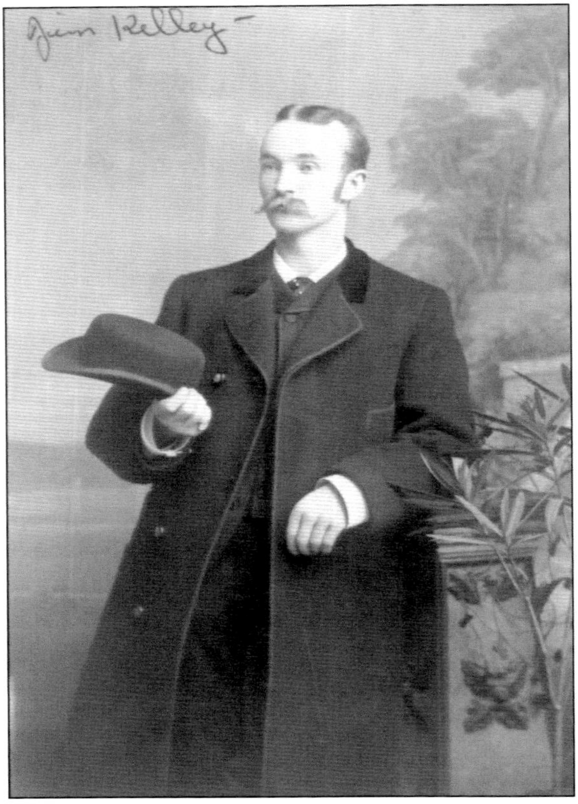

Jim Kelley, who was probably employed by one of Wauseon's men's clothing establishments, was considered to be one of Wauseon's best-dressed men. He is seen here proudly posing for a local photographer in one of his suits in 1888.

The Haumesser & Dolf Meat Market dates back to 1879. The local butchers processed local beef, hogs, and poultry. They often would slaughter livestock in the woods across from the present-day Fulton County Health Center and then bring the carcasses into town for butchering. Henry Dolf was a tailor who partnered with his brother-in-law Frank Haumesser in the popular Depot Street market.

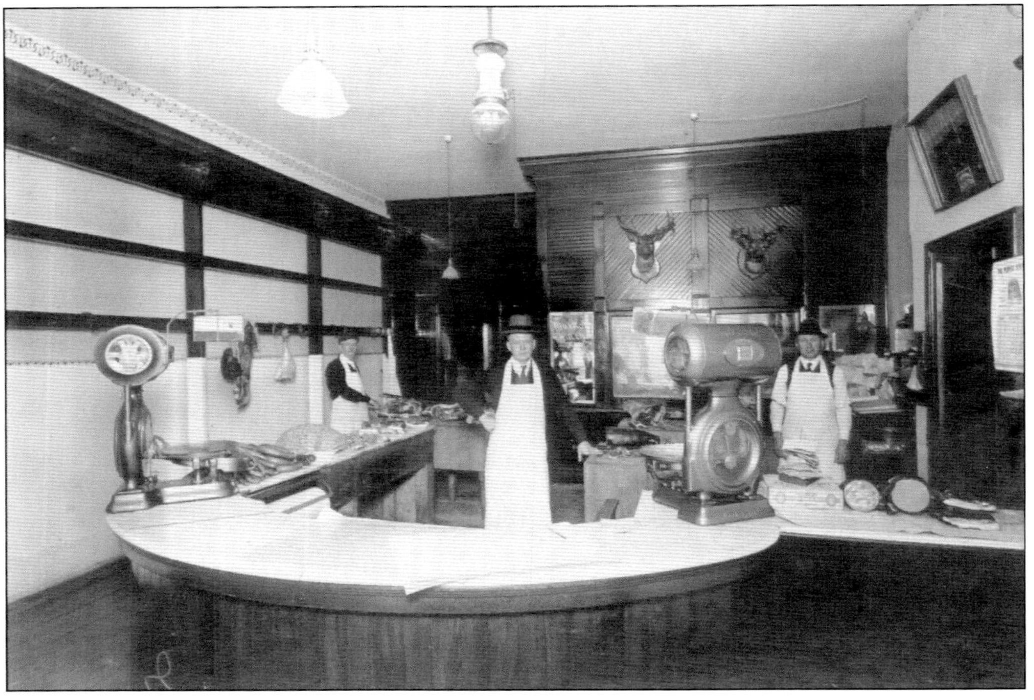

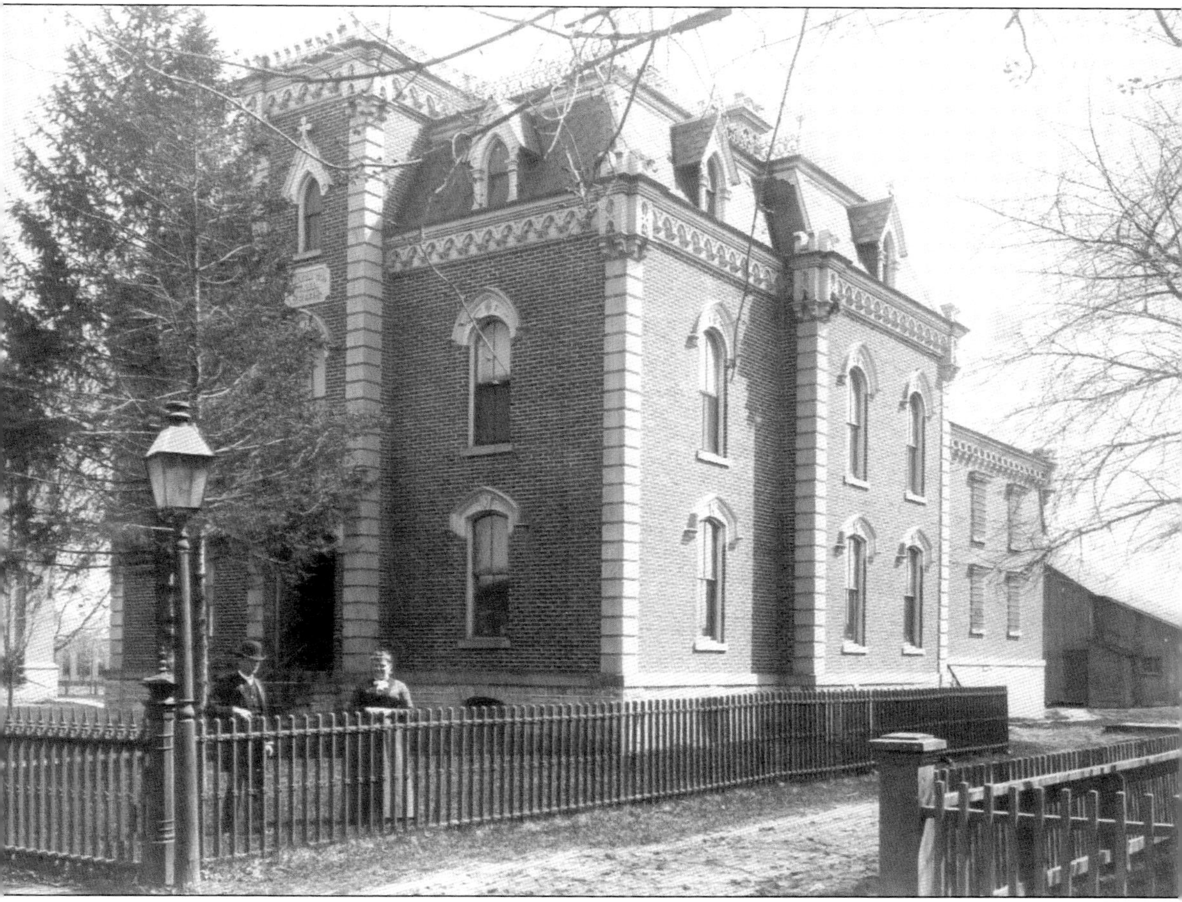

Fulton County's jailhouse was built behind the county courthouse in 1874. Mr. and Mrs. Albert Deyo, the custodians, were required to live on the first floor and were responsible for inmates' care and meals. The prisoners were housed in small jail cells on the second and third floors. The building was abandoned when the regional jail opened. For several years afterwards, it was used to store outdated county records, and it was eventually demolished in the mid-1990s.

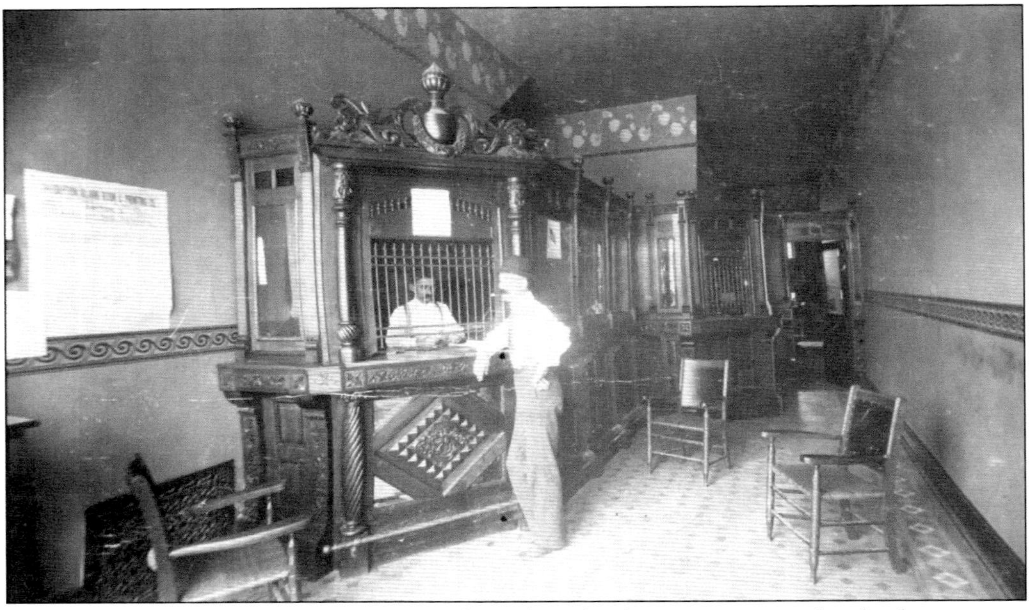

The First National Bank, on the corner of Beech and Fulton Streets, was the third to open in Wauseon. This is an early view of the inside in the 1890s. It shows the bank's single teller, protected inside a steel cage. The Bank of Wauseon was the village's first bank, founded in 1863 by E.L. Barber. The bank was a private family undertaking. Barber died in 1899. The bank closed in 1908, creating one of the worst financial disasters ever in Wauseon and the surrounding area.

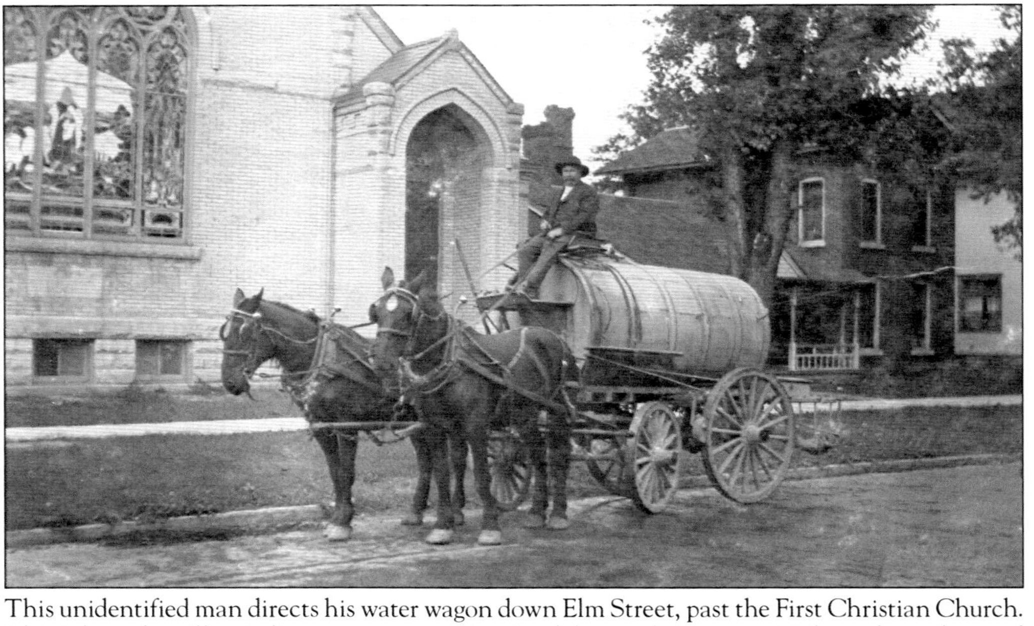

This unidentified man directs his water wagon down Elm Street, past the First Christian Church. This is how the village's dirt streets were maintained during the summer. To keep down dust and flies, which were attracted to horse droppings, the council hired several local men with large wagons to water the streets and remove droppings.

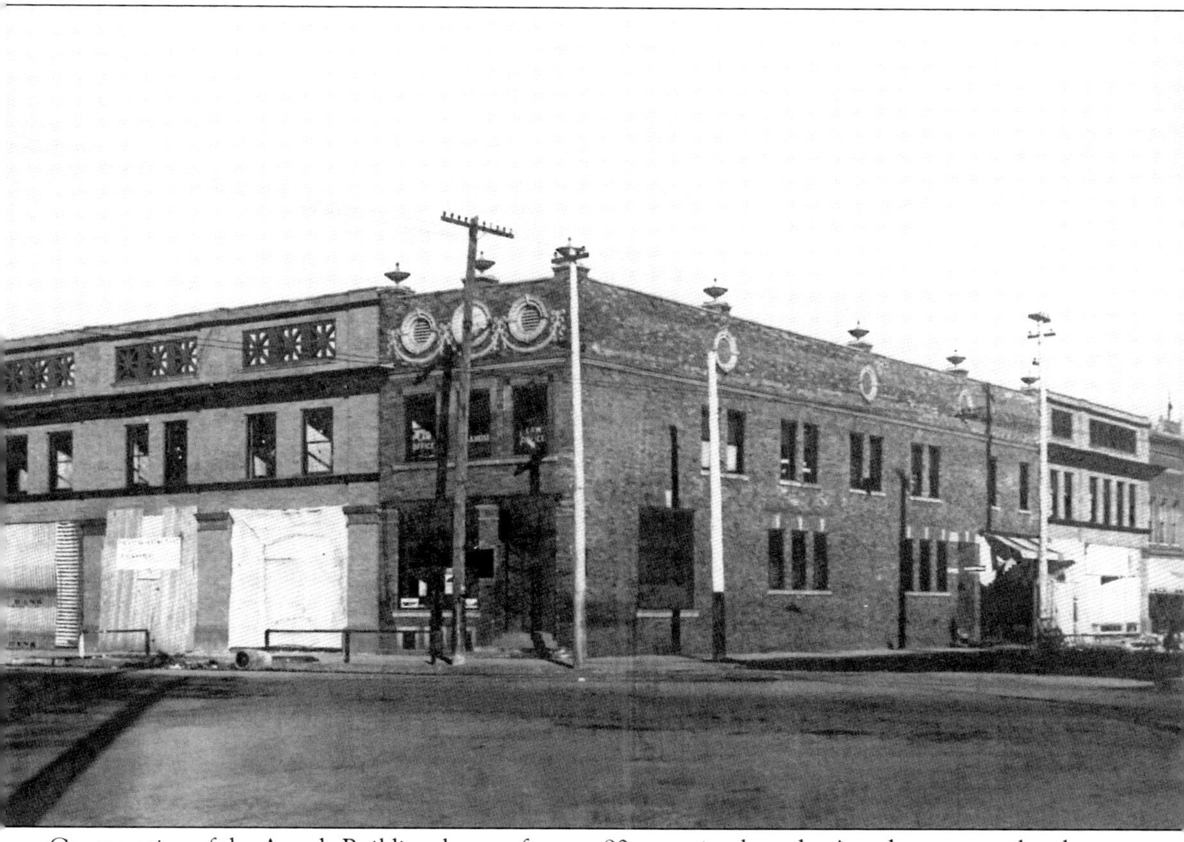

Construction of the Arcade Building, known for over 90 years simply as the Arcade, was completed in 1906 by D.K. Shoop and two partners. It was located next to the First National Bank. The two-story structure housed many small businesses, including a restaurant, a barbershop, and a ladies' boutique. Located adjacent to the railroad tracks, the building also served as the village's post office until 1936, when a larger structure was built on East Elm Street. By the early 1990s, only a few businesses were operating out of the structure and the second floor had been converted into small apartments. In 2003, the Arcade was destroyed in a fire that required the assistance of 11 area fire departments to contain. Over one million gallons of water were used to extinguish the fire and protect adjacent structures.

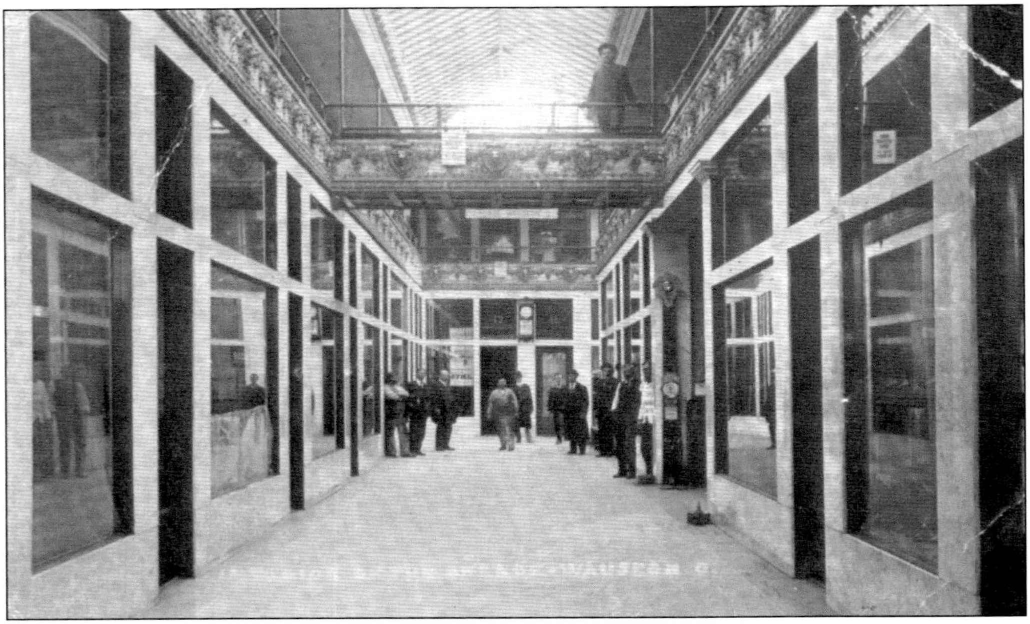

Here are two interior views of the Arcade's interior. The view from the first floor shows the intricate detail and marble that greeted shoppers. The first floor contained the post office, in the rear, and an assortment of small shops. The view from the second floor was breathtaking. There were several professional offices leading off from the mezzanine. The Arcade dazzled shoppers with its impressive rooftop skylight, one of the first in the region.

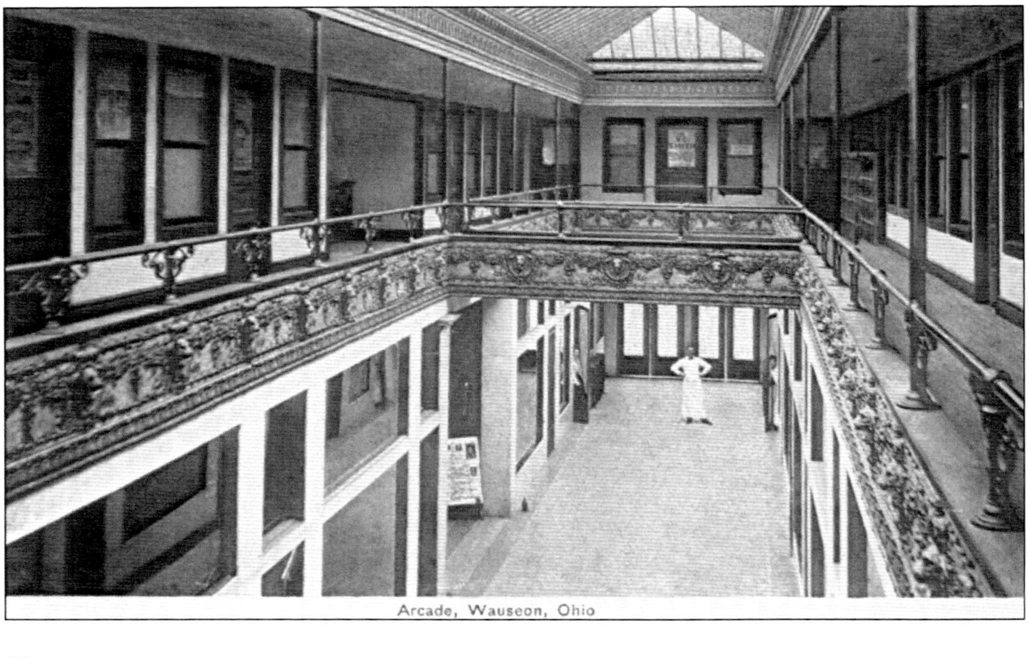

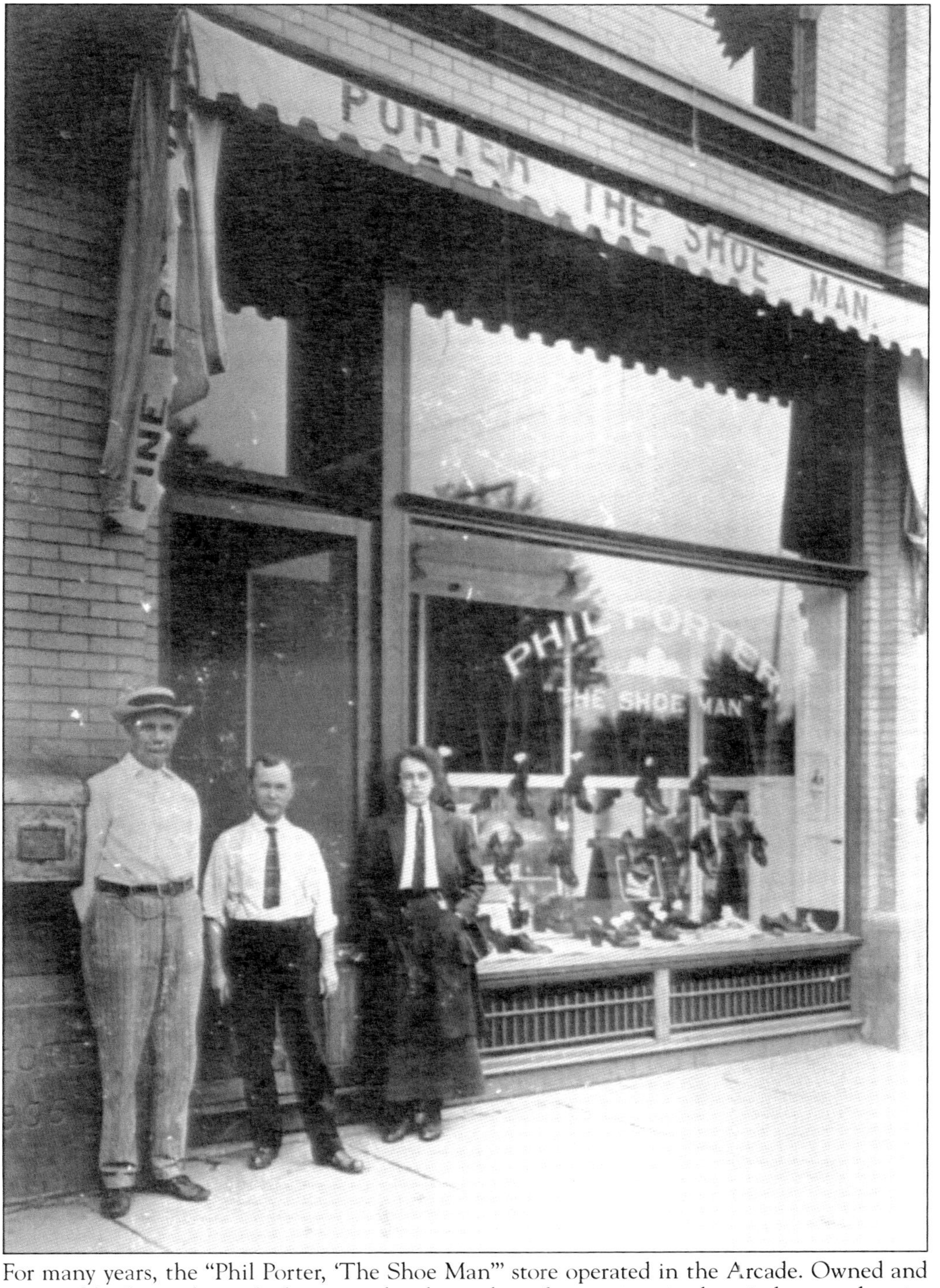

For many years, the "Phil Porter, 'The Shoe Man'" store operated in the Arcade. Owned and operated by Porter (center), the store often hung shoes from strings in the window to advertise the latest fashions. This photograph was taken in the 1950s.

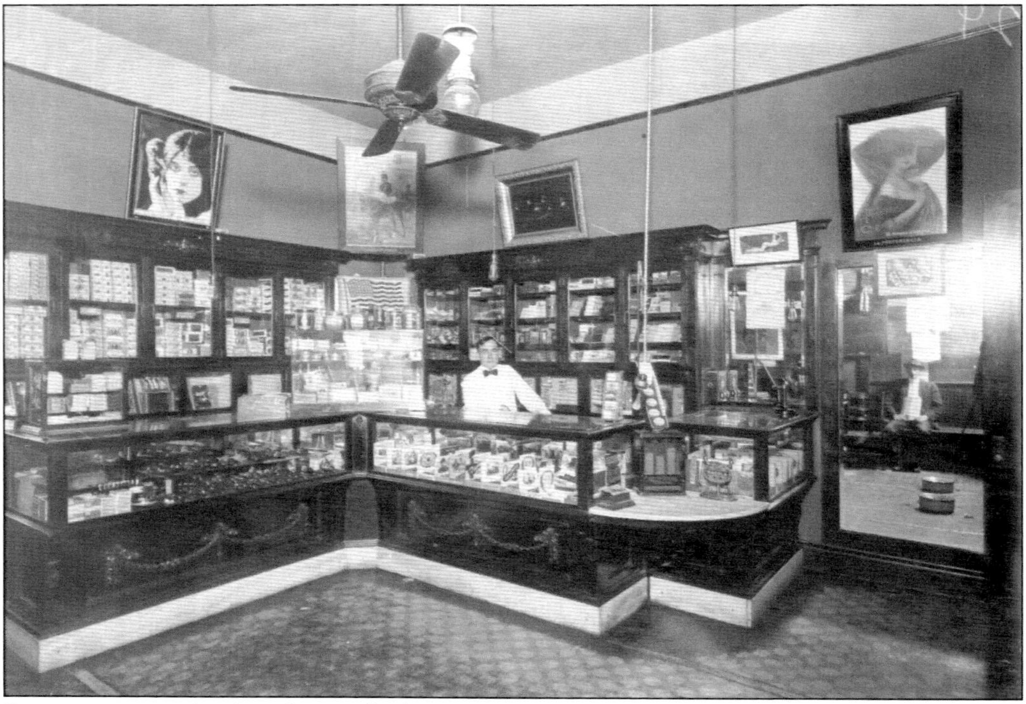

For many years, the Arcade was the busiest place in town. At the far end was the post office, and across from it was the Smokery, run by proprietor Lonnie Harriman, which received baseball scores before the radio. On either side were shops, including a floral shop, a restaurant, shoe store, and a barbershop.

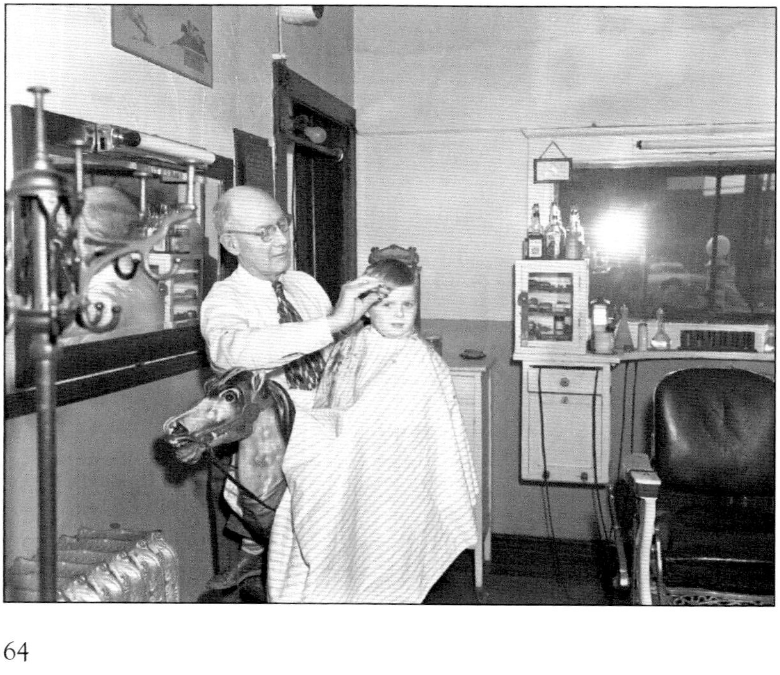

Several barbers conducted business in the Arcade in the nine decades it was open. This photograph from the early 1960s shows barber Al Harrison trimming a youngster's hair in a barber chair shaped like a horse. The horse chair was purchased several years ago at auction by a local couple and is on display at Tomahawk Printing.

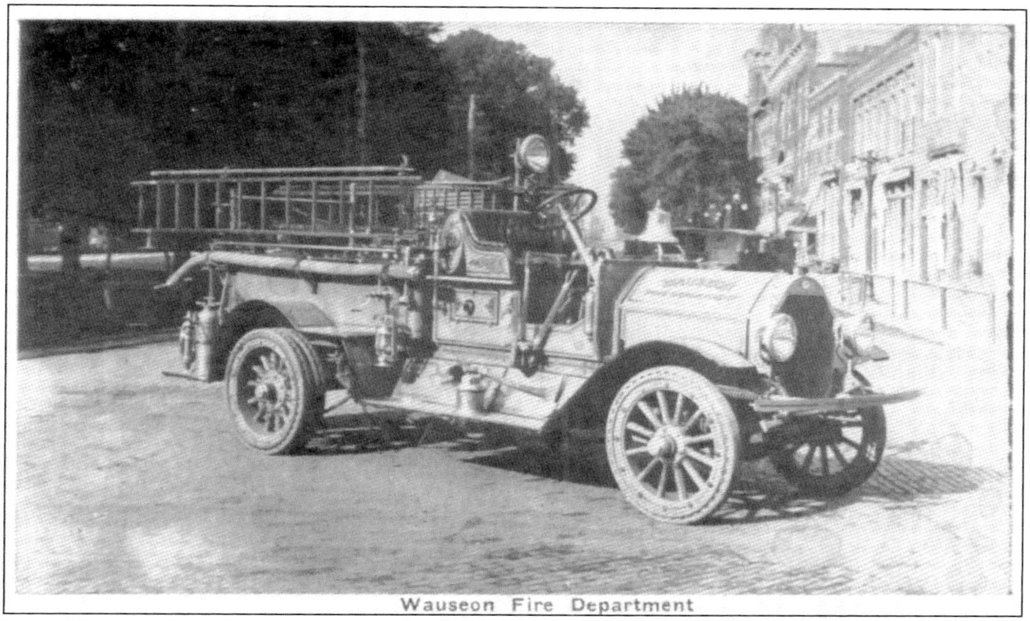

The Wauseon Fire Department was organized in January 1862, and $50 of village funds was appropriated to build a "Fire Engine House" to serve the approximately 400 village residents. With the installation of a water system and the spread of motorized vehicles, the way was paved to purchase a Seagrave pumper in 1916. It is currently being restored by department members and is on display in the Wauseon Fire Department. Wauseon volunteer firefighters gathered during a firemen's convention hosted here in the 1920s. The hose cart, seen here was an early piece of equipment purchased in about 1863 and pulled by hand. Water came from cisterns located along Fulton Street. For areas out of reach of the cisterns, private cisterns and open wells were used. A bucket brigade was established, which involved private citizens in the battle against the flames. (Both, courtesy of the Wauseon Fire Department.)

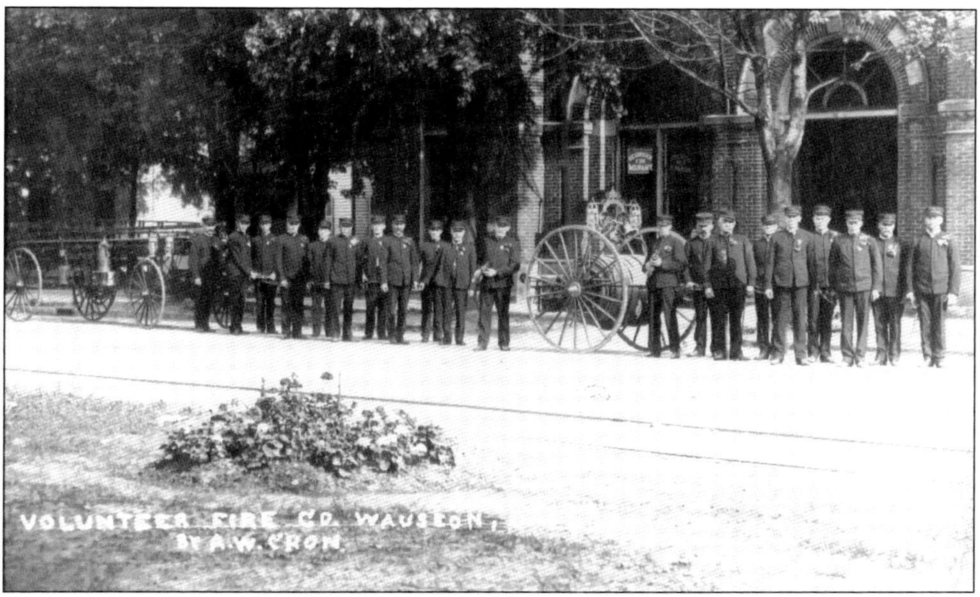

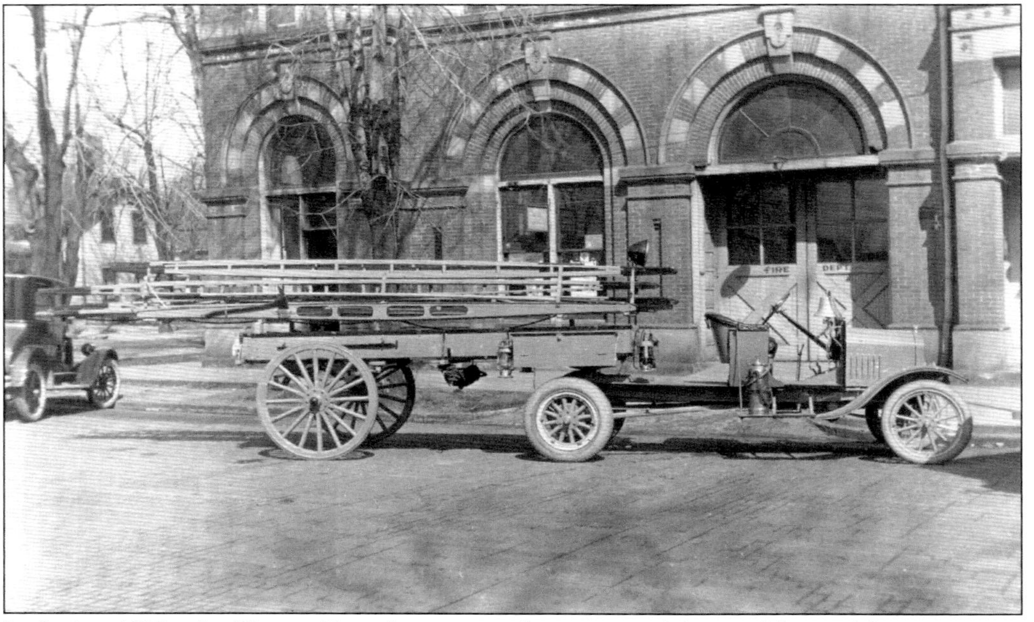

In the late 1920s, the Clinton Township trustees first organized the need for rural fire protection. As a result, in conjunction with the Wauseon Fire Department and the village council, a fire truck was purchased. The township trustees delegated the Wauseon Fire Department to man the truck, which was housed at the Wauseon Fire Station, located at Clinton and Depot Streets. This was one of the first efforts of rural fire protection in the state of Ohio.

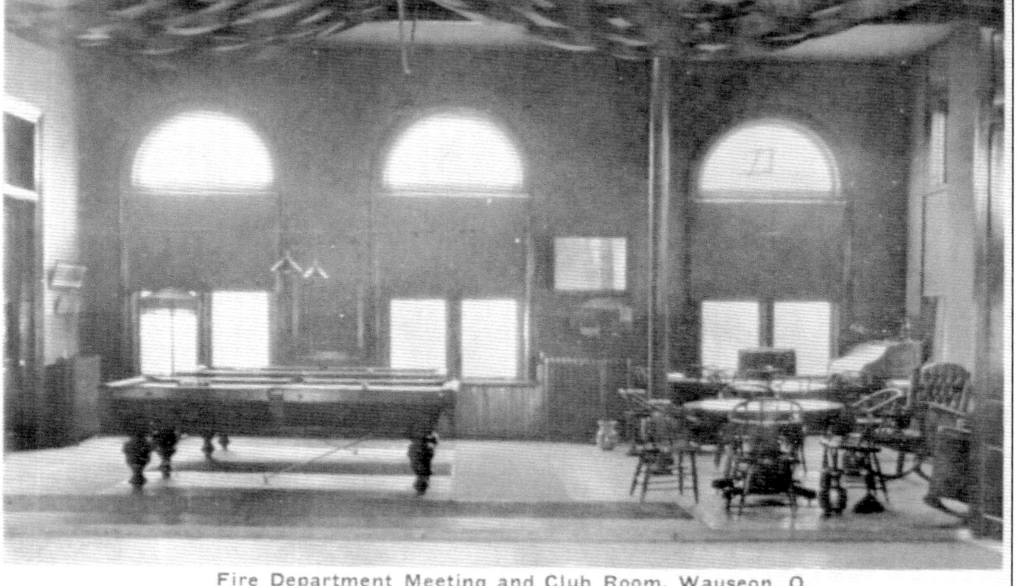

Fire Department Meeting and Club Room, Wauseon, O.

In the late 1890s and early 1900s, the Wauseon Volunteer Fire Department was housed in a building on the corner of Depot and Clinton Streets. Several of its vehicles were on the ground level facing Clinton Street. On the second floor was a meeting room where firemen conducted business meetings and training sessions and gathered for social activities.

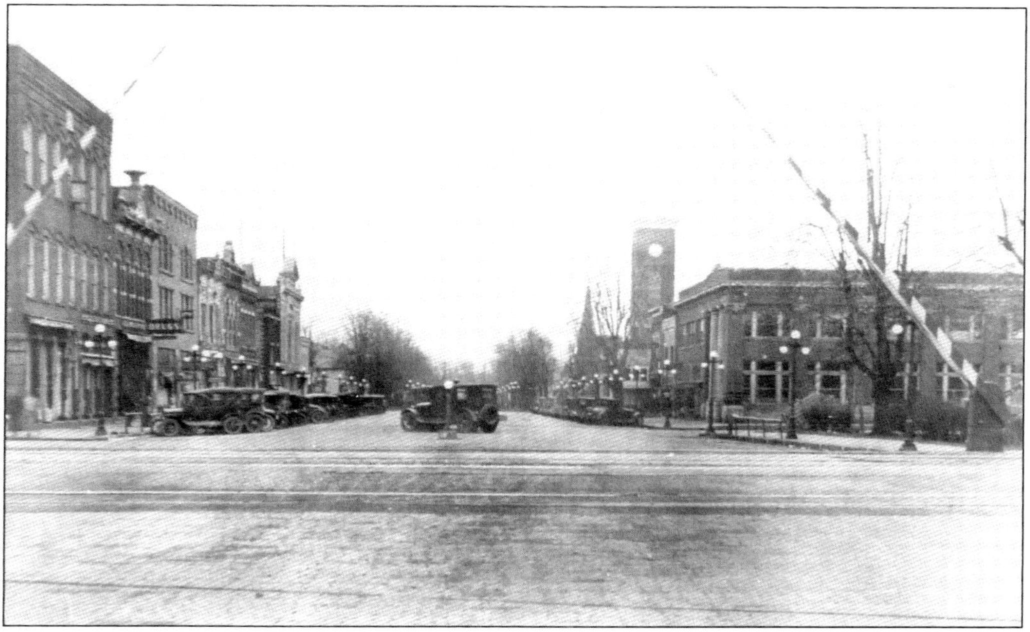

Installation of railroad crossing gates was made the responsibility of railroads by the National Safety and Transportation Board in the 1940s. Prior to this time, communities were responsible for installing and maintaining gates. This 1930s view of South Fulton Street shows the gates, which were operated by electric motors. The gates also had pedestrian arms that lowered across the sidewalks.

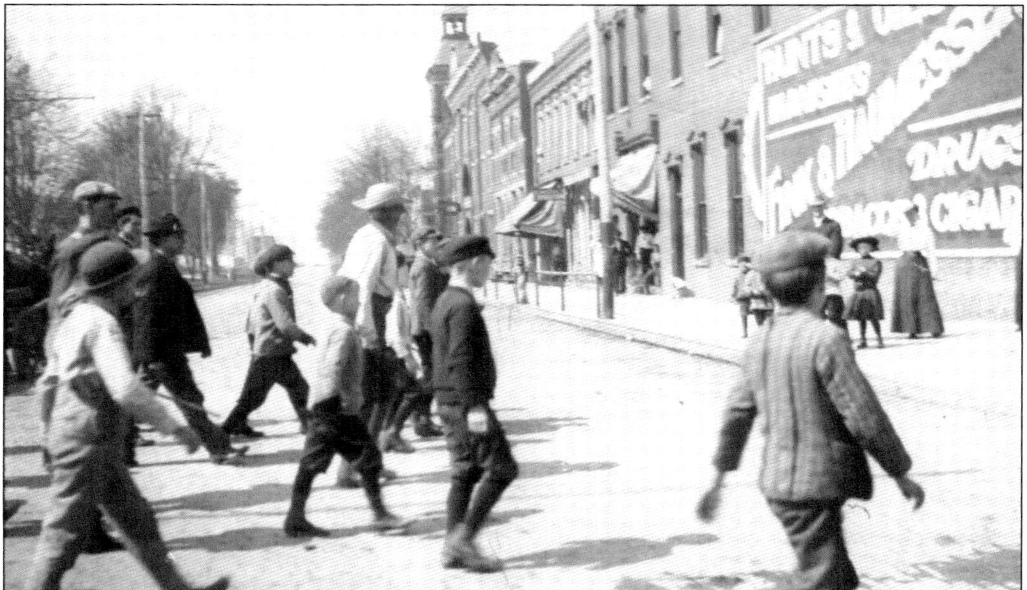

A fashionable lady holding a parasol watches from the sidewalk as a group of neatly dressed youngsters strolls across Depot Street, most likely in the early 1910s during a street fair. Everyone in this scene is wearing hats, which did not fall out of favor until the 1960s. Hitching racks were still in abundance but seldom used, as cars took over the streets.

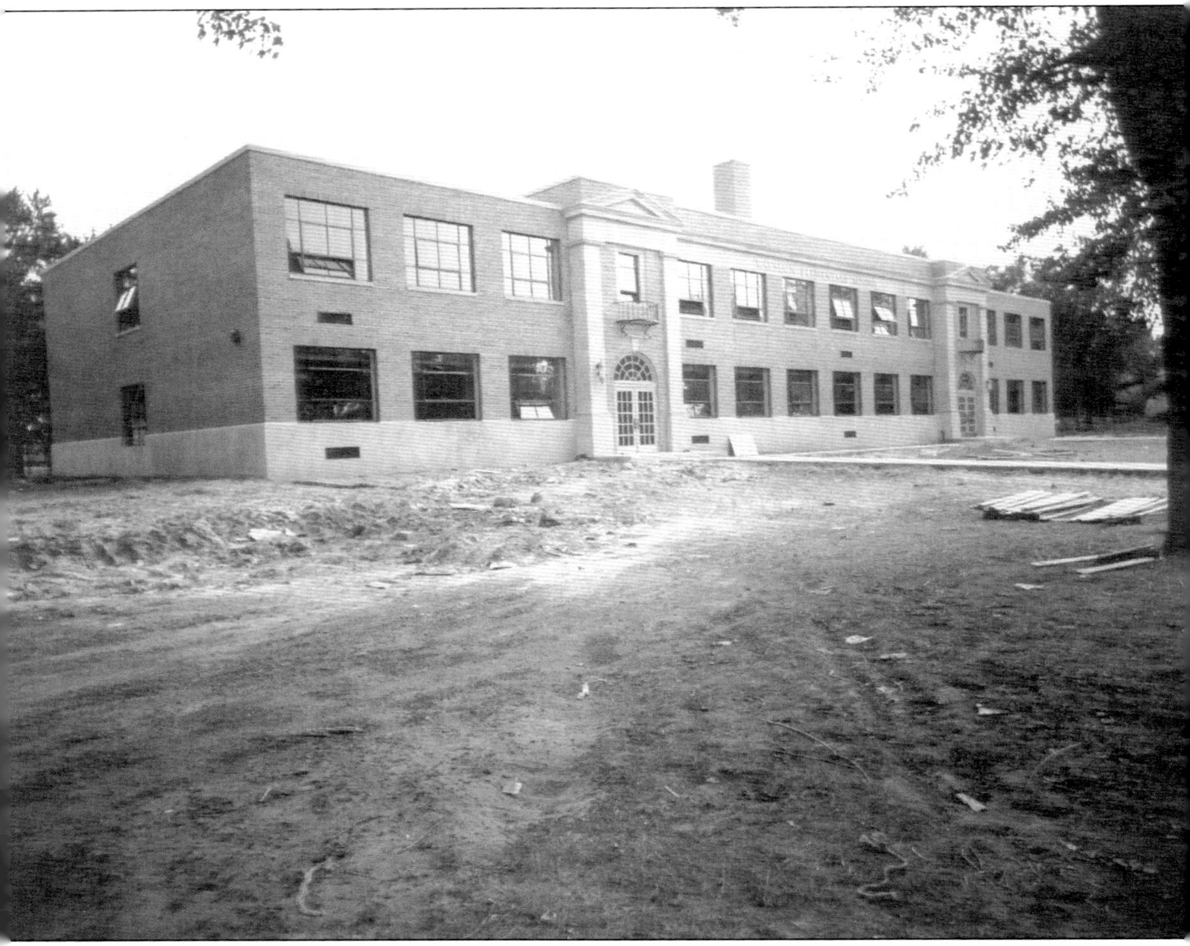

Elm Street Elementary School, seen here under construction in 1938, stood on the corner of Shoop Avenue and Elm Street. The building was remodeled and expanded several times to meet the needs of a growing population. Between 2006 and 2010, the district undertook a $44 million state-supported construction program. In that time, Wauseon Elementary/Wauseon Middle School was built, Wauseon High School was extensively renovated, and Wauseon Primary School received minor upgrades. The Elm Street school building was vacated and then demolished in 2012, after the school board's efforts to find a buyer failed.

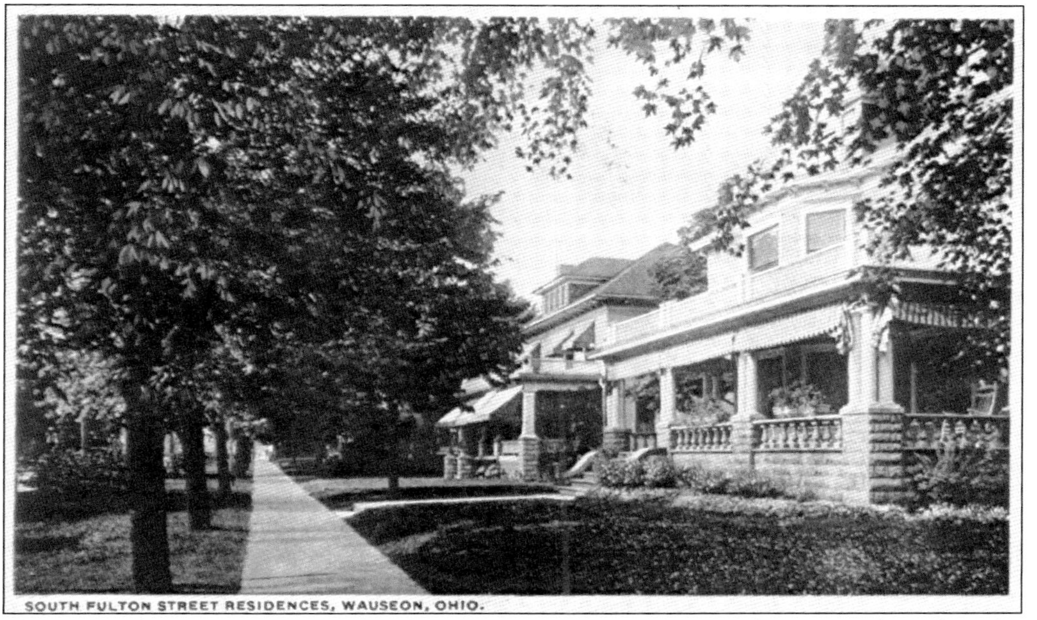

This postcard is a scene from South Fulton Street, across from the courthouse. On the right is the home built by E.H. Harrison, which included quarters for a live-in maid. Throughout Wauseon, efforts are being undertaken to preserve these old homes, which reflect the grandeur that early residents invested in their homes. (Courtesy of Hal and Jayne Bailey.)

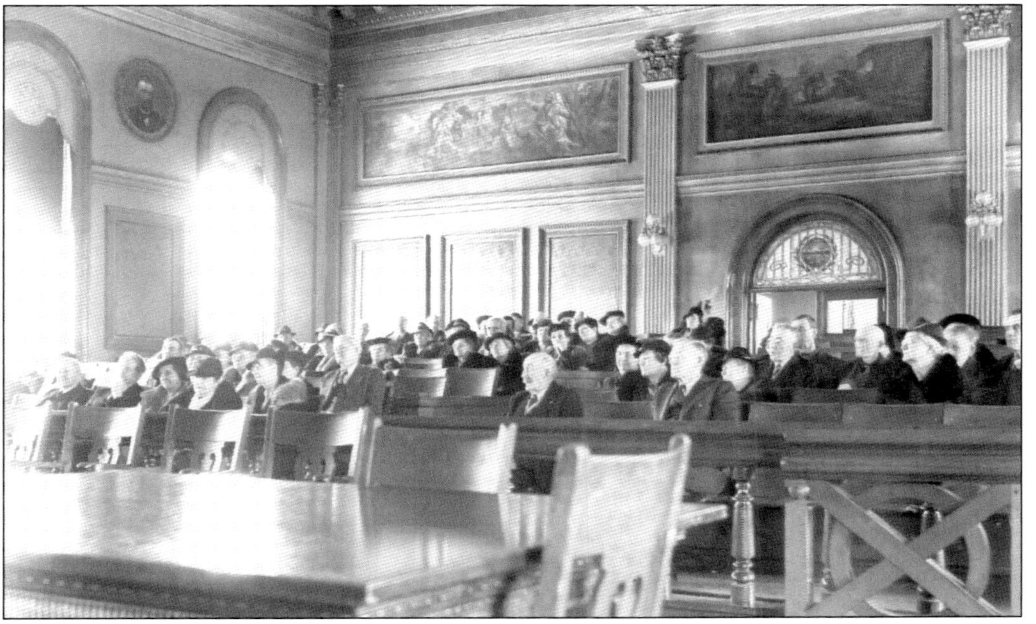

The first trial held in the county's courthouse took place shortly after construction was completed in 1871. The elegant, second-floor common pleas courtroom included murals depicting important Biblical events. Later, however, some of the murals' figures were "touched up" to cover some nudity. This courtroom scene was taken in the 1920s during the swearing in of several recently elected county officials.

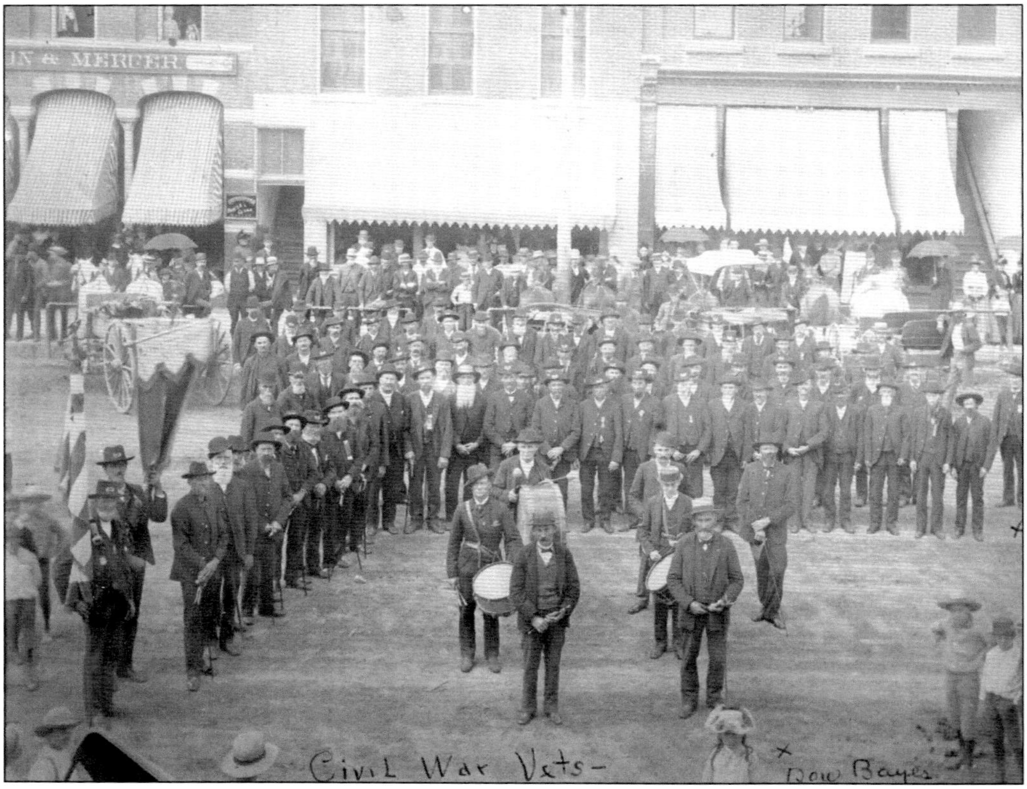

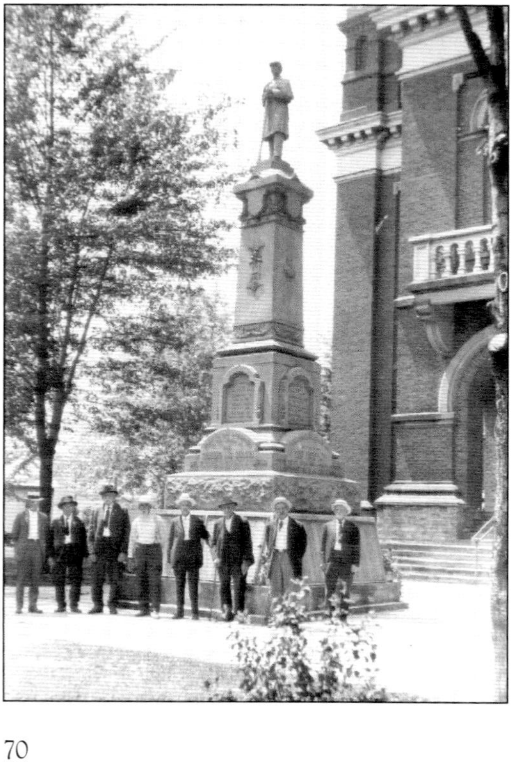

While the county's population at the start of the Civil War was only about 14,000, more than 2,200 men were drawn into the conflict. For years after the war, returning veterans of the Grand Army of the Republic would gather annually to honor those who did not make it back alive. This scene was captured in the late 1890s.

In recognition of their sacrifice and service to the nation, two Civil War monuments have been erected in Wauseon. The earliest was in North Park (briefly called Monumental Park). Later, money was collected to erect the stately statue that stands in front of the courthouse. The monument, which has a comprehensive list of all of the men who participated in the war, was often a focal point for early Memorial Day events.

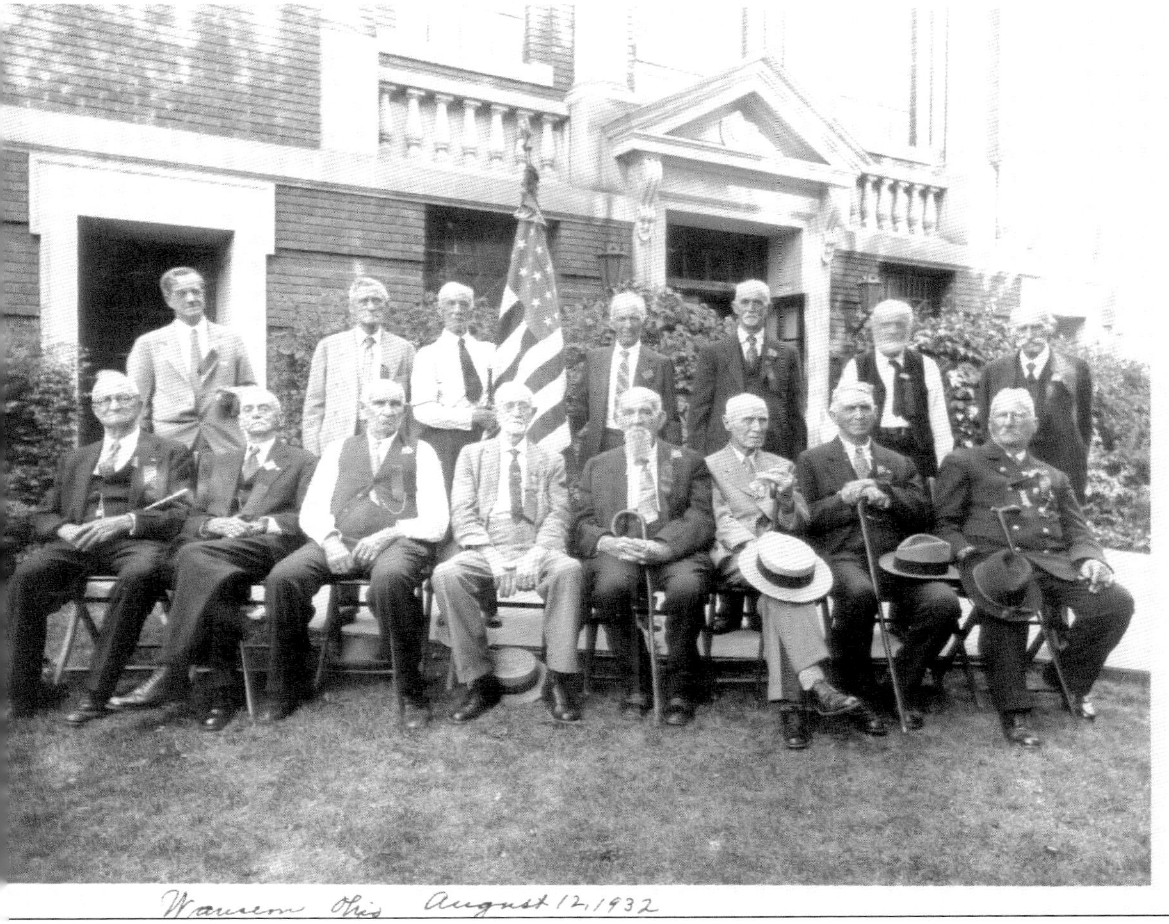

Civil War veterans gather in front of the Clinton Township Memorial Auditorium in August 1932. The auditorium was dedicated in 1925, with a $5,000 gift from the daughter of George Clement, who operated a general store here from 1864 to 1877. The second floor of the structure was a combined auditorium and gymnasium with seating for 1,000. The building has been used for classrooms for school students and as a YMCA. It now serves as one of several senior citizen centers throughout the county.

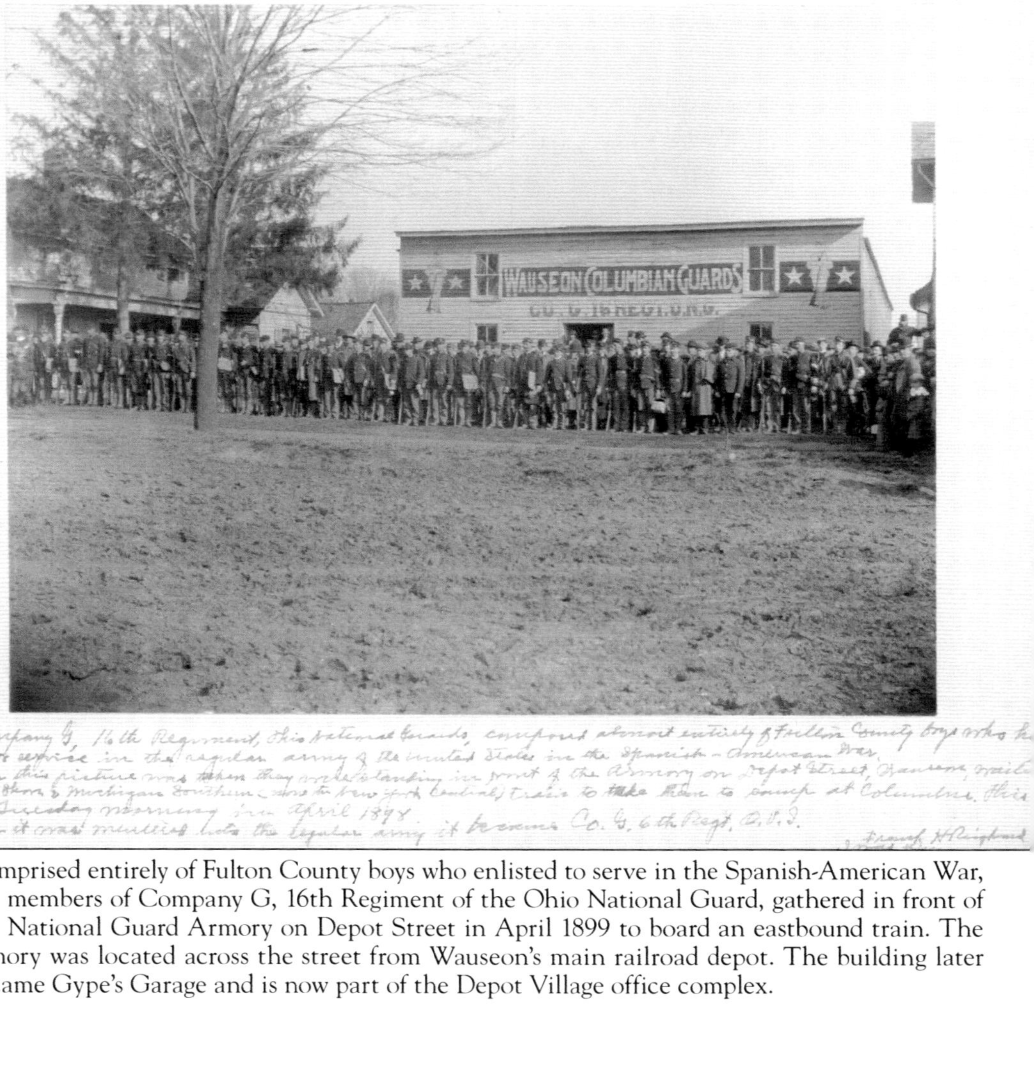

Comprised entirely of Fulton County boys who enlisted to serve in the Spanish-American War, the members of Company G, 16th Regiment of the Ohio National Guard, gathered in front of the National Guard Armory on Depot Street in April 1899 to board an eastbound train. The armory was located across the street from Wauseon's main railroad depot. The building later became Gype's Garage and is now part of the Depot Village office complex.

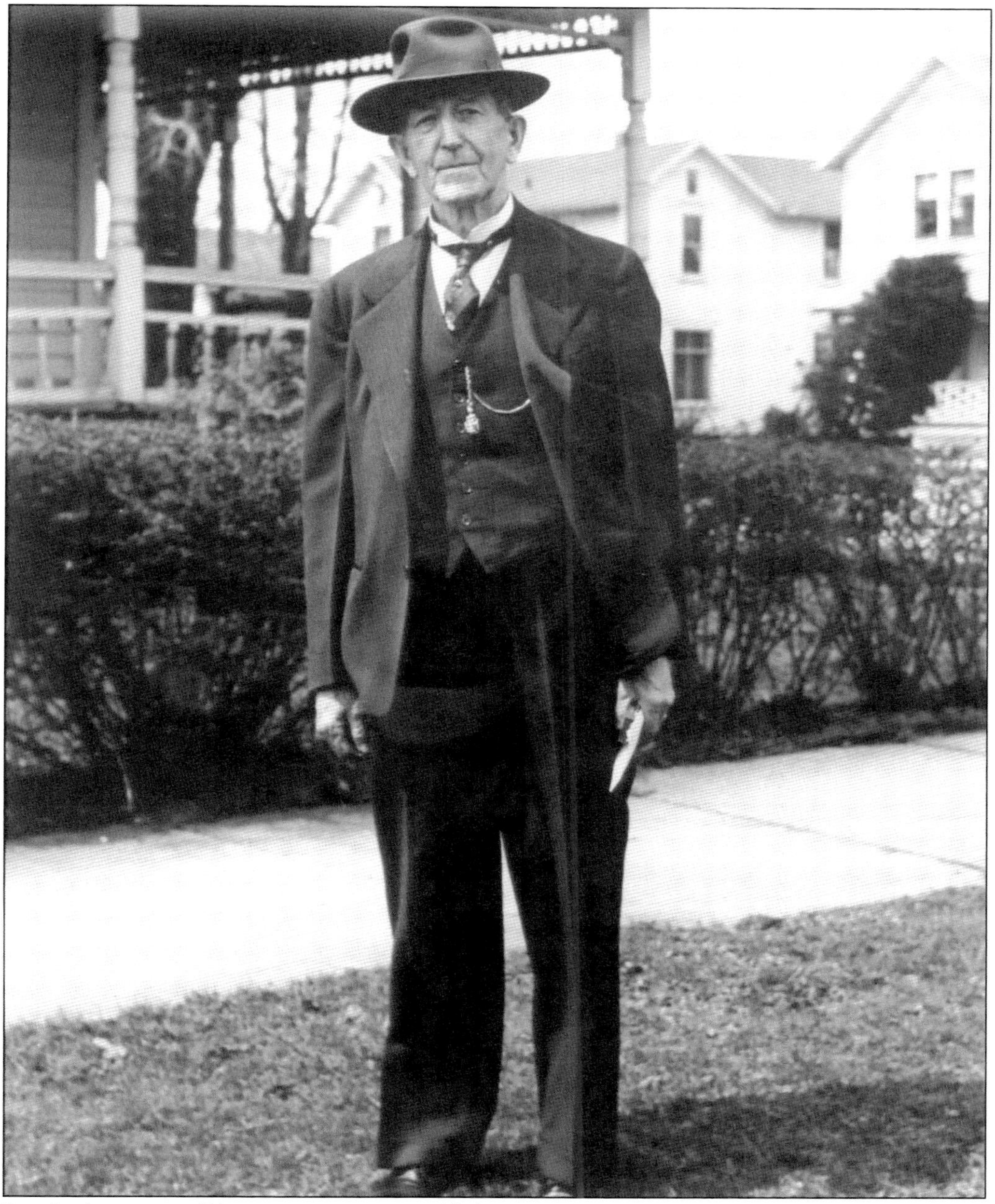

Besides being a well-known newspaper publisher, Frank Reighard also served in several public offices. In the late 1890s, he held the position of county surveyor. In 1910, he entered county politics by running and winning a seat in the state legislature. He served one term before returning to Wauseon to continue running his newspaper. Still later, in the 1920s and early 1930s, Reighard served on the Wauseon school board. He was known for his outspoken opinions on country affairs, including taxation and public spending. In 1938, Reighard, with the financial assistance of the Wauseon homecoming committee, purchased a portion of Shoop Woods, to be used as a new park. He sold his newspaper, the *Wauseon Republican*, in the 1950s, having served as the longest-tenured newspaper editor and publisher in county history.

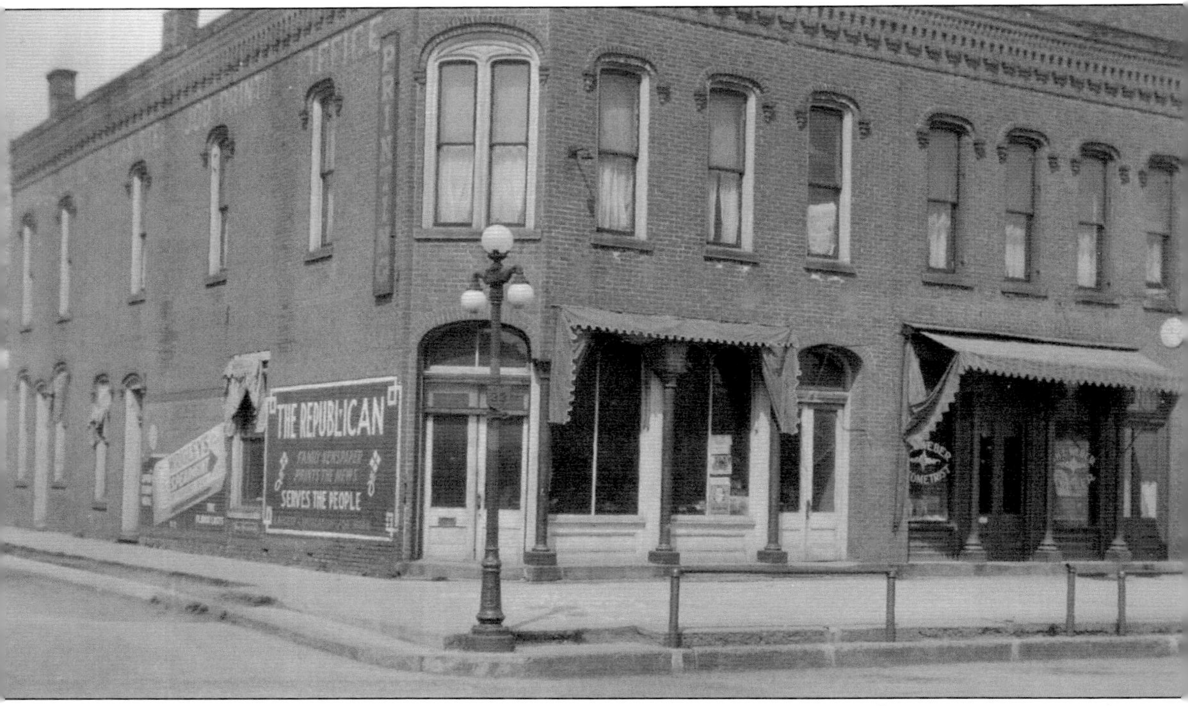

Wauseon has supported several weekly newspapers, including the *Fulton County Union*, the *Northwestern Republican*, the *Wauseon Republican*, and the *Fulton County Expositor*. There was also the short-lived *Fulton County Tribune*. This building was constructed for the *Wauseon Republican* in about 1872 on the site where the village's first church originally stood. The newspaper operated on the second floor, and a saloon was on the first floor. Publisher Frank Reighard was a teetotaler, so he kicked out the bar and rented the space to a tinsmith. Later, the newspaper offices were moved to the ground level. In 1959, the publisher at the time, Gordon Smitley, built an addition on the back, which was initially used for a bookstore. Later, the addition served as a mail department for his newspaper. For several years in the 1960s, the second floor was used as business offices for German Village Noodles. In 1971, Smitley remodeled the outside of the structure. The newspaper vacated the building in 2012, moving its operation to Shoop Avenue. In 2013, the building was purchased by a local investor and is being restored to its original appearance.

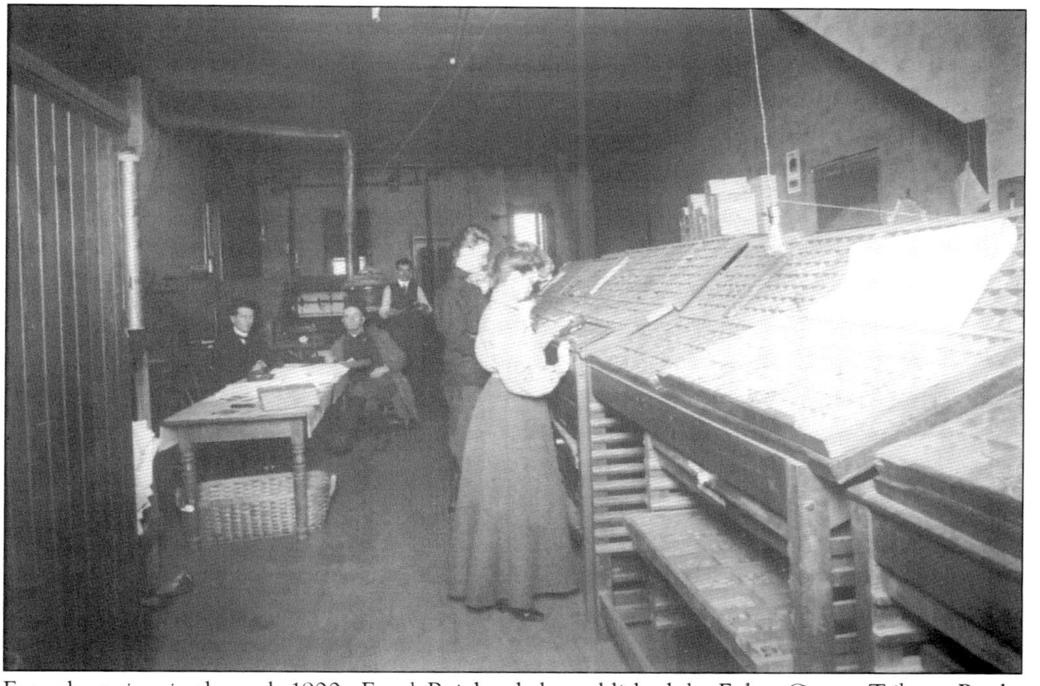

For a short time in the early 1900s, Frank Reighard also published the *Fulton County Tribune*. Banks of type cases were filled with thousands of pieces of wood and lead letters used to handset news copy and advertising. Slanted tops served to lay out the pages, an extremely time-consuming process that usually limited smaller papers to six or eight pages an issue, in order to meet deadlines.

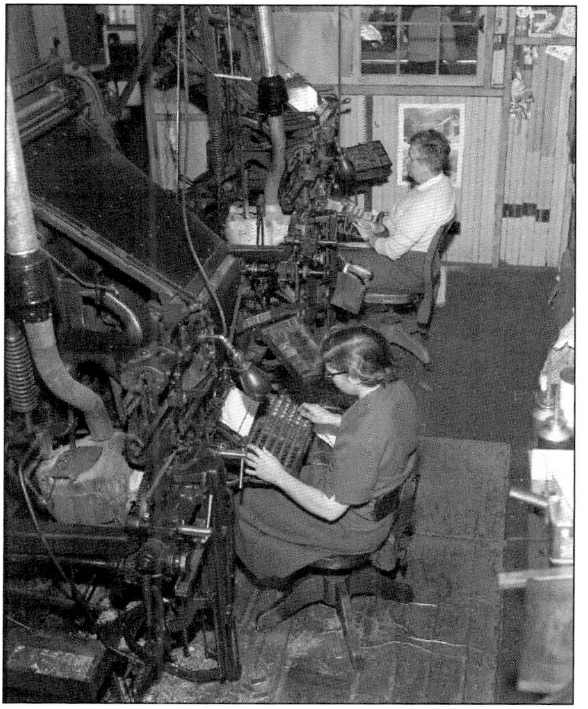

In the early 20th century, newspapers, even small weekly newspapers with limited financial resources, were able to purchase Linotypes. The complex devices used melted lead ingots to form lines of type. They were much faster than setting type by hand and increased the number of pages a paper could produce. Some Linotypes used natural gas—and others, electricity—to melt the lead, which occasionally burned the typesetters with hot metal.

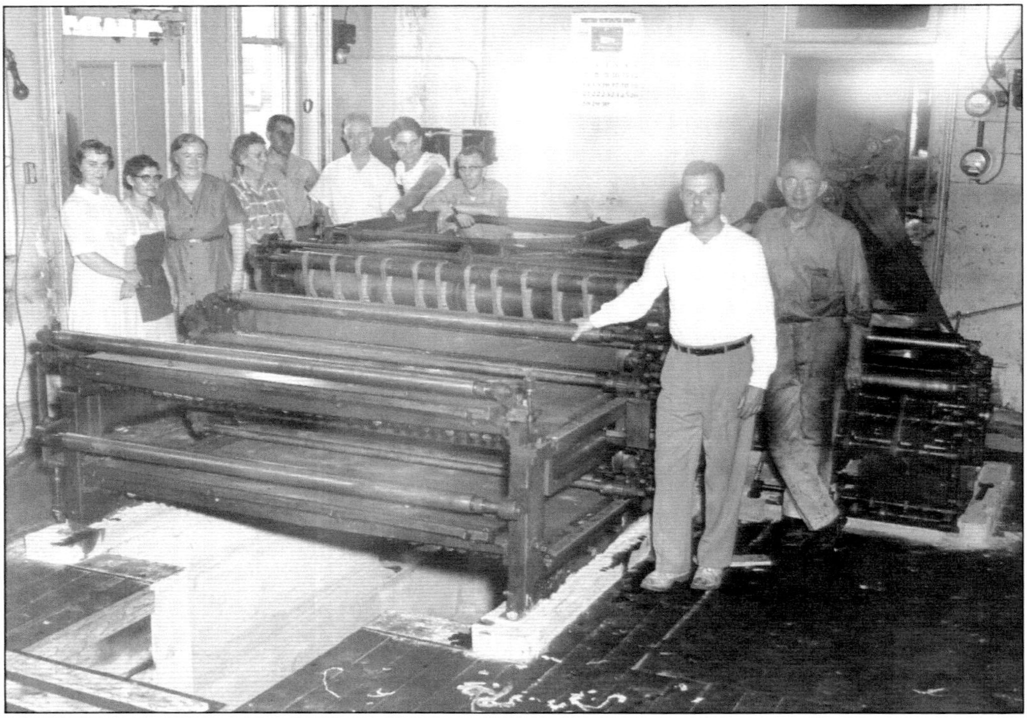

After Reighard's retirement, several new publishers followed in his footsteps. The village's two newspapers, the *Wauseon Republican* and the *Fulton County Expositor*, merged in 1959, with Gordon Smitley and Jim Fernanberg as publishers. Printing was moved from its offices several doors down the block to Mustang Printing. The slow and cumbersome sheet-fed press, shown here, was replaced with a high-speed web press. Photograph-based typesetters replaced the Linotype typesetting machines.

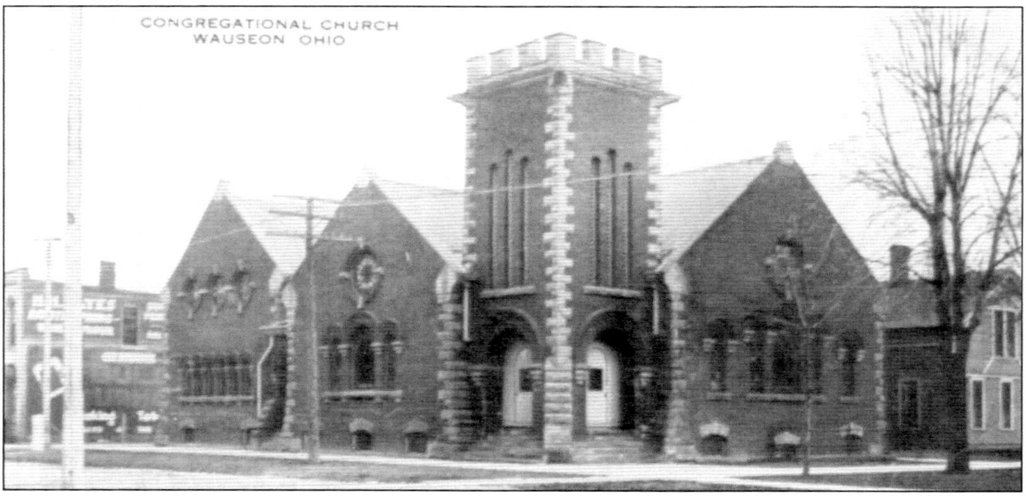

The First Congregational Church was organized in 1861. It began with 12 charter members. In 1863, their first house of worship was built on South Fulton Street. The cornerstone of their second building, located on Elm Street, was laid in February 1904. The stained-glass window, entitled *Christ Knocking on the Door*, is a memorial to Col. Dresden Howard. (Courtesy of Carol Krieger.)

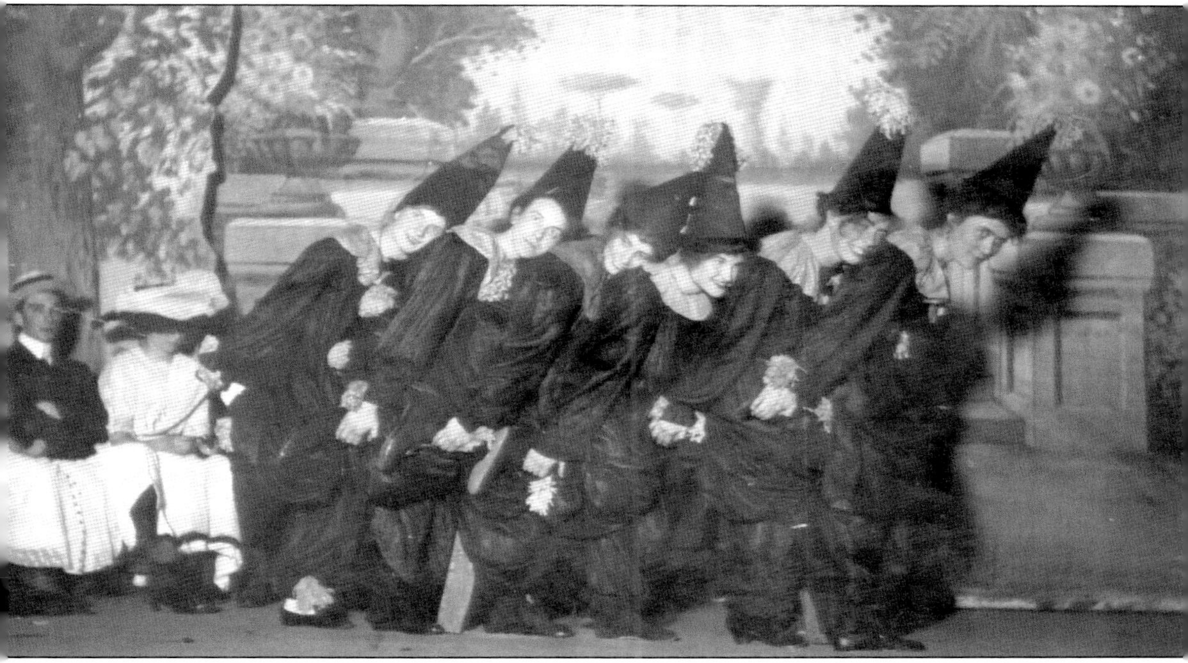

High schools were often austere buildings offering classrooms and a small library. For school plays, graduation ceremonies, and other activities, Wauseon schools relied on private buildings, such as Scott's Opera House. This scene, taken from an 1882 play, was captured by an early Wauseon photographer on the stage at the opera house.

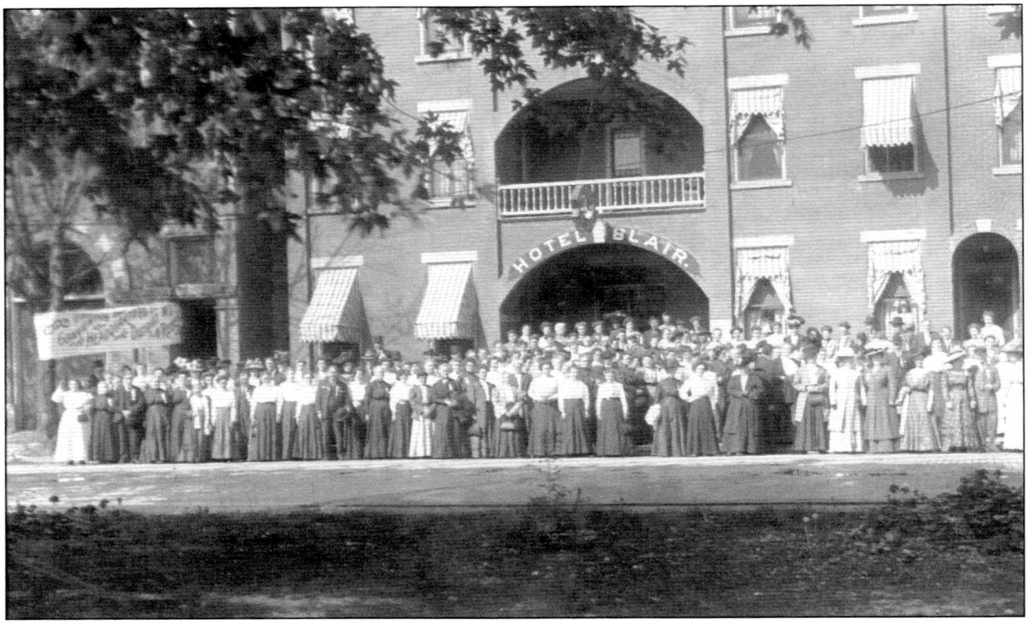

The Hotel Blair provided a large capacity room for conferences and banquets. The hotel served as convention headquarters for the large gathering of women above around 1900. The three-story building operated under several names, including the Avery Inn. The postcard below shows the front of the building, which was remodeled to include a sheltered portico entrance and second-floor porch, where guests could sit to watch the arrival of trains at the depot across the street.

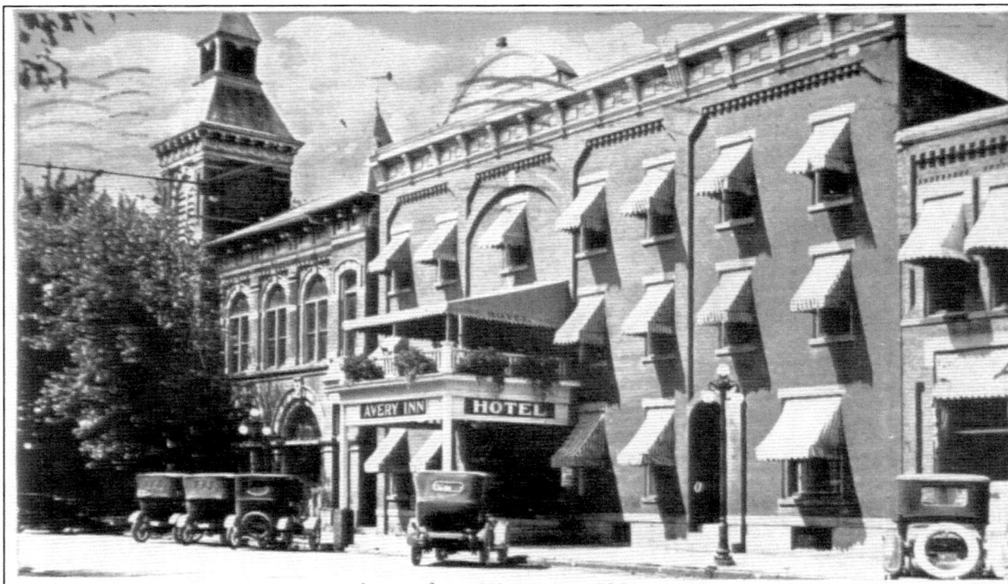

Avery Inn, Wauseon, Ohio

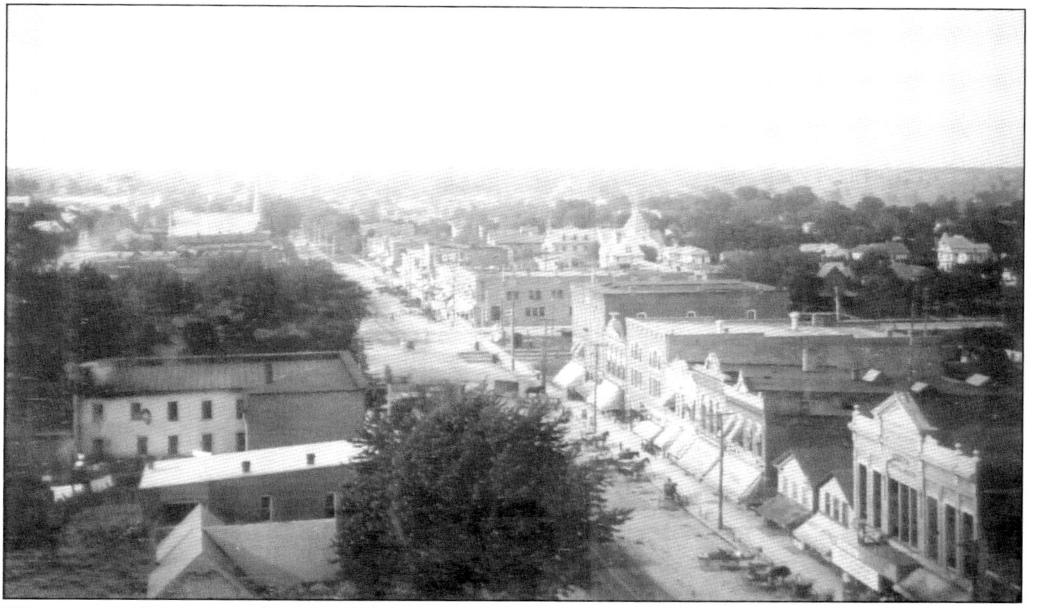

This wonderful postcard view of the community looks north from downtown. This was taken in about 1905 from a popular photography platform, the courthouse clock tower, just prior to automobiles making their appearance in the village. Horses, buggies, and wagons still dominate the street. Early electrical poles are beginning to make their appearance, as some of the businesses and homes were beginning to convert from kerosene and acetylene gas. (Courtesy of Carol Krieger.)

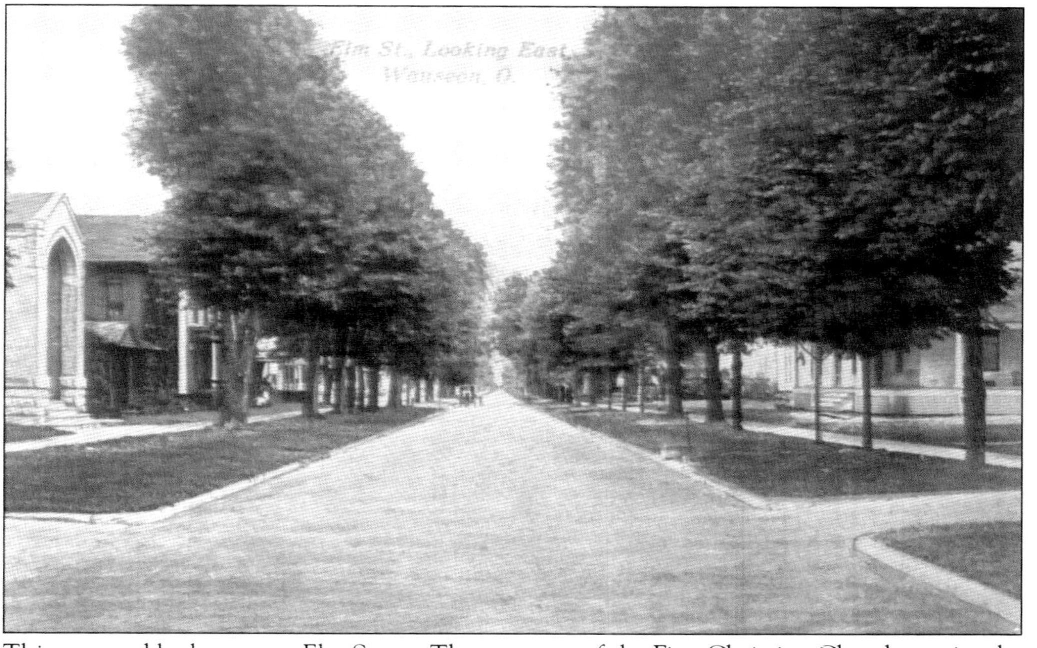

This postcard looks east on Elm Street. The entrance of the First Christian Church can just be seen on the left, and farther down the street, a horse-drawn carriage approaches. Curbs, first made from sandstone, were beginning to be placed along the streets, although it is not clear from this 1905 photograph whether the street had been paved yet.

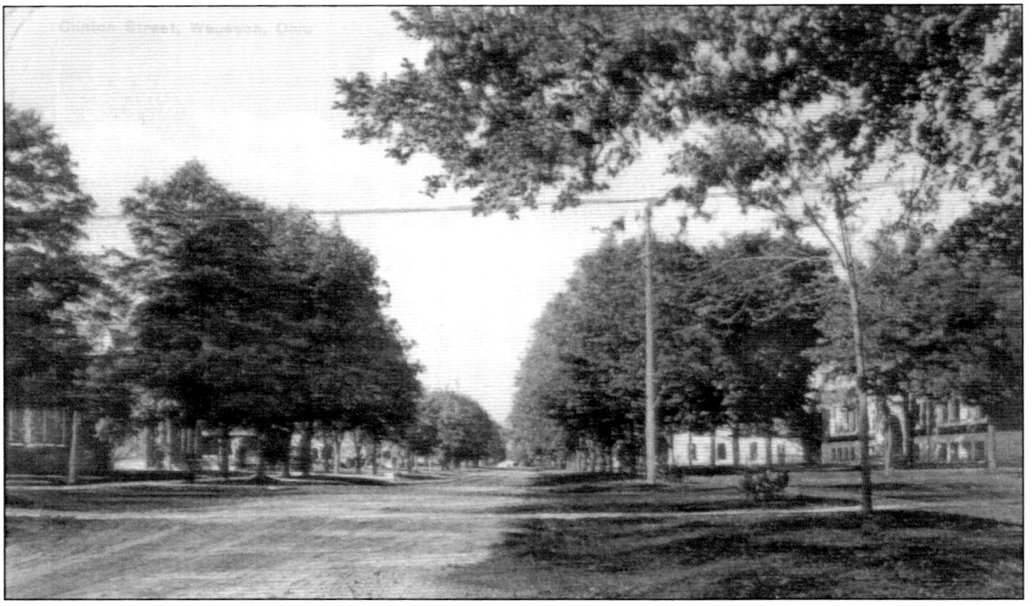

This view of Clinton Street looks northward around 1905. On the right is the entrance to the high school, situated on the corner of Elm Street. Crossing overhead are electrical lines from the generating plant on Brunell Street. (Courtesy of Carol Krieger.)

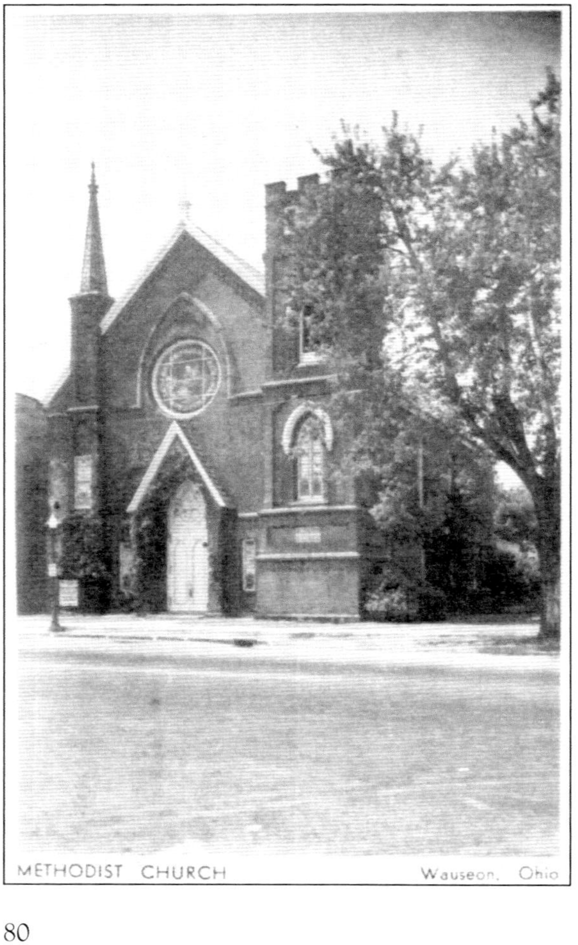

Christ United Methodist Church was the first church established in the community. The first house of worship was a wooden structure on the northwest corner of North Fulton and Elm Streets, next to the first school building. Its present sanctuary, several doors to the north, was built in 1874 and remodeled and expanded in the 1950s and again in the early 1970s. The church features a large pipe organ, installed in 1915. (Courtesy of Carol Krieger.)

Blaisdell Kull offered studio settings for local family and high school graduation photographs during the 1950s and 1960s. His South Fulton Street studio contained thousands of negatives accumulated from years behind the camera. Kull, a perfectionist, once spent an entire week trying to photograph a local man in a way he deemed suitable for the newspaper, but the gleam from the subject's head prevented him from producing anything he would acknowledge as being his work.

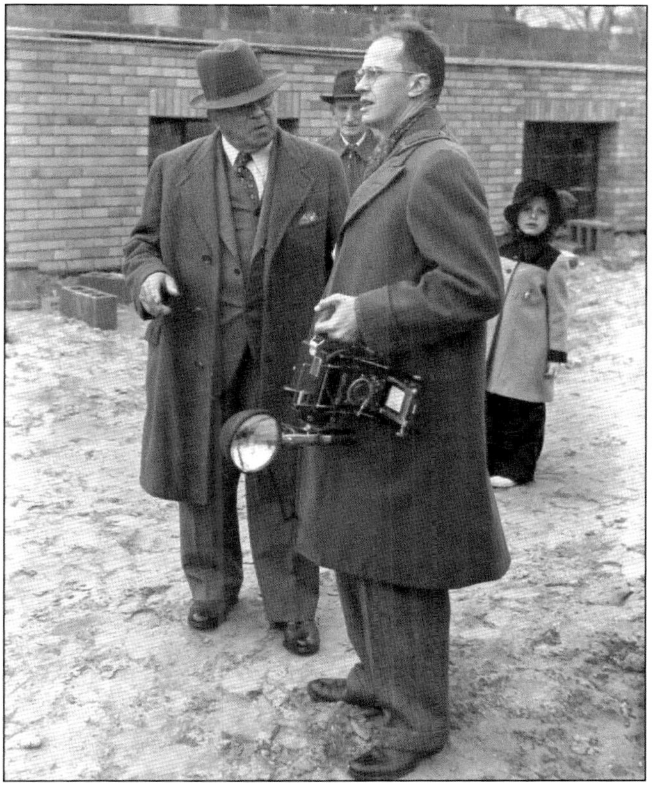

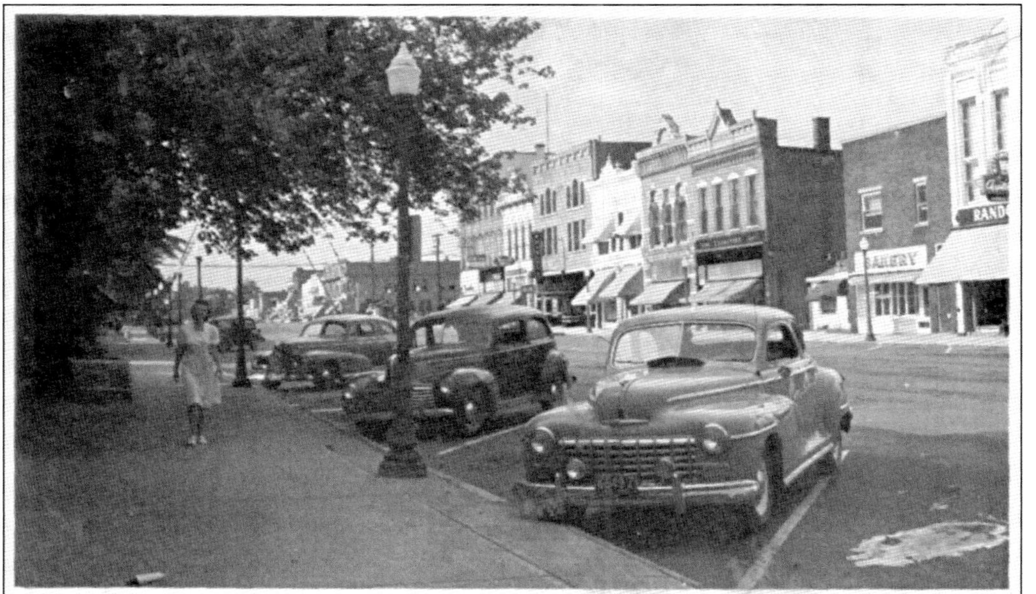

VIEW OF BUSINESS SECTION Wauseon, Ohio

This postcard shows Fulton Street, south of the railroad tracks, in 1959. The Princess Theater was located on the east side, down the block from the former Scott's Opera House. By this time, the large, two-story building had been converted into Randolph's Furniture.

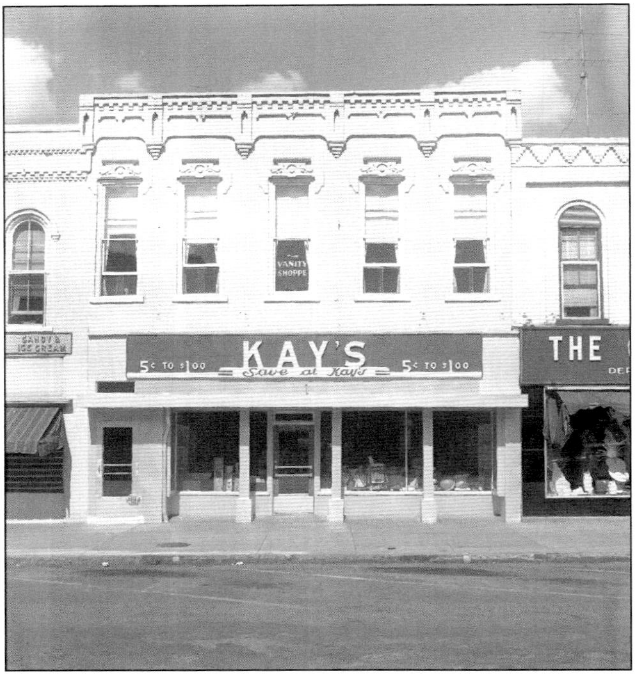

In the 1950s, Kay's offered merchandise ranging in price from 5¢ to $1. It was located next to Kolb & Son, a variety store with a popular soda fountain where folks gathered after watching movies across the street at the Chief Theater. On the second floor was the V5op.

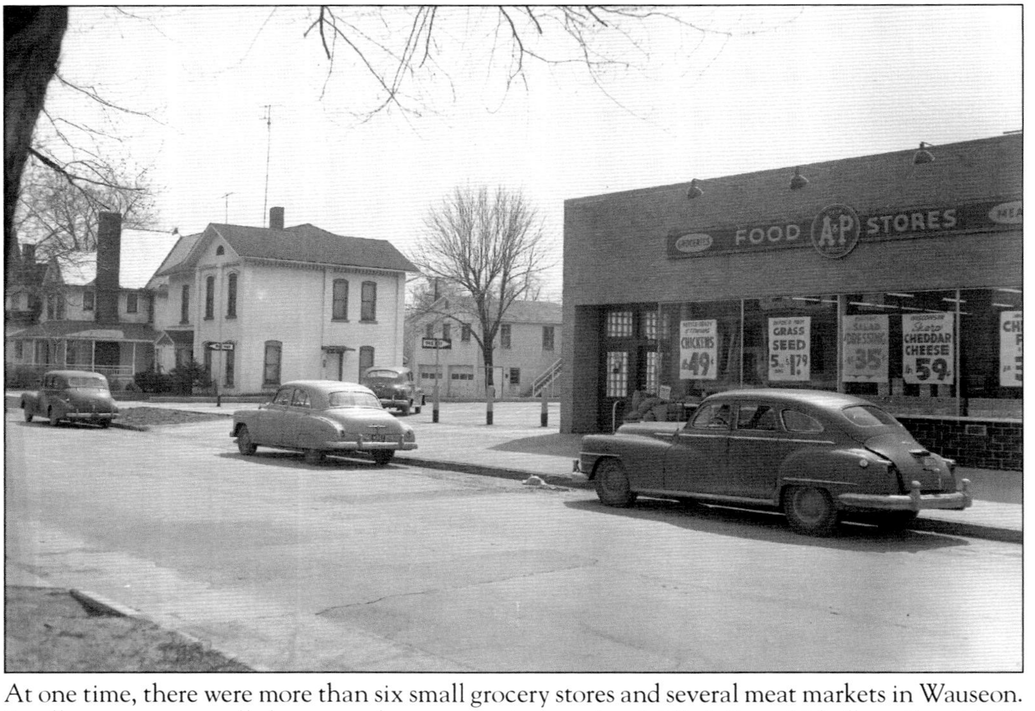

At one time, there were more than six small grocery stores and several meat markets in Wauseon. Smaller stores eventually lost out to larger operations, such as Miller's Super-Valu (later Bernicke's), the A&P, Chief Grocery, and eventually, Wal-Mart. The A&P was located on Elm Street, east of the post office. Today, the building is used by the Fulton County Health Center for physical rehabilitation.

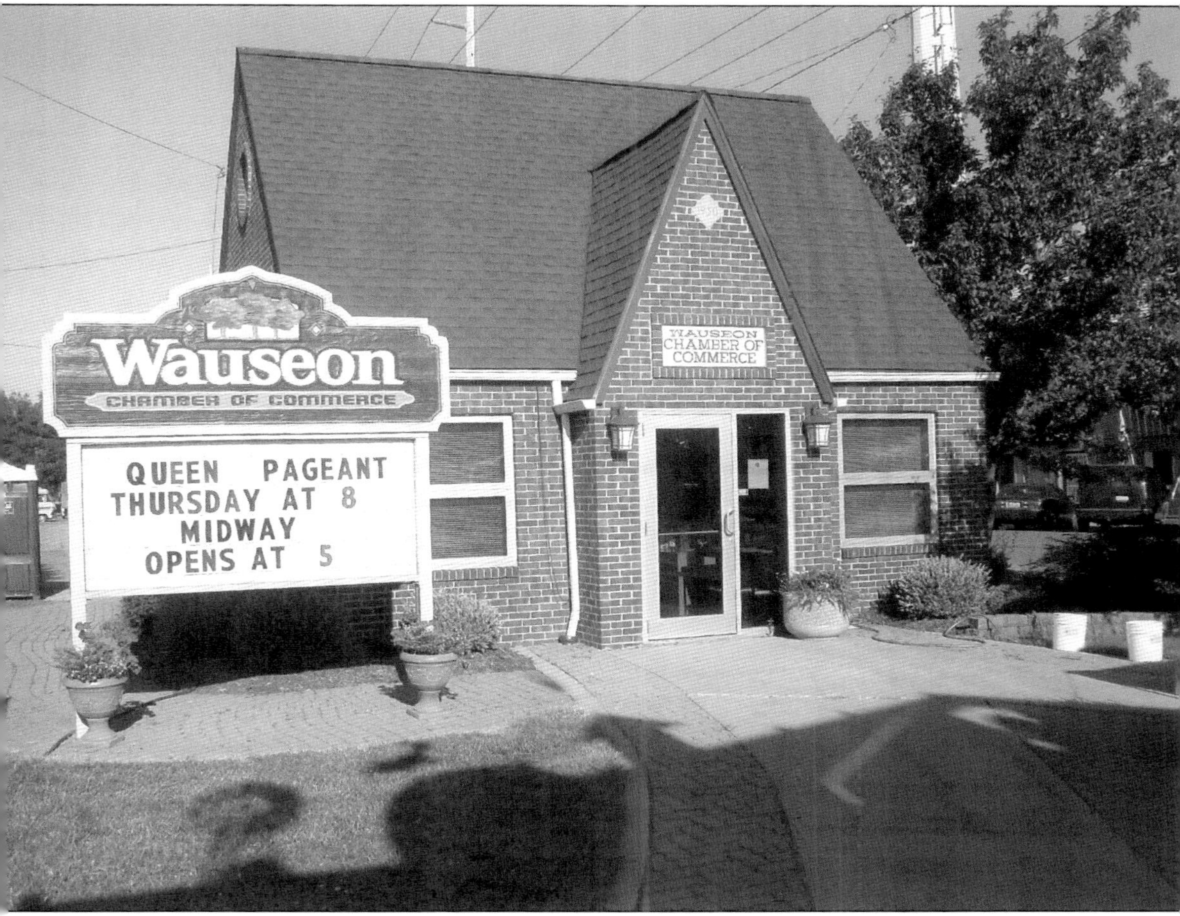

In the late 1920s, merchants began looking for a way to assist the hundreds of people who came to town, some whom needed to use restrooms while shopping. The business leaders collected funds and built a public restroom, which was completed in 1930. In 1956, the Wauseon Chamber of Commerce was founded, and the restrooms were converted into an office and visitor's center for the organization. (Courtesy of Mish Arlo.)

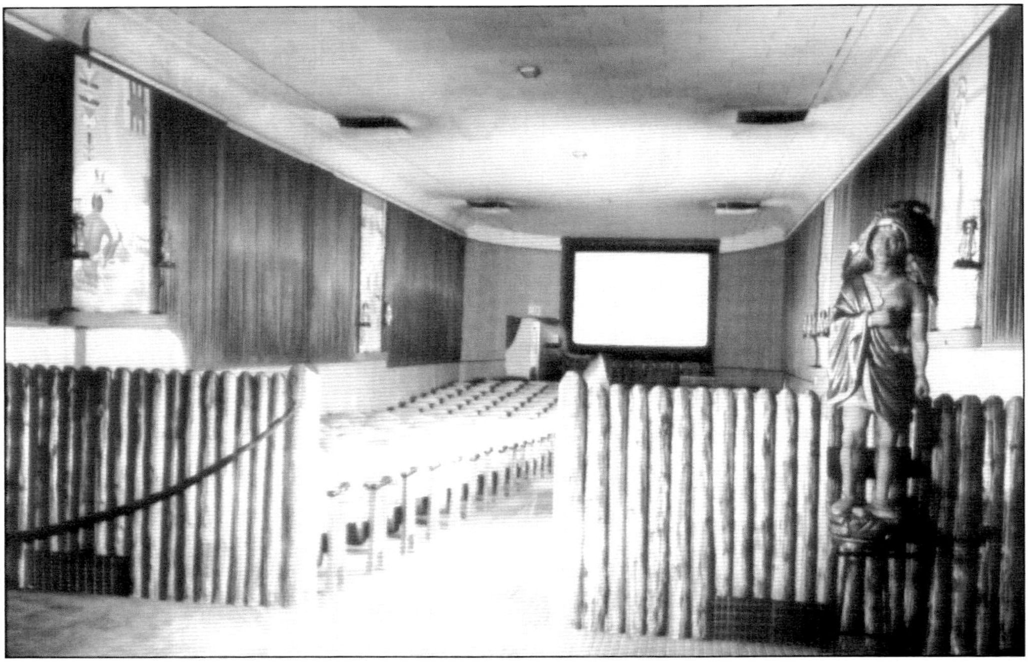

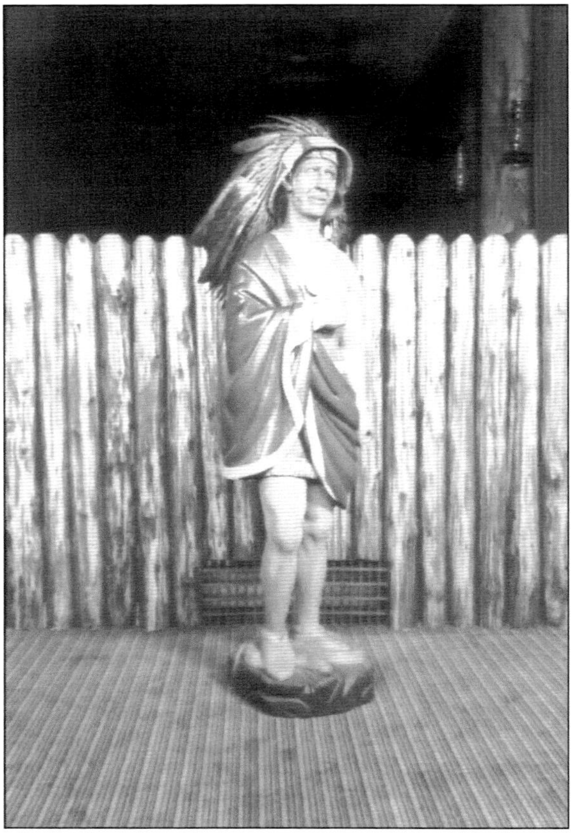

The Chief Theater, the larger of the village's two movie theaters, closed its doors in the 1960s. The Chief offered viewers comfortable seating. One of the movies featured in 1938, as reported in the *Wauseon Republican*, was *Boys' Town*, with Mickey Rooney and Spencer Tracy.

For years, a carved statue purportedly resembling Chief Wauseon greeted and guarded moviegoers to the Chief Theater. After the theater closed, the statue disappeared from public view until the late 1990s, when it was sold at an auction held near Cleveland.

In 1966, a fire broke out in Hammontree's Appliance, threatening to destroy an entire block. Many of the buildings in the downtown area were physically connected by common walls and wide-open attic spaces. The intense flames required the assistance of five fire departments, which saved adjoining buildings. The appliance store, however, was completely destroyed and had to be rebuilt. (Courtesy of the Wauseon Fire Department.)

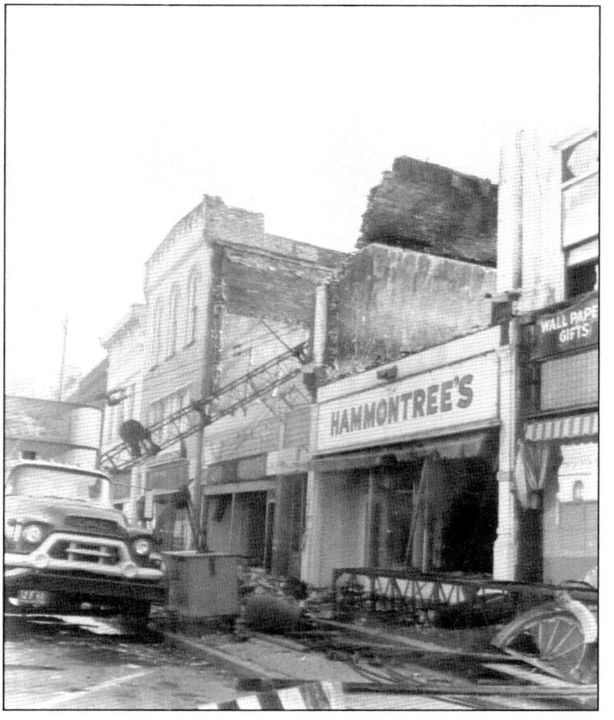

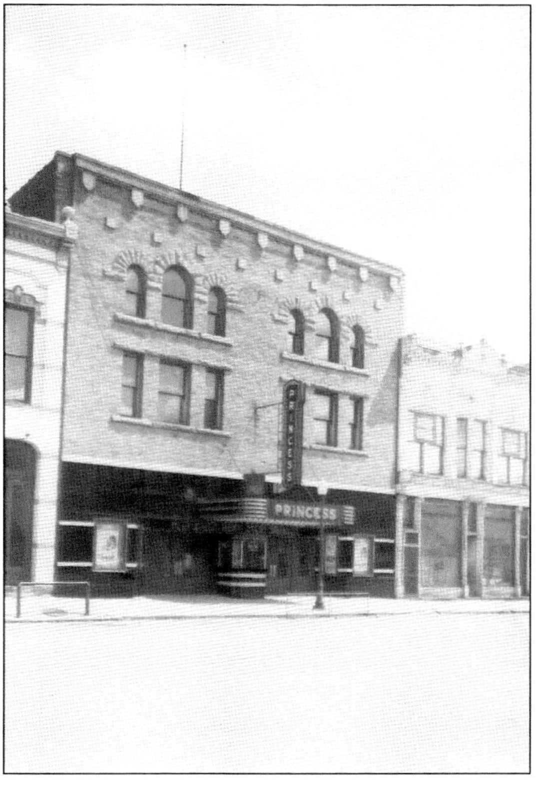

The Princess Theater was on the south side of the tracks. The lobby leading to its silver screen was about 10 feet wide and 20 feet long. A glass-block wall separated it from the seating area. After the theater closed, the building was remodeled and served for many years in a different capacity. First, it was Osborne Pharmacy. Later, it became Yoder Pharmacy. It closed several years ago, and the building now houses a gun shop.

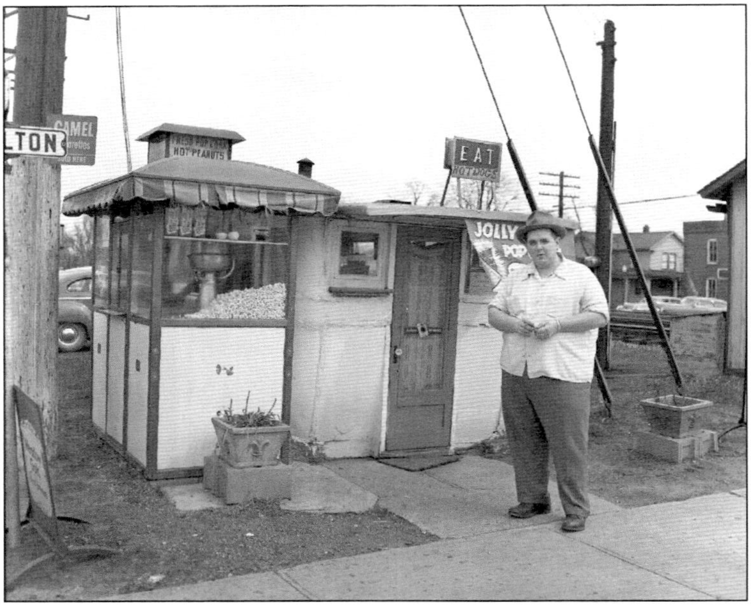

Shirley Chenoweth operated a street-side booth for many years, seen here around 1959. It was adjacent to the tracks on South Fulton Street. Customers remember purchasing, among many things, popcorn and hotdogs from the street vendor. Because the booth did not have a water supply, Chenoweth used the public restrooms (now the Wauseon Chamber of Commerce office) for water to boil his hotdogs.

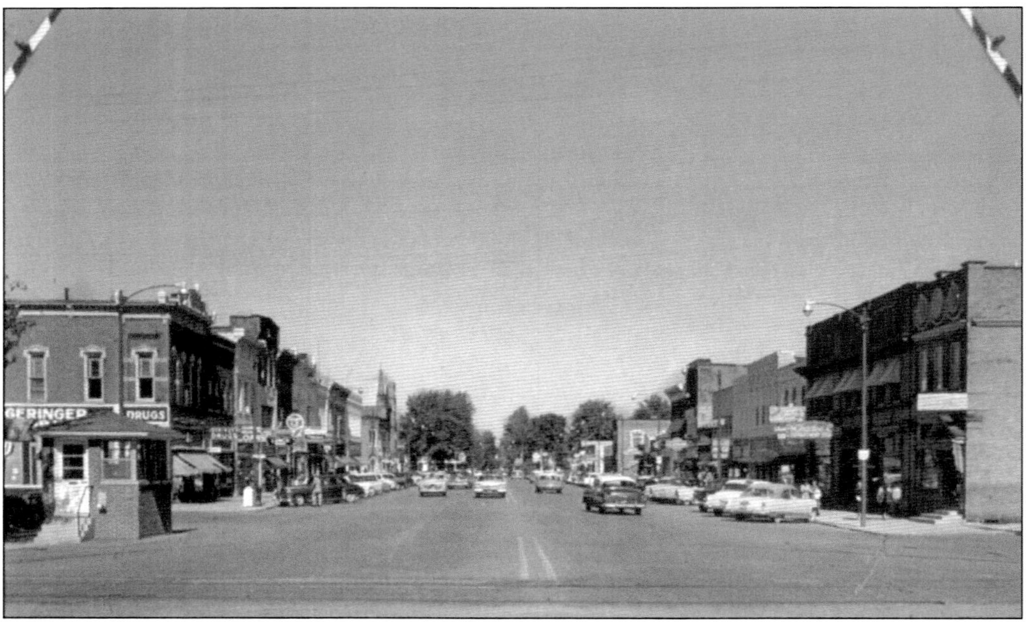

Wauseon is the uncontested center of commerce in Fulton County. The downtown was a beehive of activity until retailers abandoned it, relocating to Shoop Avenue. Adjacent to the railroad track in this 1955 view stands a small tower housing the village's police department. It served as a shelter and office for police on location, who likely helped raise and lower the railroad crossing gates on Fulton Street.

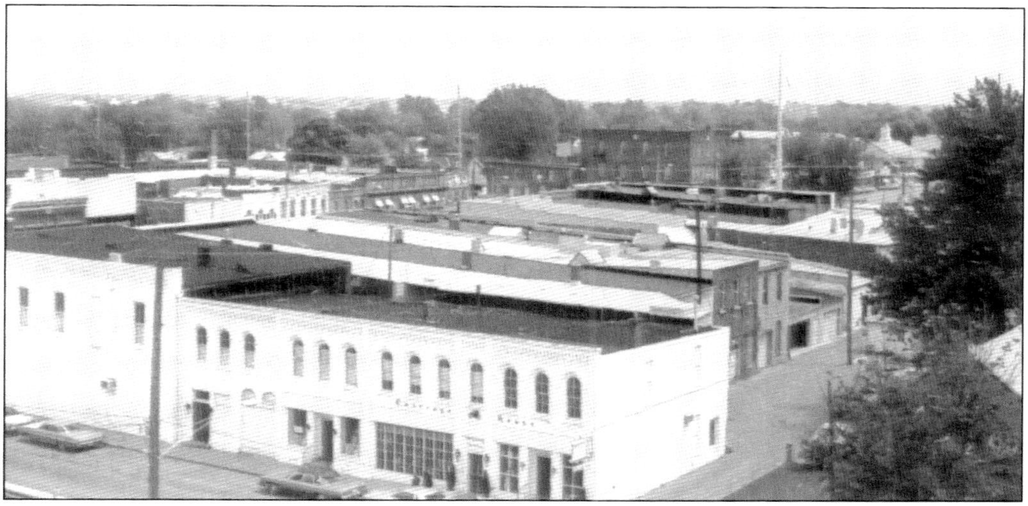

The Carriage House was on East Elm Street. This photograph was taken from the top of the extended Wauseon Fire Department's aerial ladder in the early 1990s. Many retail businesses operated within the structure during its 100-year history. These included Waldeck's, a popular five-and-dime department store; a Christian bookstore; an early video rental outlet; a computer repair shop; and the Coachlight Room (a women's clothing store). The building was demolished following a devastating downtown fire in April 2007.

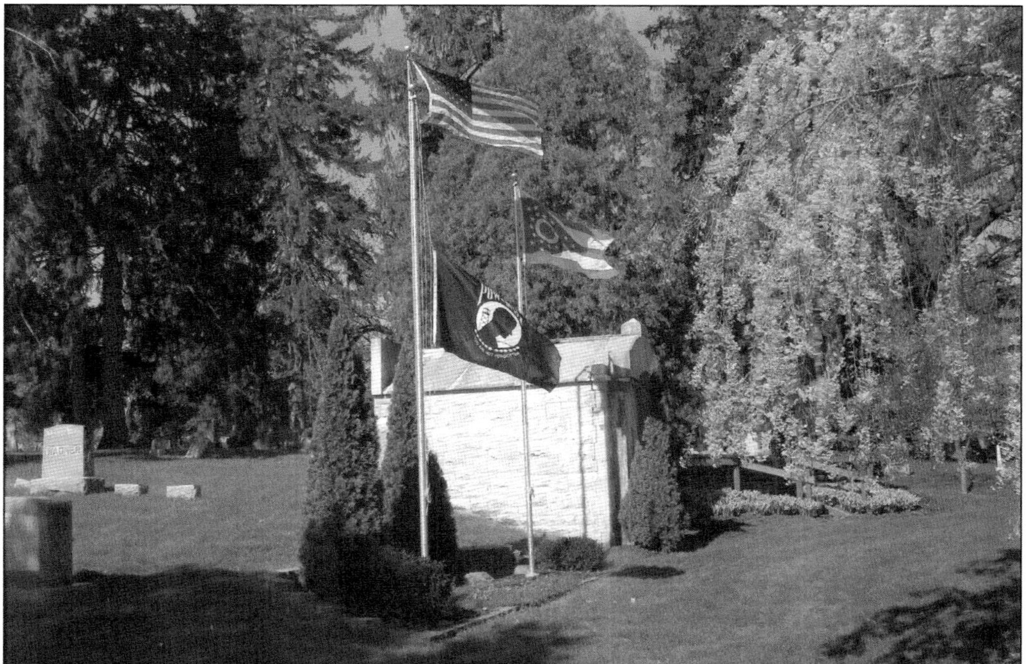

Wauseon Union Cemetery was established in 1862, following Nathaniel Leggett's death. His grave is located at the highest point in the cemetery, which is operated jointly by the City of Wauseon and Clinton Township. The mausoleum is no longer used, but it was originally built to store caskets during winter months. (Photograph by the author.)

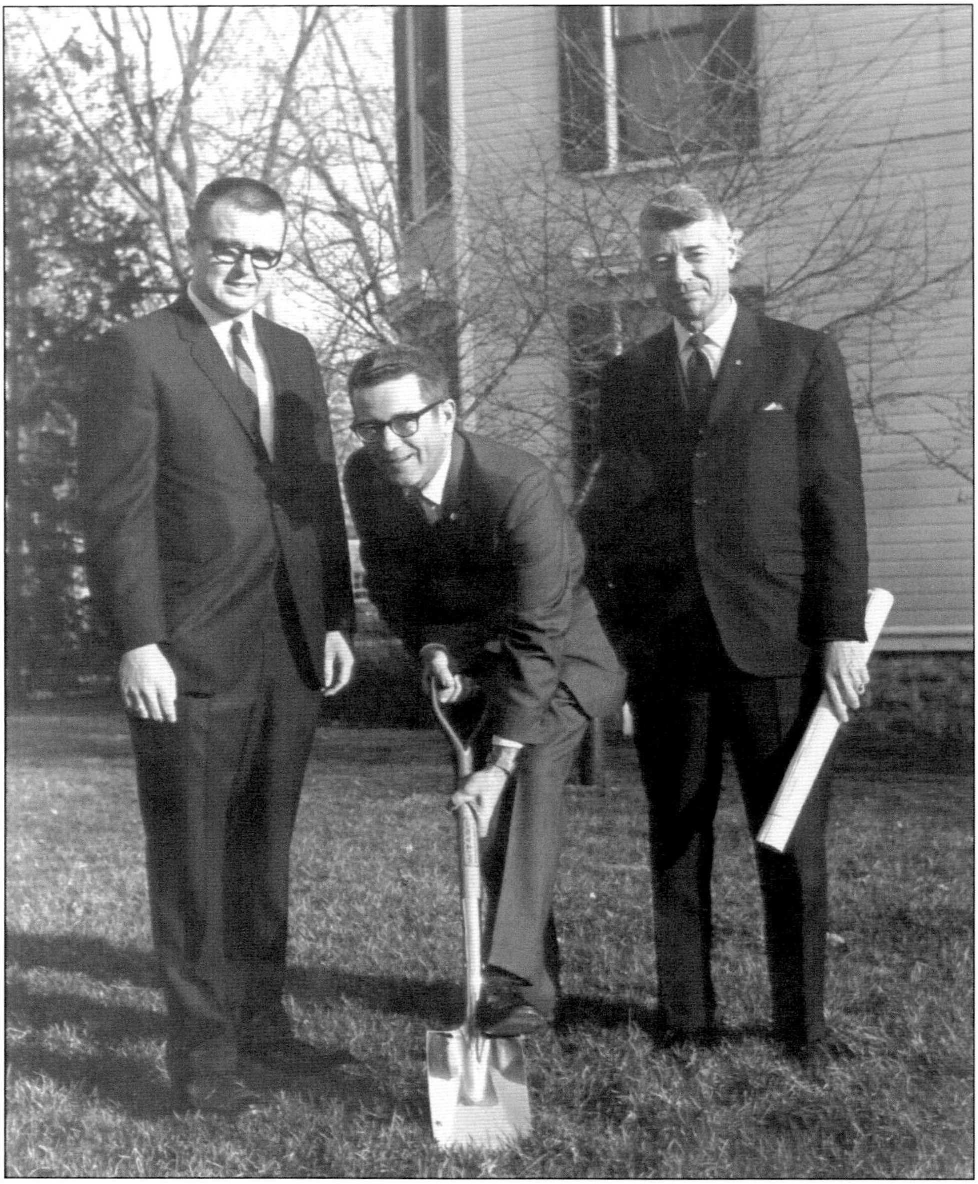

Freemasons have always been an active group in Wauseon and remain so today. Wauseon Lodge No. 349 of the Masons was chartered in 1864. The first meetings were held in an unfurnished room over Springer's Dry Goods. Annual dues in 1880 were $2, and the lodge had 143 members. They built a third-floor meeting room in the building on the corner of Fulton and Birch Streets. Their logo can still be seen on the north and west sides of the structure. In June 1874, about 3,500 area Masons and their families attended the grand opening, traveling here by rail, wagon, and horseback. As time passed, more of the most prominent men joined the fraternal order. By 1969, the Masons needed a larger building—at that time, the lodge was located on a third floor, making it difficult for older members to access the meeting rooms via two long stairways. Land was acquired on the corner of Clinton and Elm Streets, and a ground breaking took place there on April 11, 1969.

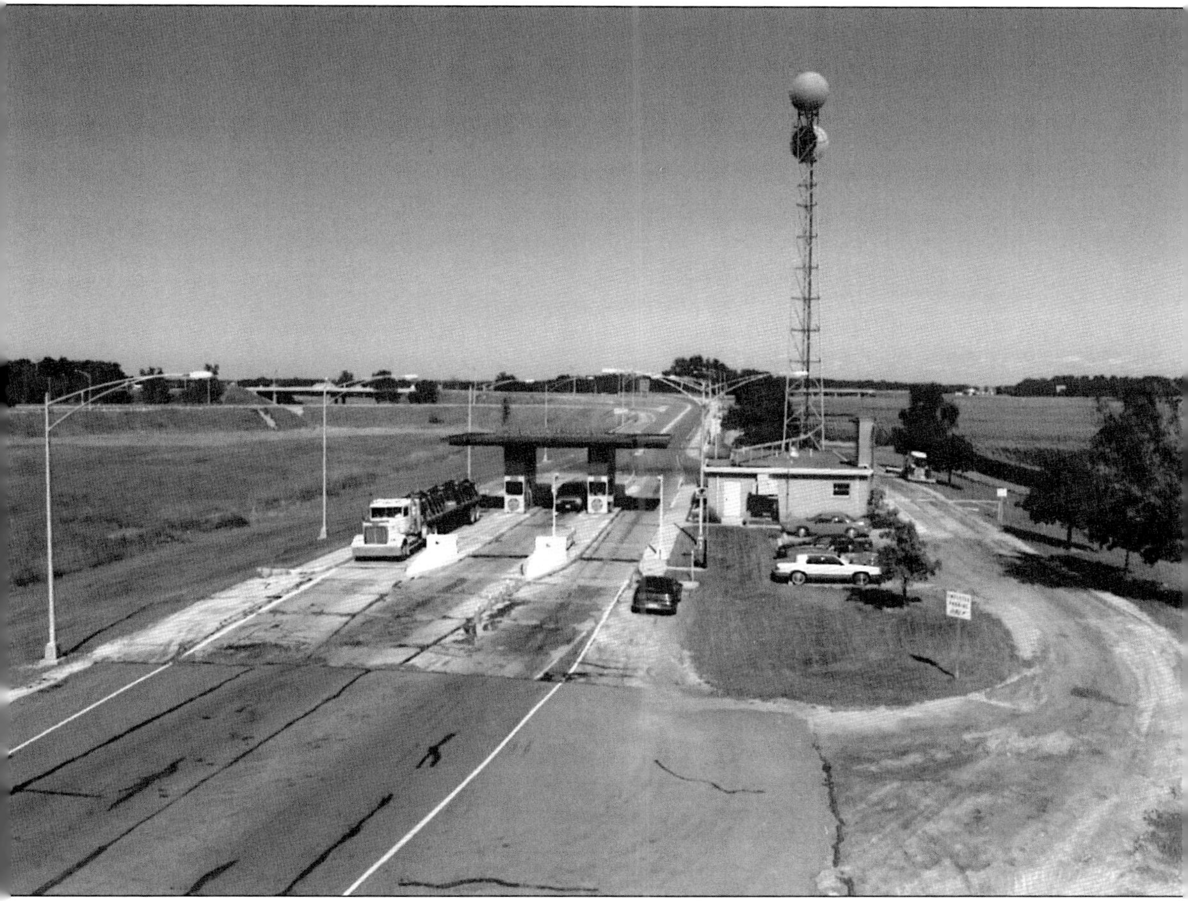

Construction of the Ohio Turnpike was completed in 1955. It created a new access point for Wauseon and provided many local construction jobs. It gave the community's industry easy access to major markets, including Chicago, Detroit, and Cleveland. There were initially only 18 access points, including Exit 3, several miles north of town. (Courtesy of Joseph Horwath.)

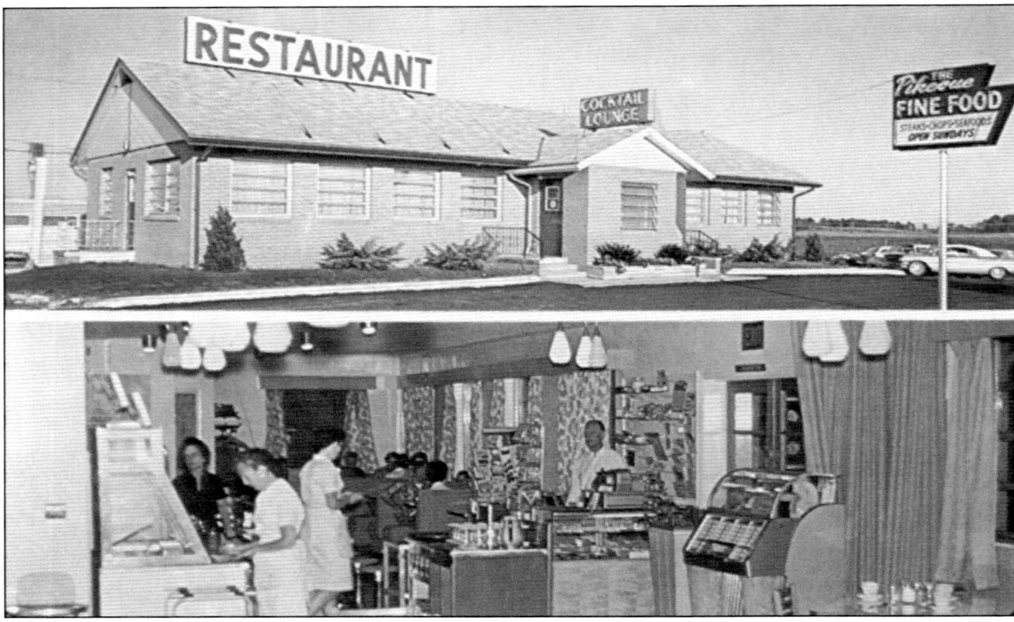

Shortly after the completion of the turnpike, construction began on several motels and a restaurant. This restaurant, one of the oldest still operating in Fulton County, was first known as the Pikeque Restaurant and Cocktail Lounge. Later, it became Smith's Restaurant, which was managed by Al Kruez and, later, his son Mike. In 2013, the restaurant was remodeled and changed its name to Kruezers & Smith's Catering. (Courtesy of Hal and Jayne Bailey.)

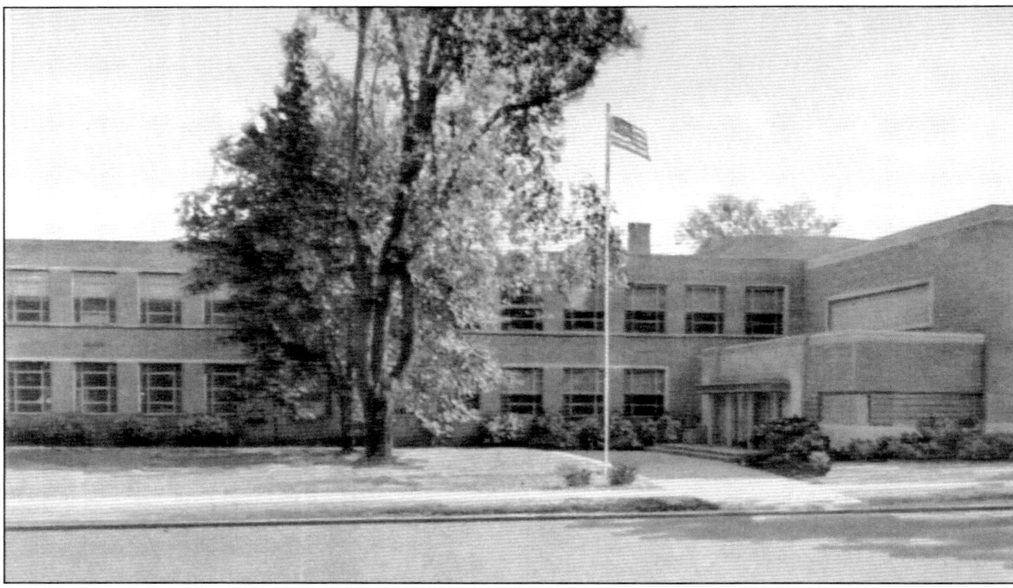

In 1943, local men serving overseas were shocked to read in letters from home that their beloved high school had been destroyed by fire. Although never proven, many suspected the fire was intentional, because an attempt was made the next week to burn the Memorial Auditorium. In 1946, a new high school, seen here, was dedicated. Less than 14 years later, fire would again strike the school district. (Courtesy of Carol Krieger.)

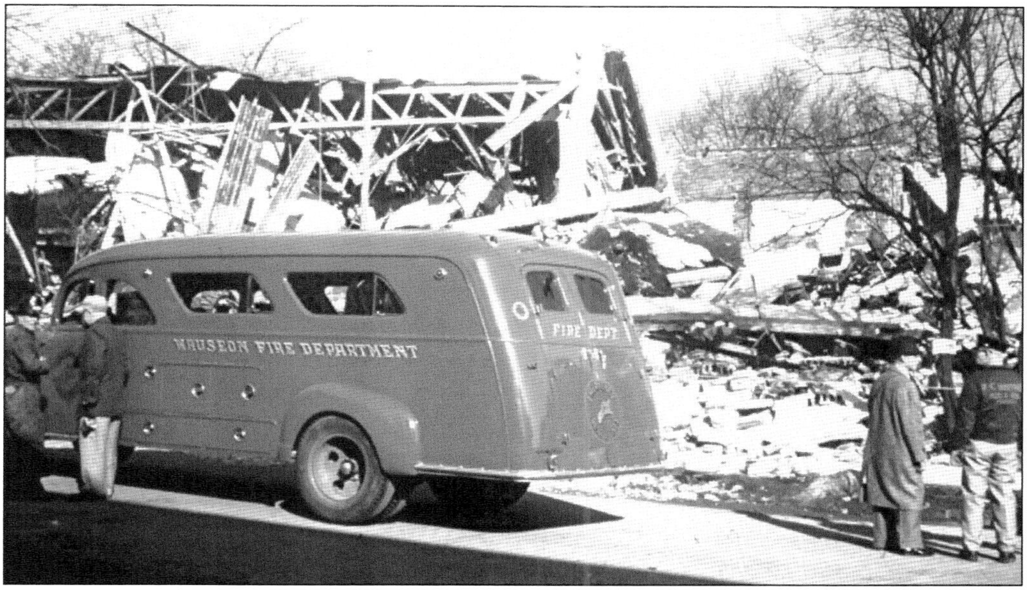

In 1958, the school district opened its third high school building on the corner of Parkview and Glenwood Streets. The Clinton Street building became a junior high school. On Saturday, March 19, 1960, an explosion rocked the school. A gas leak is suspected to have been the source of the explosion, which destroyed the school's gym and adjoining classrooms. Amazingly, no one was seriously injured. (Courtesy of the Wauseon Fire Department.)

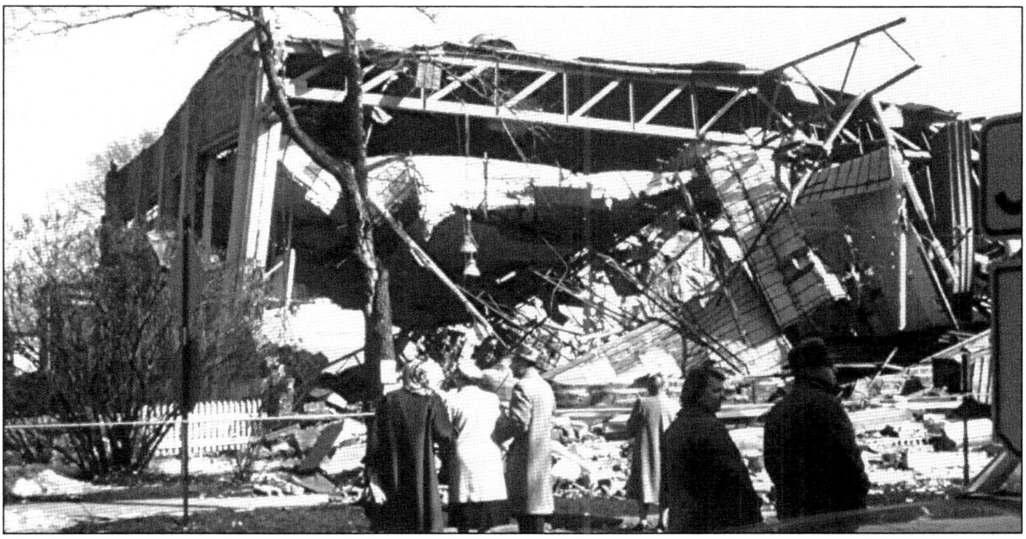

The *Fulton County Expositor* and the *Wauseon Republican* reported that the day after the explosion, thousands people traveled to Wauseon from as far away as Indiana and Michigan to view the destruction. The two newspapers wrote that streets throughout the village were congested with lines of cars of sightseers. School students were forced to attend classes in churches and at Memorial Hall until a new junior high school was completed on Burr Road. While many believe a natural gas line leak resulted in the explosion, no blame was ever laid. However, the Ohio Gas Company made a voluntary $200,000 donation to aid in construction of the new junior high school. (Courtesy of the Wauseon Fire Department.)

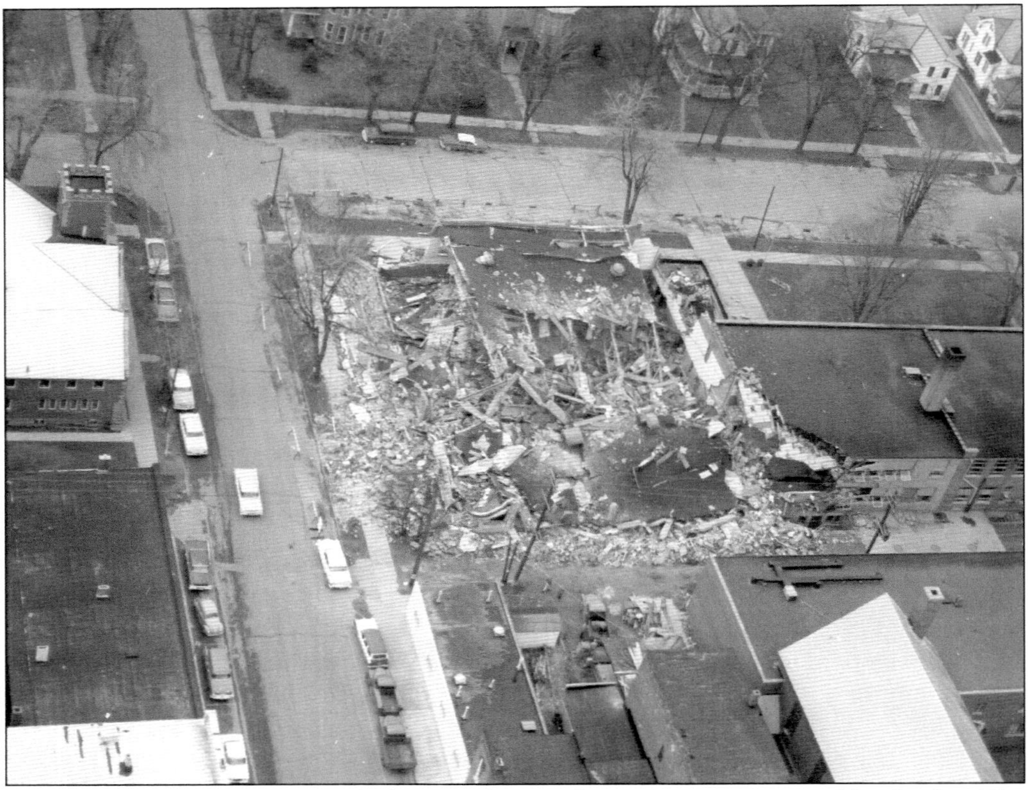

Above is a rare aerial photograph showing the significant destruction caused by the fire. The story made national headlines. Television stations from Toledo and Fort Wayne, Indiana, rushed crews to the scene with film cameras (live transmissions were not possible in that era). Only part of the school, including the gymnasium, as seen below, was destroyed. Fortunately, although several men, including the school system's superintendent, William Pees, were in the building investigating the leak when it exploded, they were virtually unharmed. The explosion was so violent that surrounding buildings suffered broken windows and cracked plaster. Some residents thought an earthquake had occurred, while others thought a bomb had exploded. (Both, courtesy of the Wauseon Fire Department.)

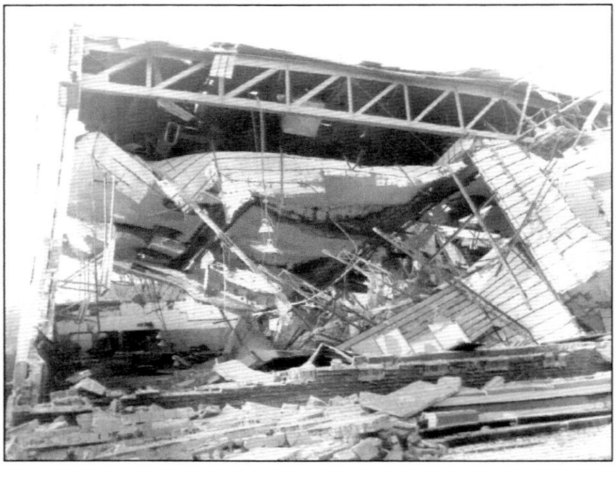

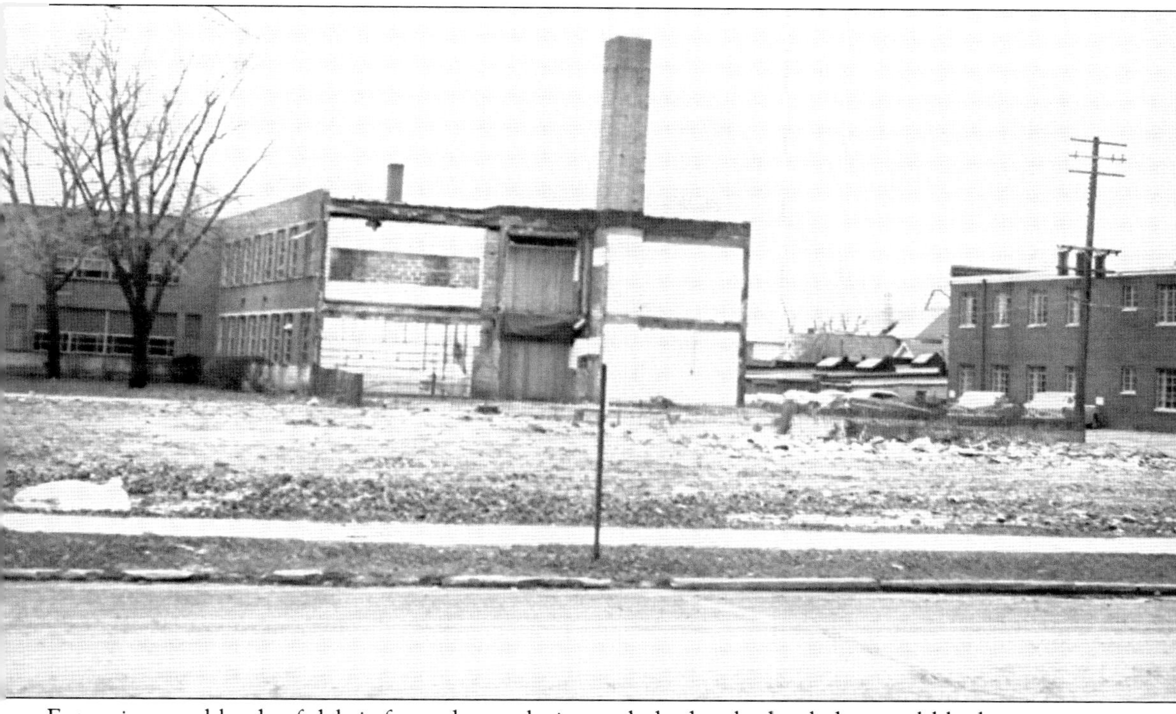

Extensive truckloads of debris from the explosion only had to be hauled several blocks away. The village used the waste as fill-in for a pond and rat-infested area near the railroad tracks on Brunell Street. Part of the school area eventually became a parking lot for the city. The rear of the United Methodist Church can be seen on the right.

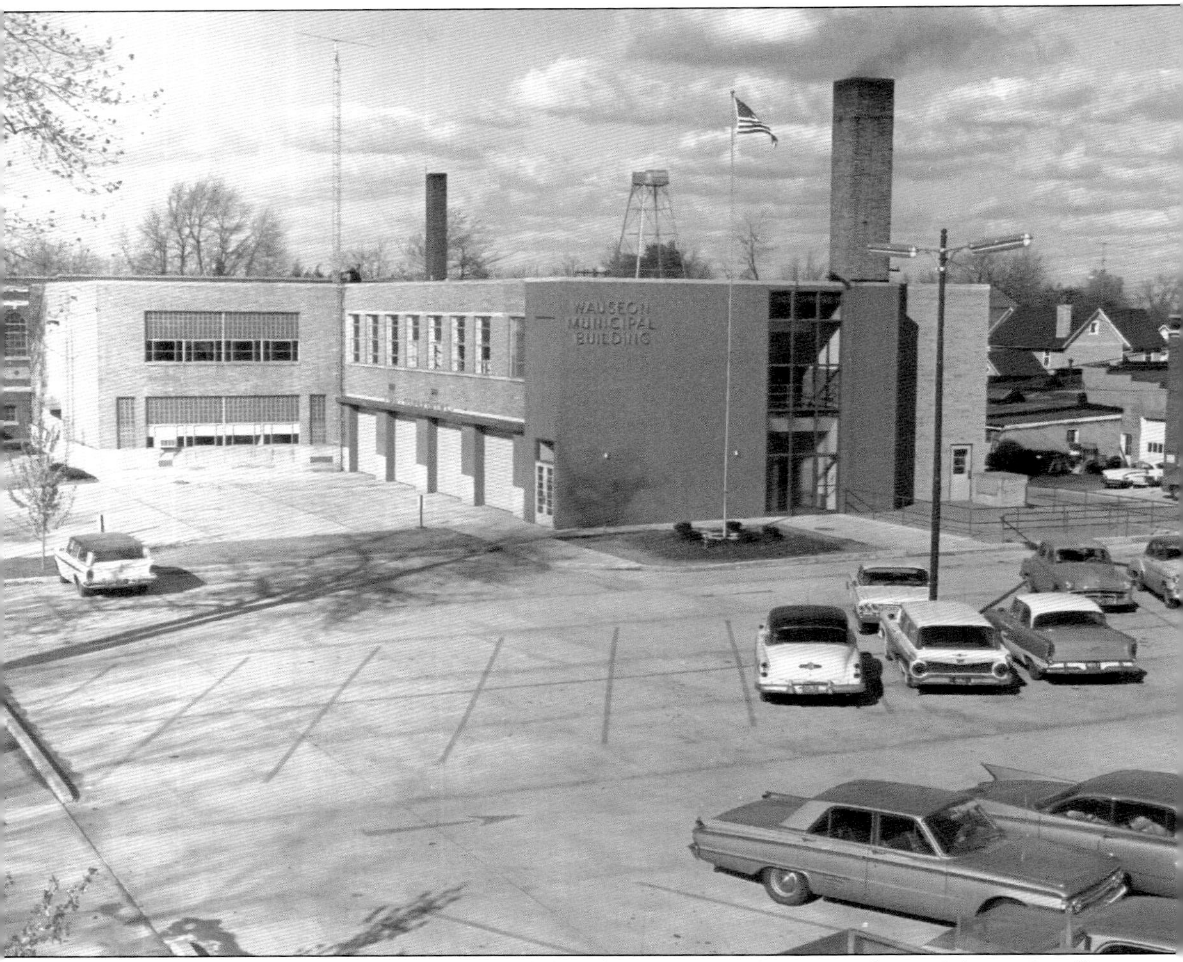

The village council purchased what was left of the structure, salvaging and remodeling it for offices, a second-floor community room, and police and fire departments. A new municipal parking lot encouraged business owners and their employees to park off the street and provided additional parking for two neighboring churches during Sunday morning services.

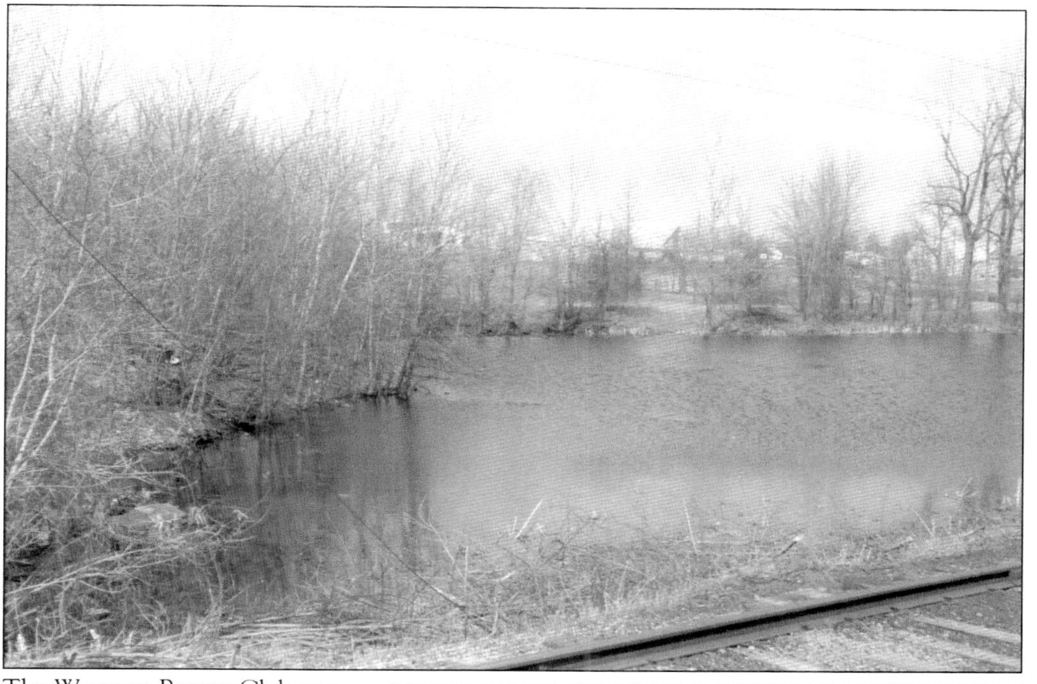

The Wauseon Rotary Club was started in 1962. It has a long history of leading crusades to improve the city's extensive park system. The organization's first major project was the development of Rotary Park in 1971. Located along the Wabash Railroad was an old pond, often referred by locals as the Old Frog Pond, or the "mosquito-infested swamp." When Wauseon was a fledgling community, the pond was used to collect ice for the hot summer months. An icehouse stood along the shoreline. In later years, it became a site for dumping trash, until the club purchased the property, drained the pond (right), cleaned up the trash, restored the pond, and built a shelter house. Once completed, the park was donated to the community. Over the years, the club, which meets weekly in the shelter house, has maintained and improved the park. (Both, courtesy of the Wauseon Rotary Club.)

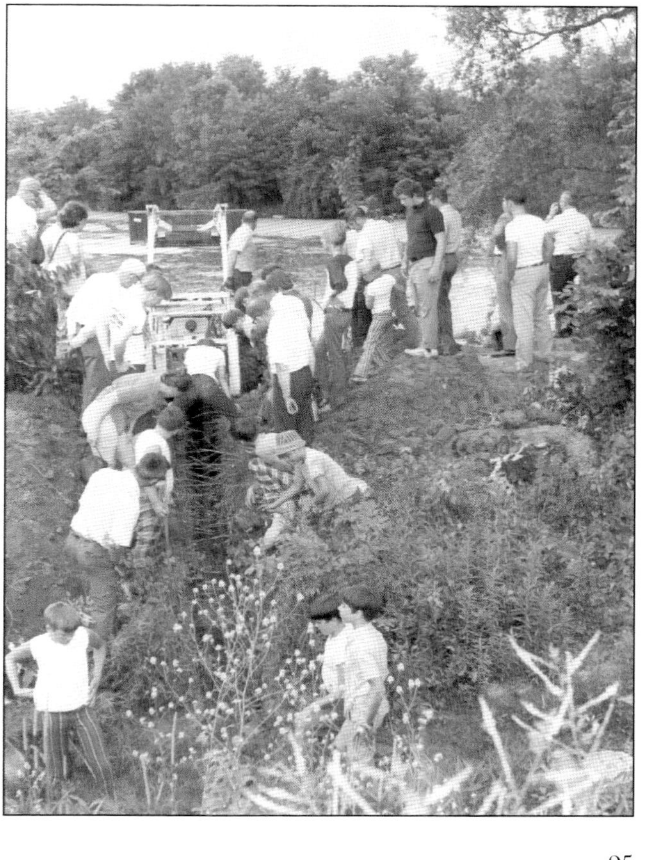

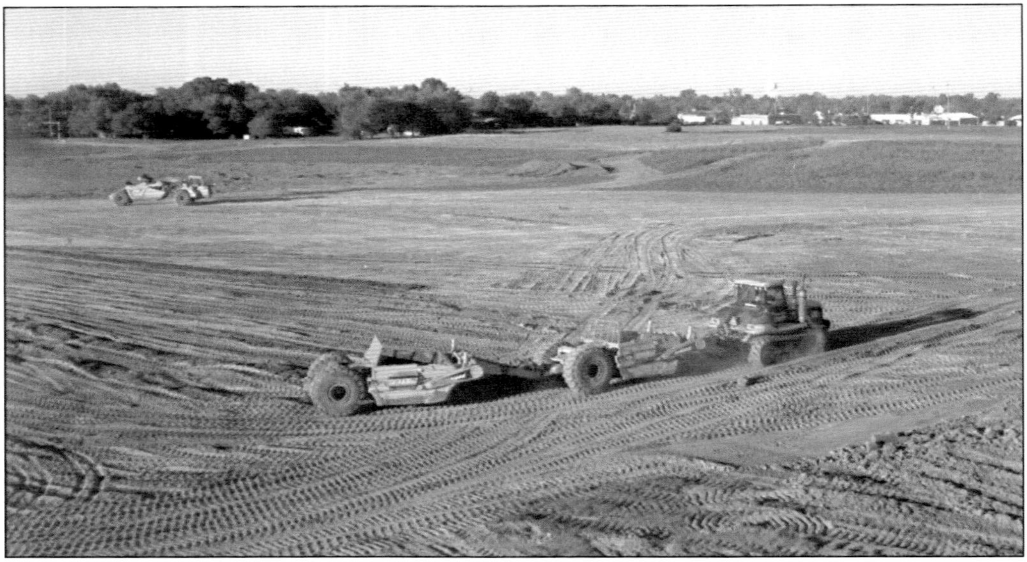

The Wauseon Rotary Club's latest project has been the years-long development of a 78-acre sports complex on Wauseon's northeast edge. The club purchased the property in 1999. It began working with a sports complex design company from Cleveland to draw up plans. With an estimated cost of $3.8 million, many residents, including some club members, never thought they would see the project completed in their lifetimes. This all changed in 2003 with three substantial donations, including a $1.2 million gift from resident Dorothy B. Biddle. The ground was soon cleared (above), and the first of several concession/announcer stands was built. On May 29, 2009, the nearly completed complex was turned over to the Wauseon Parks and Recreation Department. Installation of the final few ball fields is currently underway by the club. (Both, courtesy of Dan Ross.)

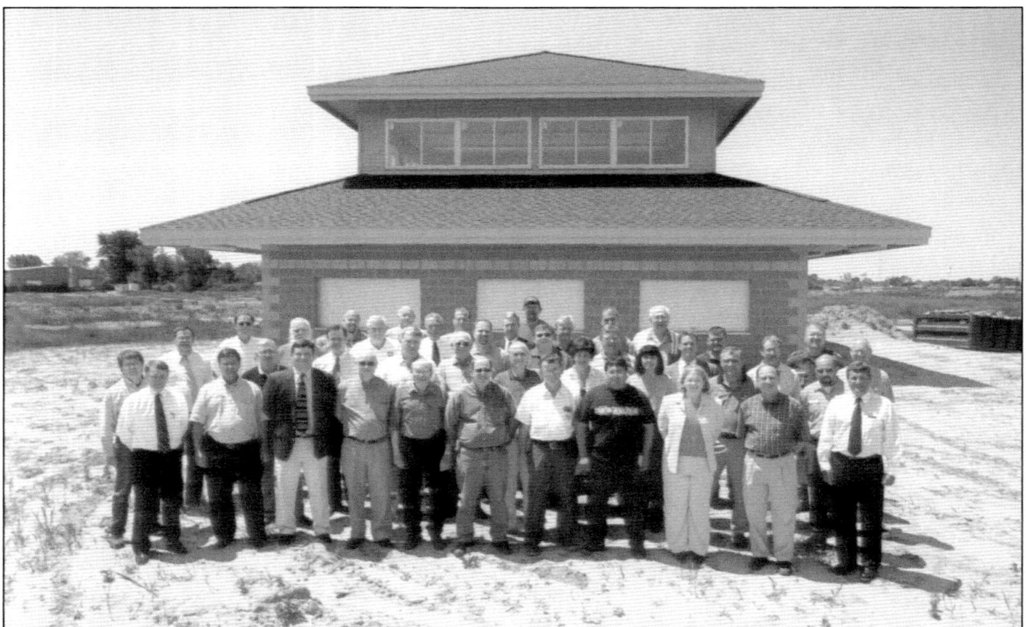

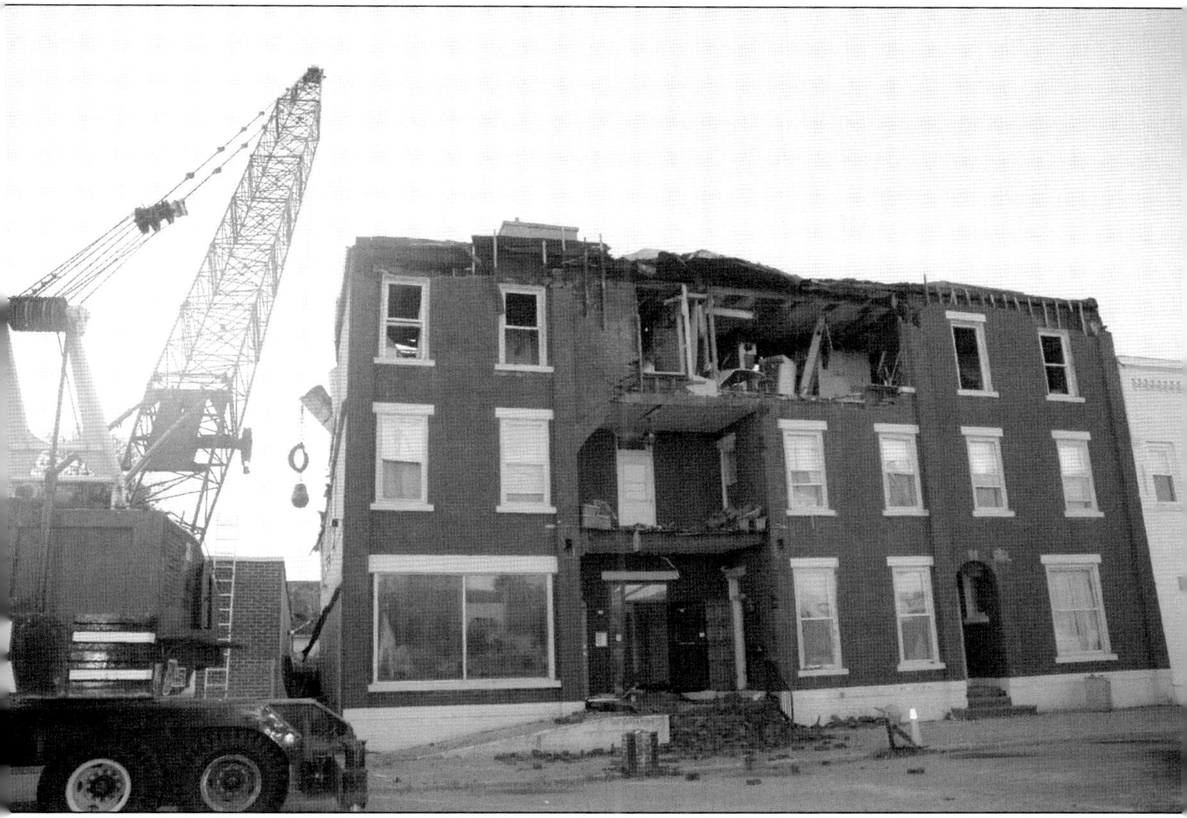

Built in 1896, the Avery Inn, later renamed the Blair House and then Clairmont Manor, was a popular hotel with a spacious ballroom seating 300. The 14,000-square-foot building was converted into a 20-apartment complex and, in July 2005, destroyed by fire. The vacant lot where the manor stood was donated by its owners to the City of Wauseon, and it is now part of a large municipal parking lot. (Courtesy of the Wauseon Fire Department.)

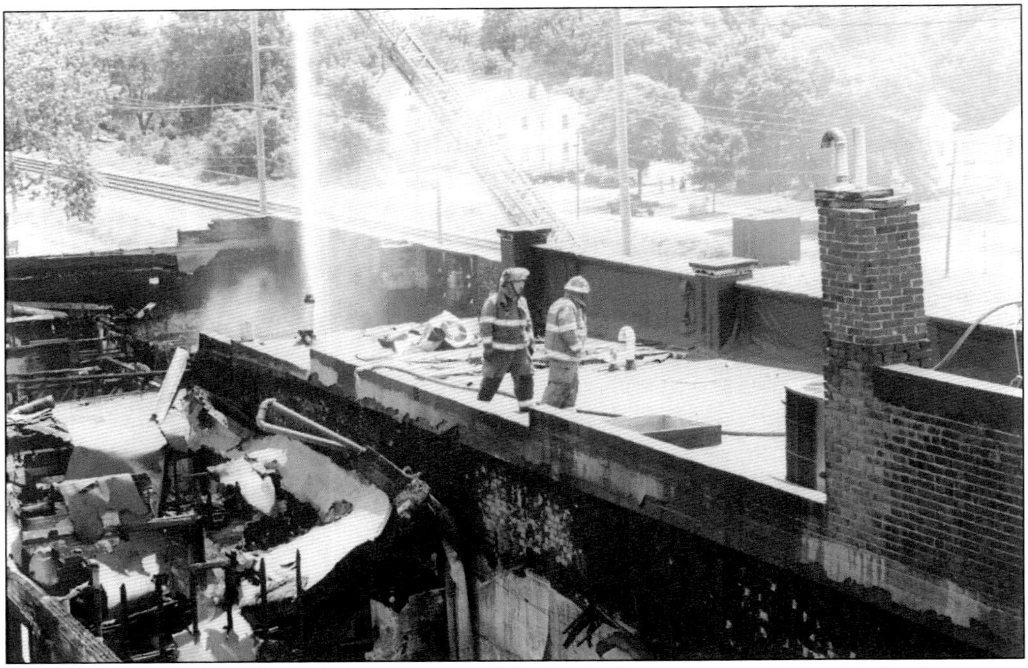

The historic Arcade Building did not age gracefully. In the later years, it, along with the downtown area, began to lose businesses to competing plazas on Shoop Avenue. Consequently, its owners converted the second-floor offices into small apartments, which offered affordable housing for residents. Except for an appliance store on the street level, most of once bustling retail space stood empty. In 2002, one of the residents was cooking on a hotplate, which caught on fire. Flames and deadly smoke quickly spread, and two residents lost their lives in the early-morning conflagration. Over 100 area firefighters responded to scene and battled the fire for nearly 12 hours. Fortunately, the adjacent building was salvaged. (Both, courtesy of Brett Kolb..)

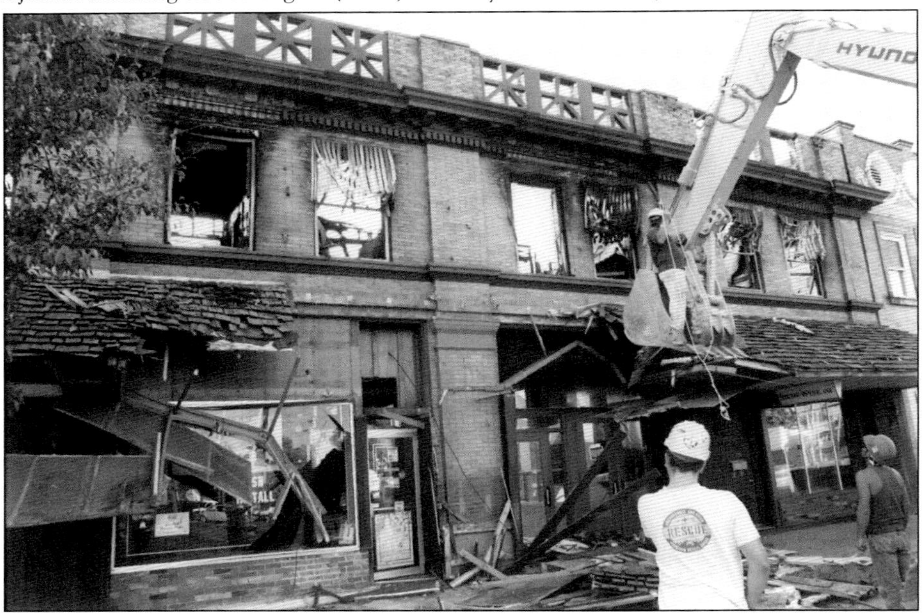

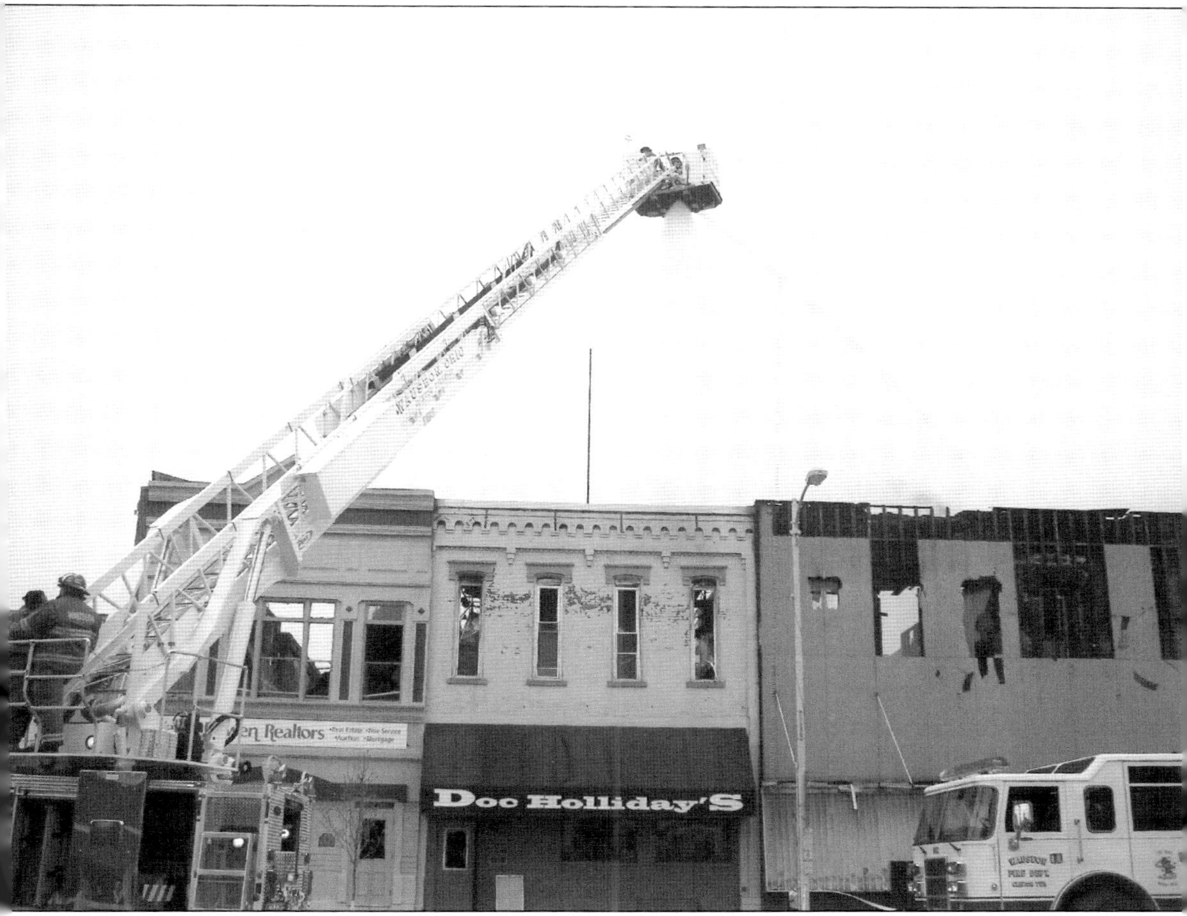

In the early morning hours of April 16, 2007, another major fire erupted in downtown Wauseon. The fire originated on the second floor of Doc Holliday's Restaurant, quickly spreading to adjoining buildings. Destroyed in the blaze were the restaurant, a real estate office, and Shaw's clothing, a popular men's and women's clothing store. (Courtesy of the Wauseon Fire Department.)

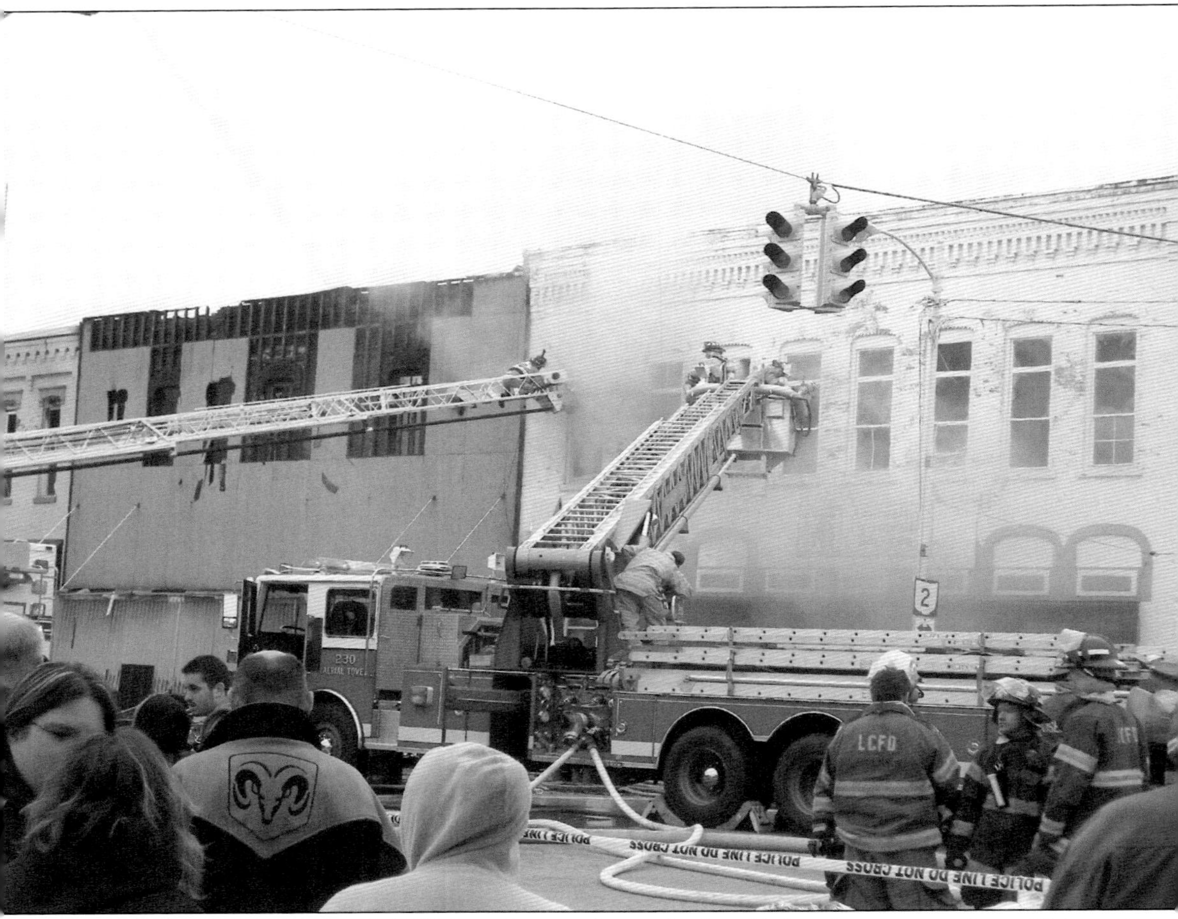

On the day of the April 2007 fire, thousands watched as 14 fire departments from Ohio and Michigan pumped over two million gallons of water on the structures. The cause of the fire was never proven. The structures were then demolished, and a new restaurant, Sullivan's, was constructed on the site. (Courtesy of the Wauseon Fire Department.)

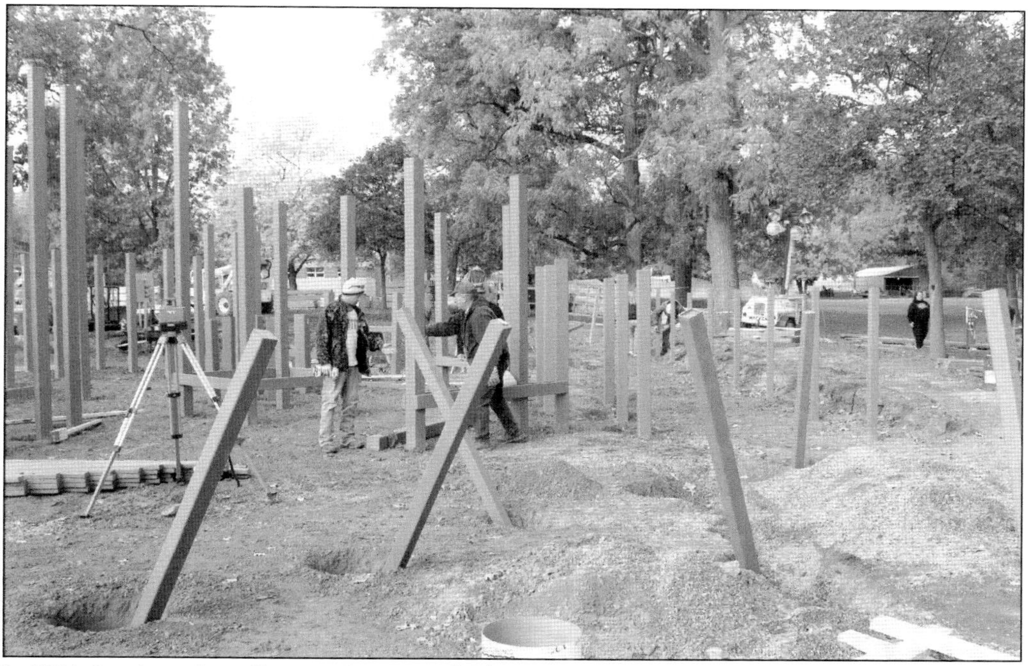

In 2011, local residents Bonnie Grisier and Gloria Gunn, along with family, friends, and a team of volunteers, undertook a campaign to raise money to build the city's largest playground. In less than a year, with fundraisers such as scrap drives and a talent show, plus donations by individuals or families (who purchased fence posts and engraved granite pavers) and large contributions by businesses from around the county, $250,000 was raised to construct the playground in Reighard Park. The park was named the Imagination Kingdom by an elementary school student. Students assisted planners in the design of the facility. During a one-week period in October 2012, hundreds of volunteers joined forces to construct the extensive complex. The project required teams, which did everything from feed construction workers, to paint the facility, to provide childcare for volunteers with children. (Both, courtesy of the Project Playground committee.)

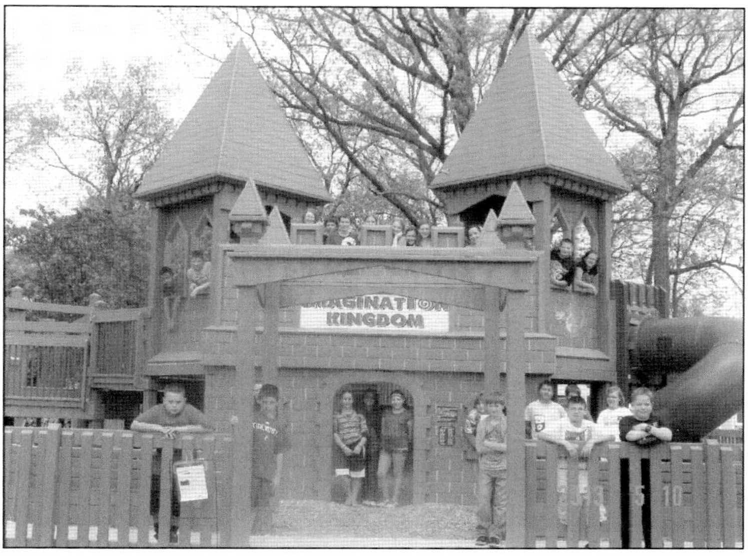

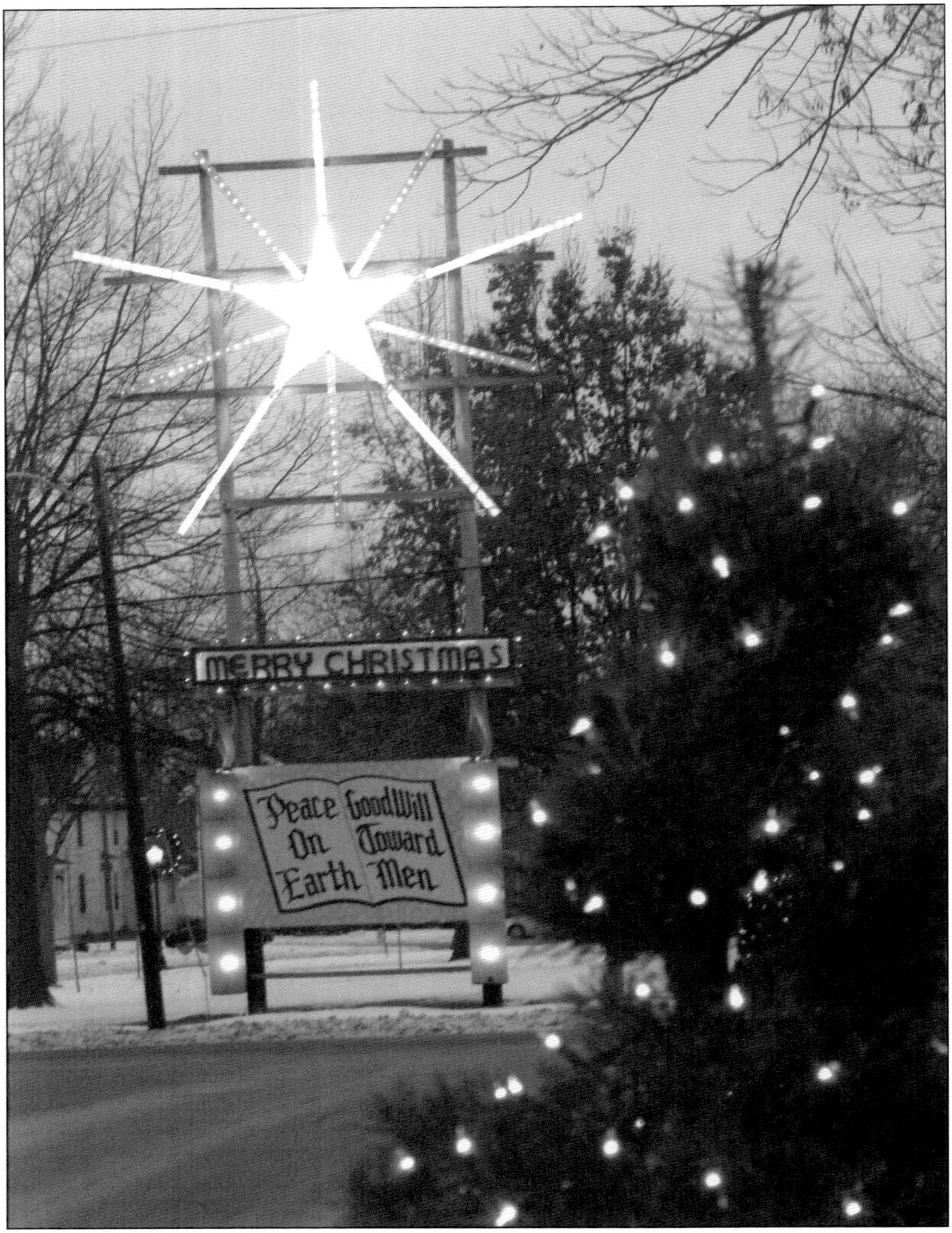

The Christmas Star has heralded the beginning of Wauseon's Christmas season for more than half a century. It burst onto the scene in 1939, built by members of the Toledo Edison Club to represent the Star of Bethlehem. It was displayed on various building before being moved to South Park. The star is about 30 feet in diameter, with 226 lights varying in intensity from 15 watts to 200 watts. The star has been lit every year since, except in 1977, during the nation's energy crisis. (Photograph by the author.)

Five

Special Events

Since the inception of the town, Wauseon residents have always found opportunities to come together for celebrations. Be it a national holiday, carnival, circus, special commemoration, street or county fair, or school play, hardworking Wauseon residents like having fun, too.

Annual events include a Memorial Day parade leading to special observances at the Wauseon Union Cemetery. At the start of summer ball season, area youth gather for their own parade leading from downtown to the ball fields. In early July, there are fireworks, followed in late July or early August with the Wauseon homecoming. Whenever Wauseon High School has a reason to celebrate—with a winning sports team, for instance—impromptu parades are usually formed.

On its 40th anniversary, in 1895, the town organized its first downtown fair, simply called the Street Fair. The annual Wauseon homecoming traces its roots back to 1934, when a group of community leaders joined forces to create the event. For the first several years, it was called the Wauseon Homecoming and Horse Show. Homecoming initially started as a three-day celebration and was later reduced to two days. In 1993, it again became a three-day event.

The Fulton County Fair, first held on the northern outskirts of the village over 150 years ago, now attracts over 250,000 visitors each year, making it one of Ohio's top four county fairs. Events continue to be agriculturally oriented, and the appearance of top entertainers and an industrious group of board members keep the fair a number-one attraction.

In 1992, a new downtown event began with the advent of the weekly Cruise-in to Wauseon, for both car owners and car buffs. Held through the summer, the Tuesday evening event fills Wauseon's downtown streets with hundreds of vehicles. Each month, there is also one evening called the Super Cruise, where free music and other special activities are offered. The largest Super Cruise attracted over 600 vehicles.

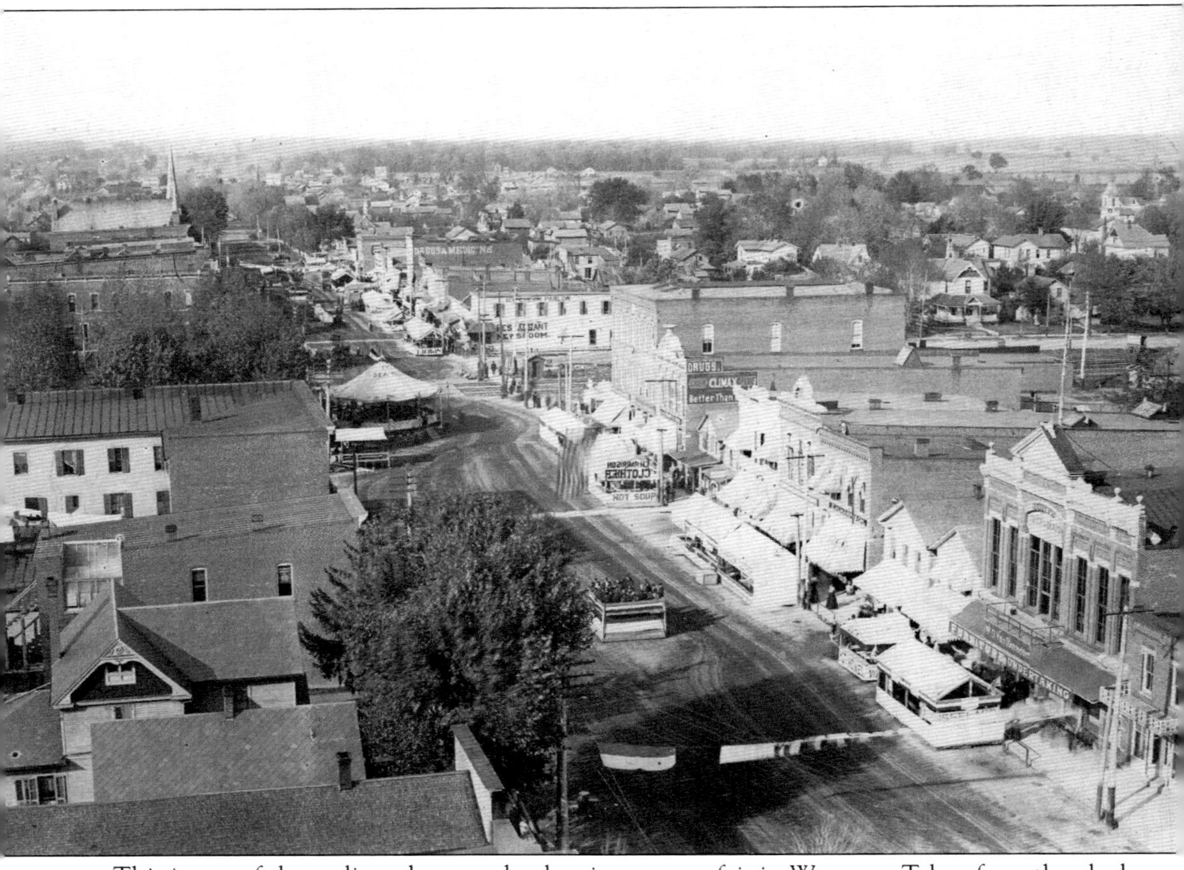

This is one of the earliest photographs showing a street fair in Wauseon. Taken from the clock tower on the county courthouse, it captures preparations for Wauseon's 1897 street fair, held October 13–15. Historical records indicate the event was called a "Homecoming and Carnival." Tickets to special events cost $2 for adults, and children attended for free.

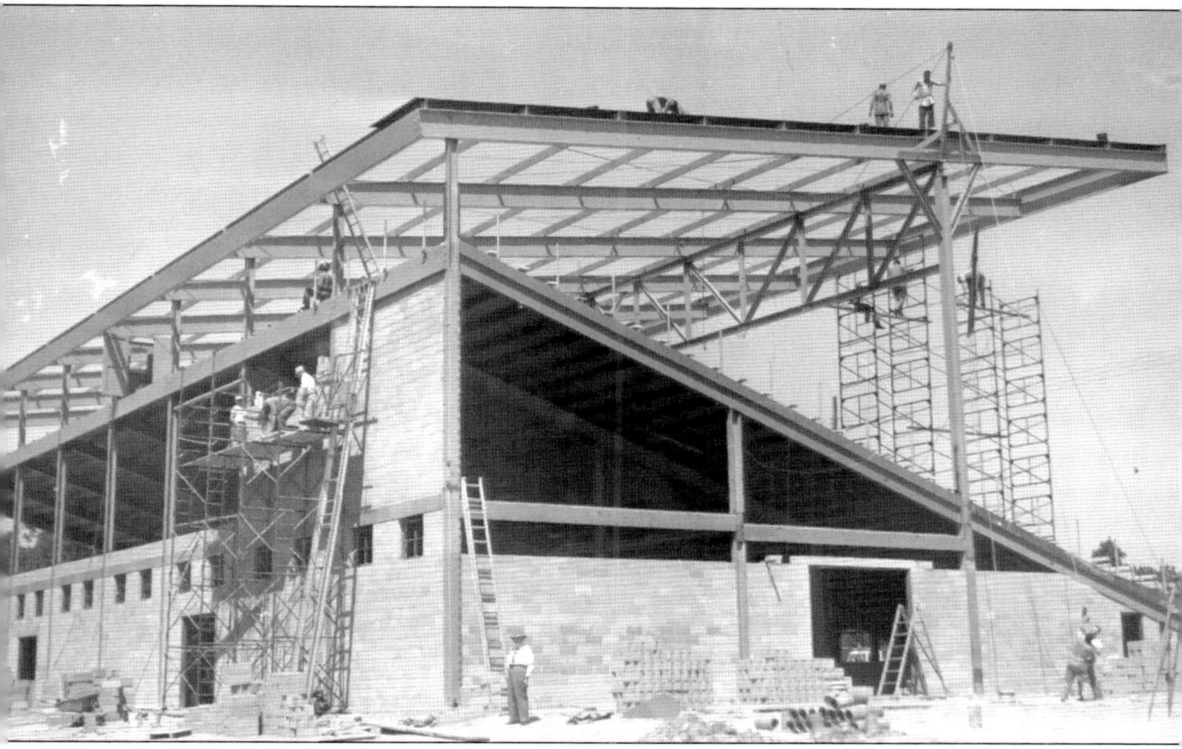

When the Wabash Railroad came through Wauseon in the late 1920s, the Fulton County Fairgrounds were forced to move several miles north of town. In August 1950, construction began on the grandstand. The grandstand offered comfortable, sheltered seating for horse racing, demolition derbies, live music, tractor pulls, and other events. Beneath the stand are restrooms, offices, ticket booths, and space for other booths. The grandstand has since undergone several expansions, as crowds at the fair continue to grow.

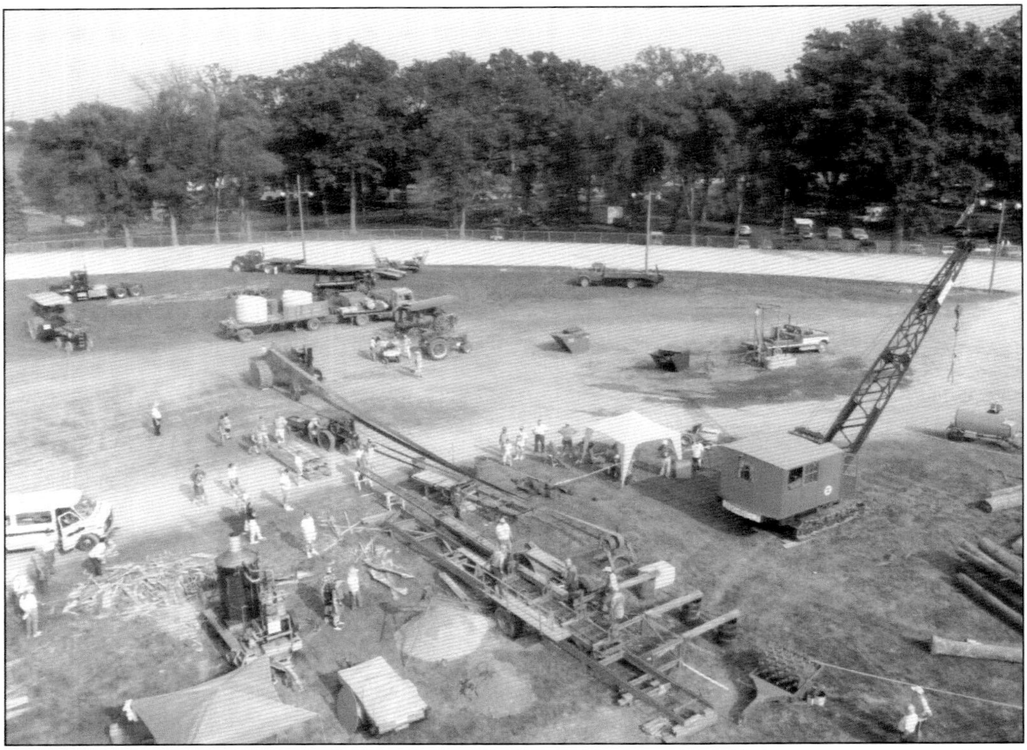

The Fulton County Fairgrounds have events taking place on virtually every summer weekend. Among them are the State Line Gem and Mineral Show, the Maumee Valley Tractor Pull, the Black Swamp Benefit bazaar, the Wauseon Rotary Club auction, National Thresher's Annual Reunion (seen in this aerial photograph), the Antique Motorcycle Show and Race, Relay for Life, the Crosley Auto Club National Meet, and much more. The fairgrounds feature a large campground for tents and trailers. (Courtesy of Joseph Horwath.)

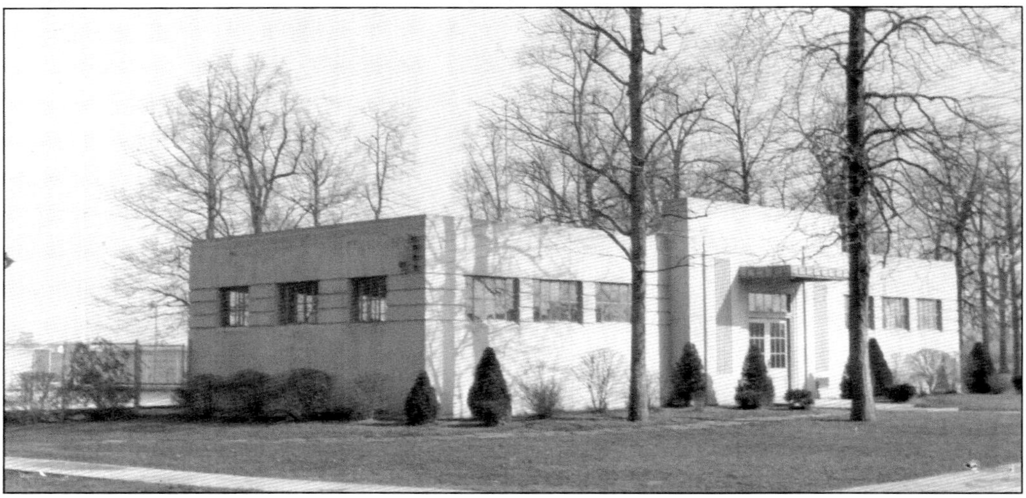

In 1941, the Work Projects Administration (WPA) built a swimming pool and this bathhouse at Reighard Park. The pool was used by area youngsters to take swimming lessons and cool off during the summers. It was also utilized by local swimming and dive teams to hold tournaments.

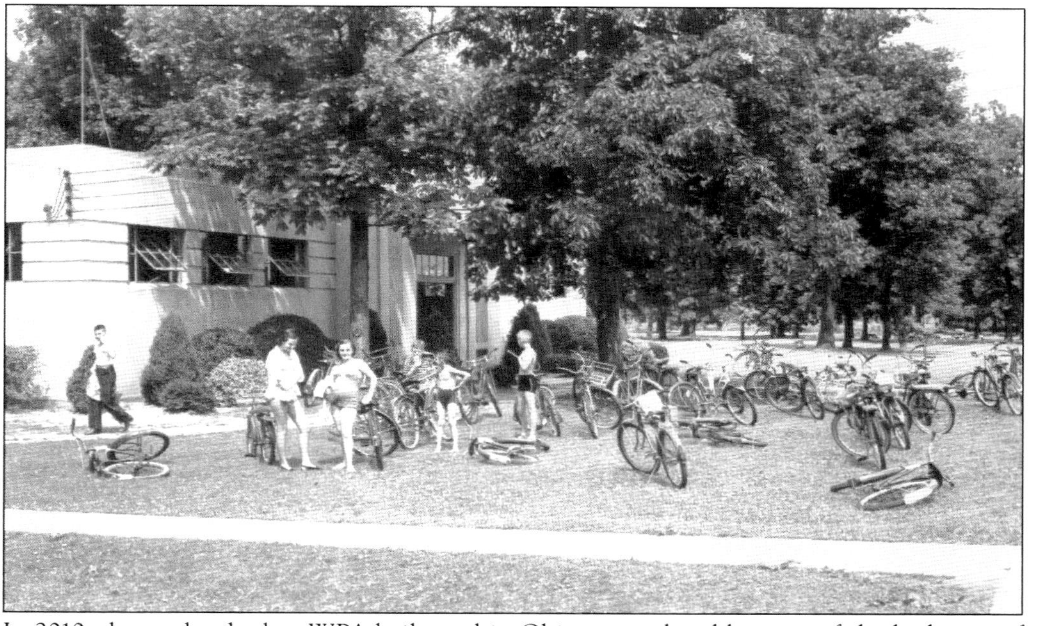

In 2010, the pool—the last WPA-built pool in Ohio—was closed because of the high cost of maintenance and repairs. The city removed the pool, but it is attempting to preserve the bathhouse for future use. Children would ride their bikes to the pool, where admission was only a couple of dollars. Season passes could also be purchased.

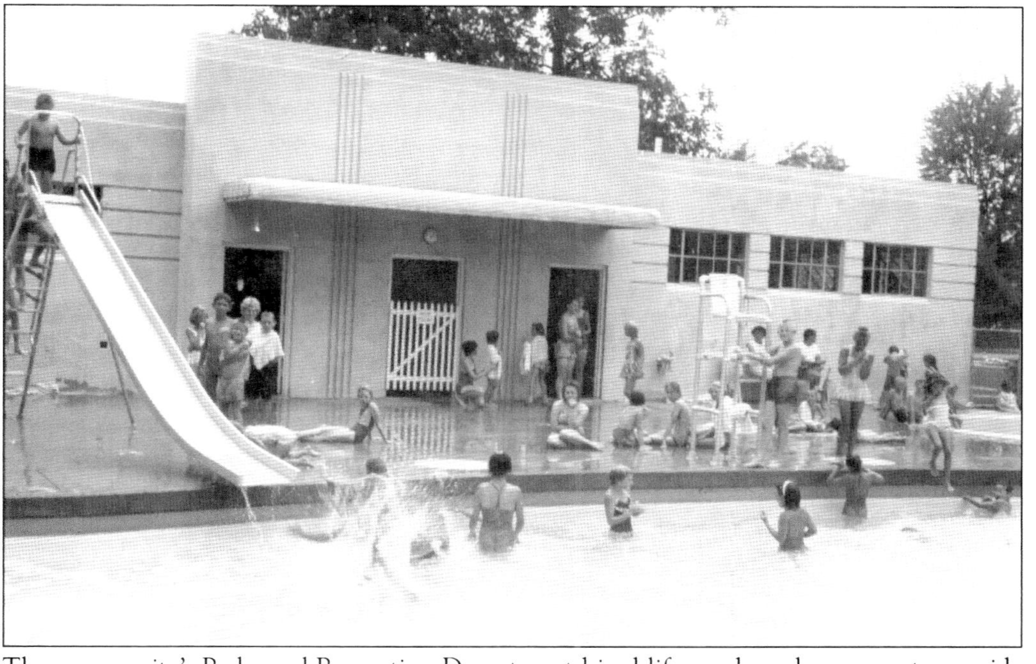

The community's Parks and Recreation Department hired lifeguards each summer to provide swimming lessons for beginners and to monitor pool activities. The pool was used by both Wauseon's residents and others. A New Pool for Wauseon committee has been formed to raise the money that will be needed to finance and operate a new pool and splash park here.

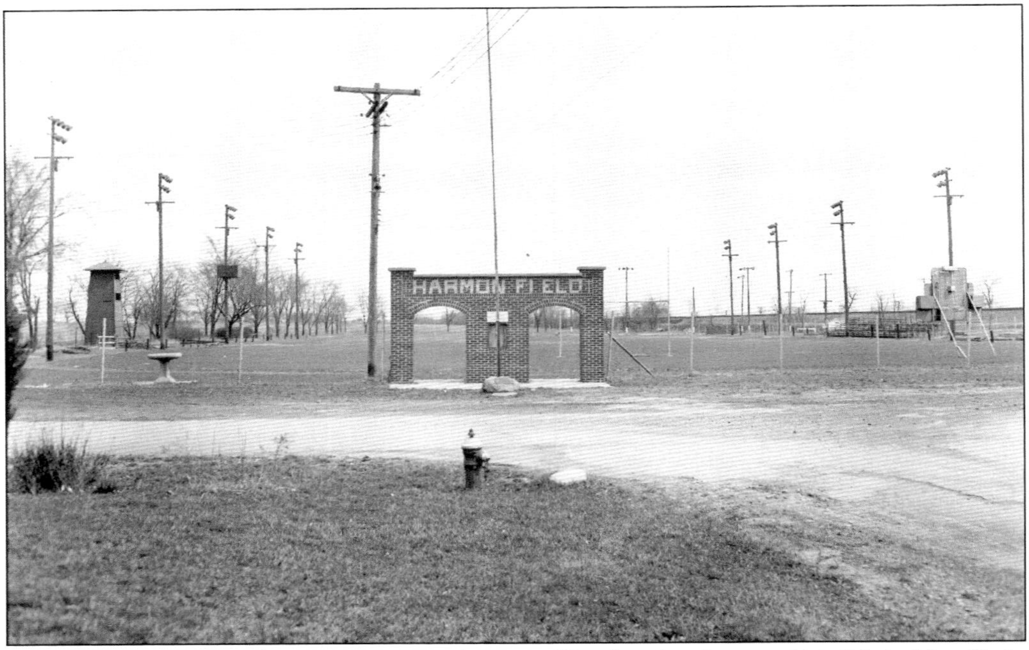

William Harmon, a real estate agent, was born in Ohio but lived most of his life in New York. He formed the Harmon Foundation, which contributed money to various interests, including playgrounds. Over 120 communities, including Wauseon, benefited from his foundation. Wauseon's Harmon Field was built in the early 1920s. Here is an early view of the main entrance.

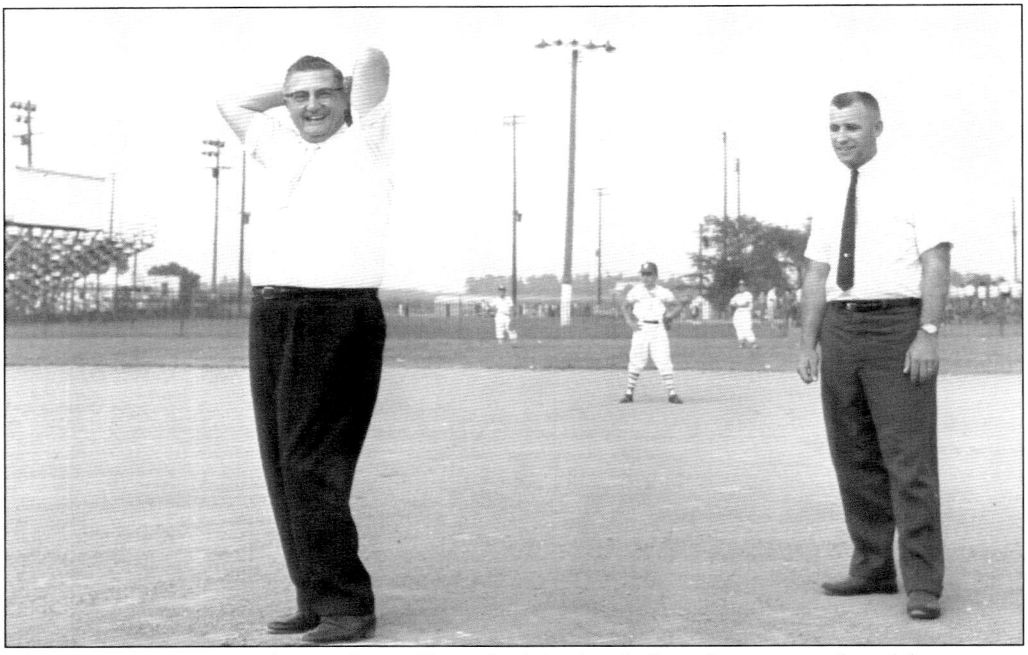

Wauseon's current mayor has traditionally pitched the first ball on the opening day of the summer baseball, softball, and Little League season. Pictured here is former Wauseon mayor Olin Dunbar (left), who served as mayor in the late 1960s until 1971.

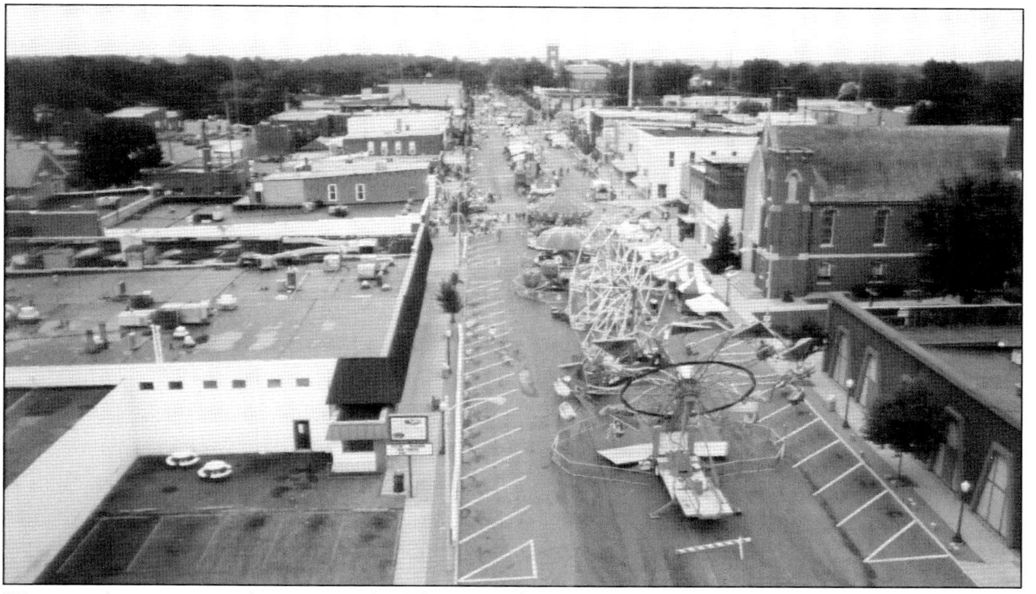

Wauseon homecoming began in 1934. The annual summer event relies on the support of hundreds of volunteers. Profits are primarily used to support the city's extensive park system. The event has also been an opportunity for former residents to visit and for high school classes to hold reunions. (Courtesy of Joseph Horwath.)

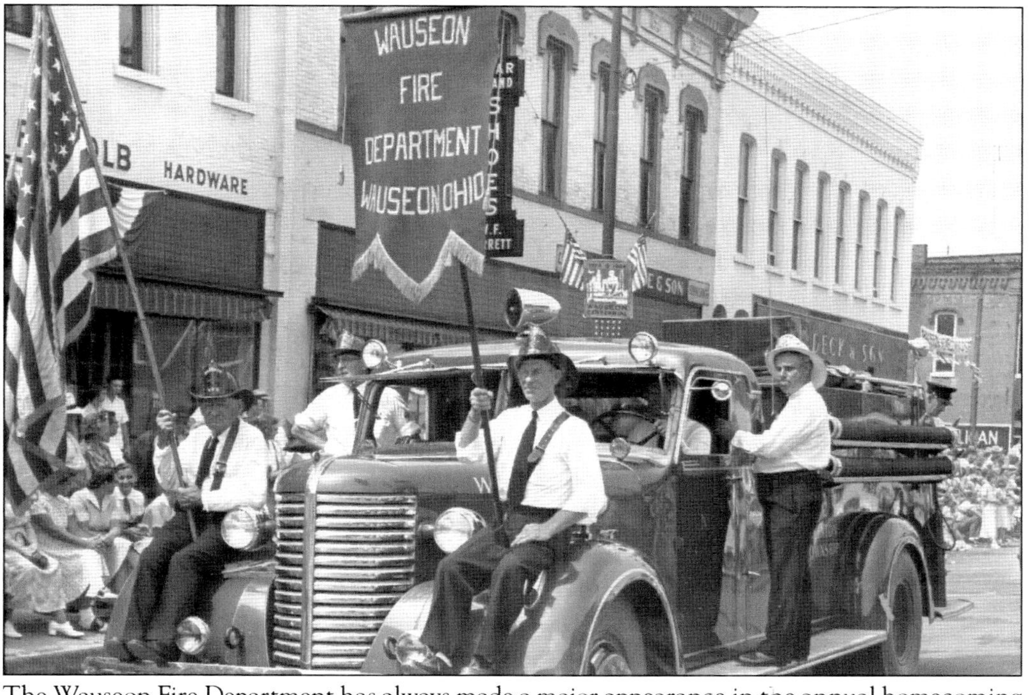

The Wauseon Fire Department has always made a major appearance in the annual homecoming grand parade. Here, firemen man one of the volunteer department's trucks in 1954. This was the 20th anniversary of the event and the village's centennial celebration. Note that the direction of the parade was south toward the courthouse at that time.

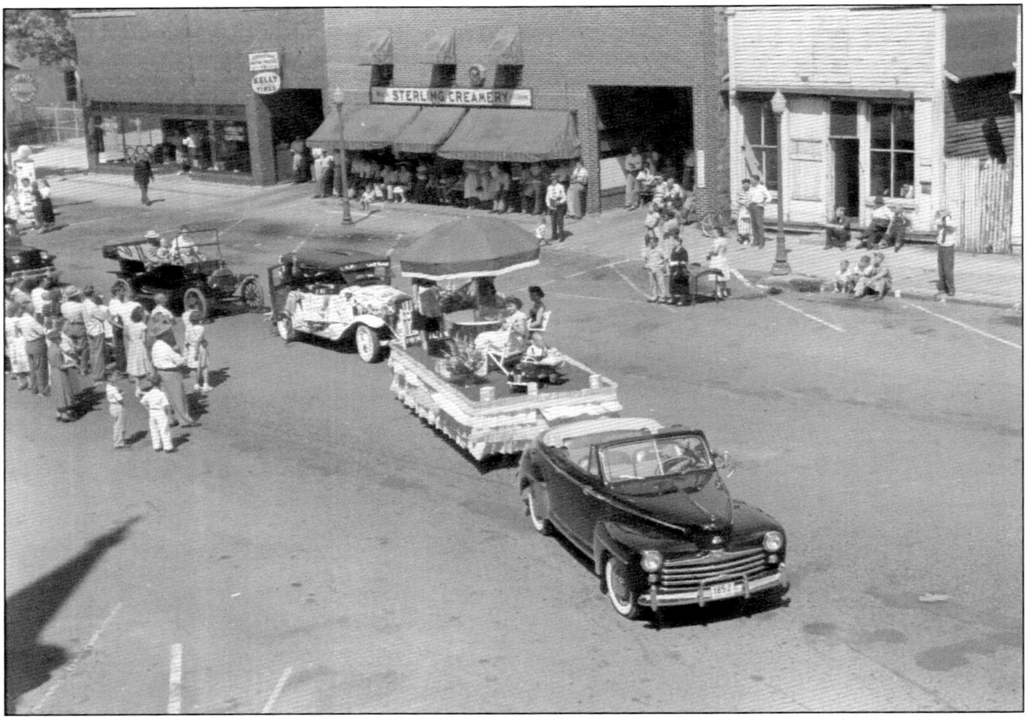

Wauseon's homecoming grand parade is seen here in 1954. The parade usually had a theme, and it hosted many area high school marching bands. At one time, there were as many as 20 bands and 120 other units in the parade. Because of the expenses associated with transportation, the number of high school bands participating in the parade has been reduced to less than five. The structure to the right of Sterling Creamery was torn down to allow room for a parking lot when the creamery expanded into a small grocery and convenience store.

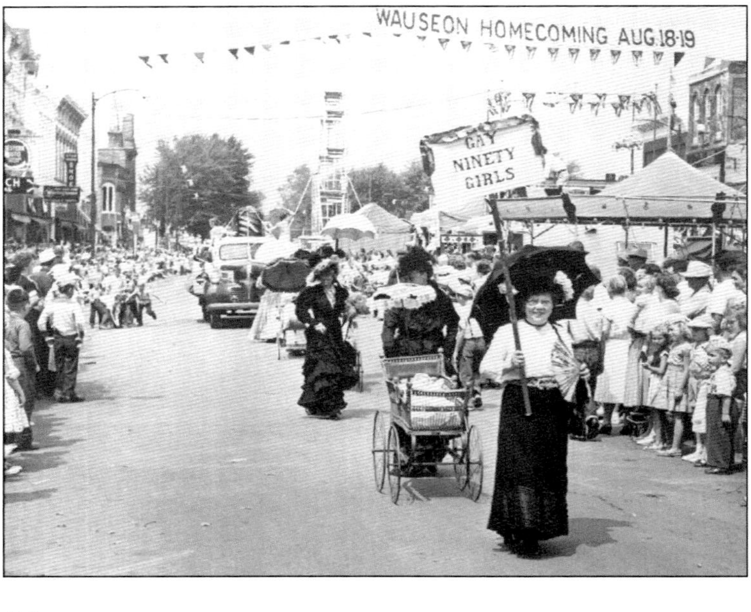

The Gay Ninety Girls were one of the entries in the 1954 homecoming grand parade. That year's event was a cause for celebration , as the community observed its 100th anniversary.

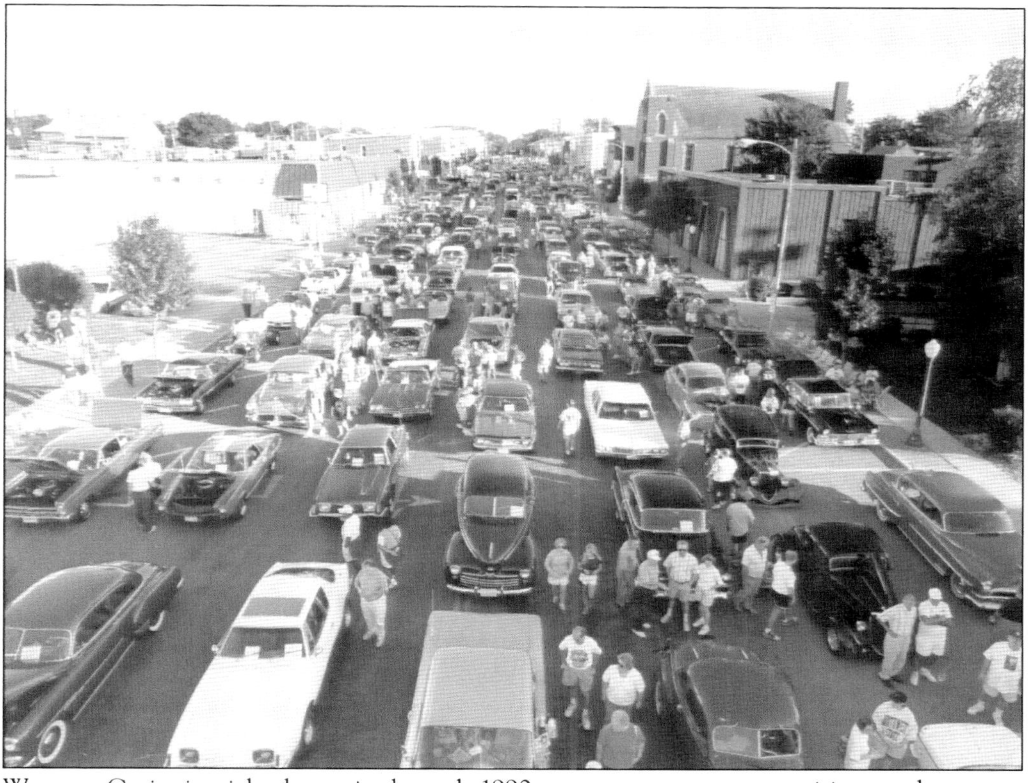

Wauseon Cruise-in nights began in the early 1990s as a way to attract more visitors to downtown and for car collectors to gather. One evening each month is the Super Cruise-in, which features live entertainment and a host of food booths. It is not uncommon for the Super Cruise-in to attract several hundred cars. (Courtesy of Joseph Horwath.)

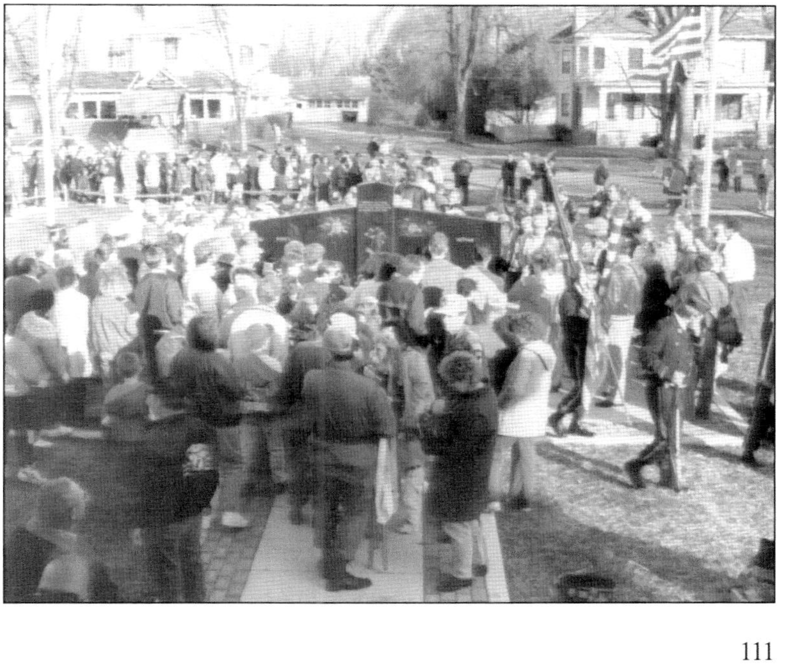

On a clear day in late November in 1992, over 1,000 residents gathered in front of the county's courthouse annex to participate in the unveiling of a new war memorial. The monument recognized the county's fallen heroes from World War I, World War II, Korea, and Vietnam. (Courtesy of Floyd Franks.)

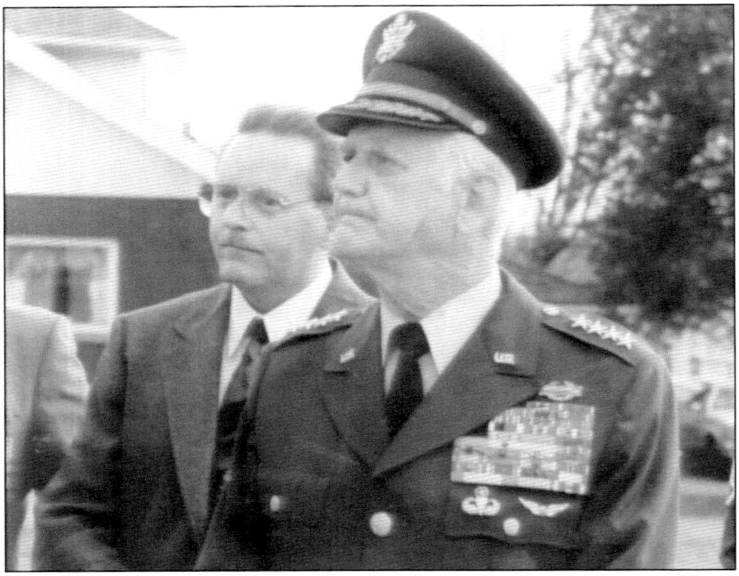

Vietnam veteran Floyd Franks (left) looks on as Gen. William Westmoreland, US Army (Ret.), views the county's new war memorial. General Westmoreland served in three wars and earned four Distinguished Service medals before retirement. He was the featured speaker during the memorial's dedication. (Courtesy of Floyd Franks.)

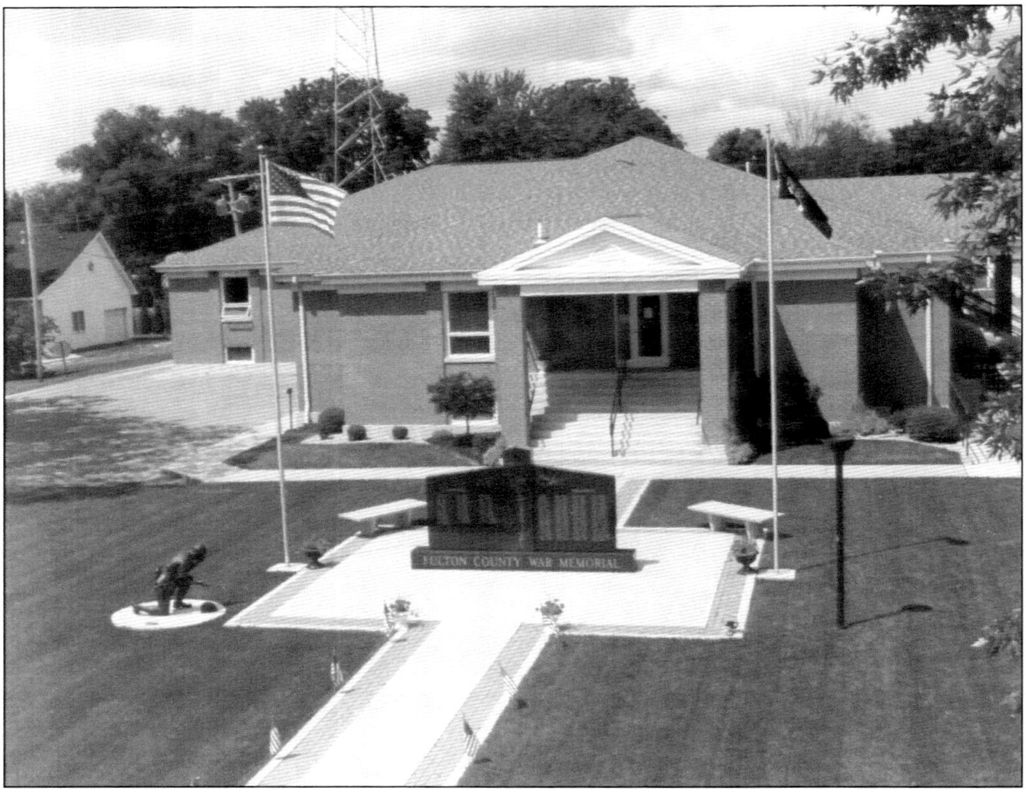

The war memorial was completed several years after its dedication with the installation of a bronze statue called the *Sky Pilot*. The kneeling figure is a life-size military chaplain, praying as he holds a pair of dog tags. (Courtesy of Joseph Horwath.)

Six

Business and Industry

In the 21st century, Wauseon has been experiencing a quiet, steady resurgence in its manufacturing base. Today, there are firms fabricating myriad items, including flashlights, custom cabinetry, insulation, custom knives, automotive parts, dairy products, powder-coated products, and garage doors.

Some of these local companies have created regional, national, and international markets for their products. They include Wauseon Machine and Manufacturing, Hill Manufacturing, the IAC Group, Perfection Finishing, Fulton Industries, E&J Demark, American Power Pull, Bussee Combat Knife Company, Northwest Ohio Foam Products (NOFP), Haas Door, and Certified Document Destruction.

Most of these companies were started or are owned and managed today by sharp-minded entrepreneurs who developed and began marketing their products and services right here.

Two of the city's largest employers are the Fulton County Health Center, with over 500 employees, and the Wauseon school system, with an estimated 600 teachers, staff, and support personnel.

Over the past century, there have also been many other profitable companies that have come and gone. These include, but are not limited to, Supreme Iron Works, Multi-Cast, Sheridan Manufacturing, the Van Camp Packing Company, Sheller-Globe (which supplied a wide variety office supplies), Sterling Dairy, German Village Noodles (which supplied noodles for Campbell's Soup in Napoleon), the Wauseon Foundry, and McCord (which packaged gaskets and other parts).

Some of the past companies were the first in the nation to provide services such as electricity and telephone service to customers. Companies that prospered early on, and those that continue producing quality products today, provide employment opportunities to many dedicated and hardworking people in the Wauseon area.

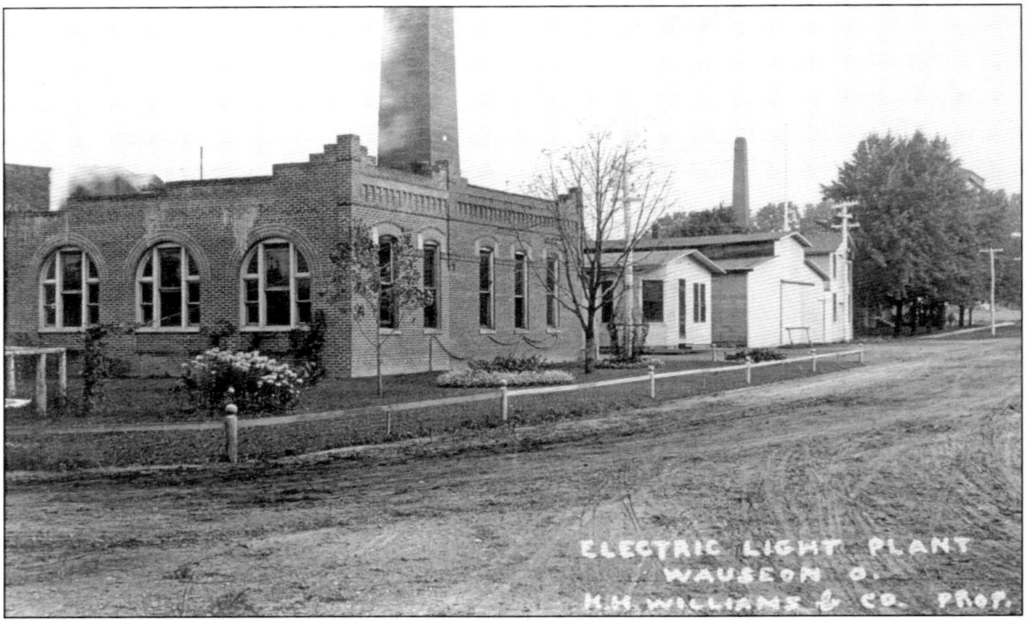

The first electricity in Wauseon was provided in the late 1890s by the Williams Generating Plant, located on the corner of Brunell and West Leggett Streets. Air Line Light & Power took over ownership in the early 1900s. The Lake Shore Power Company took over in 1924. In 1949, the Toledo Edison Company became the electrical provider. Now abandoned, the original plant used coal to fire boilers, which then turned an electrical generator.

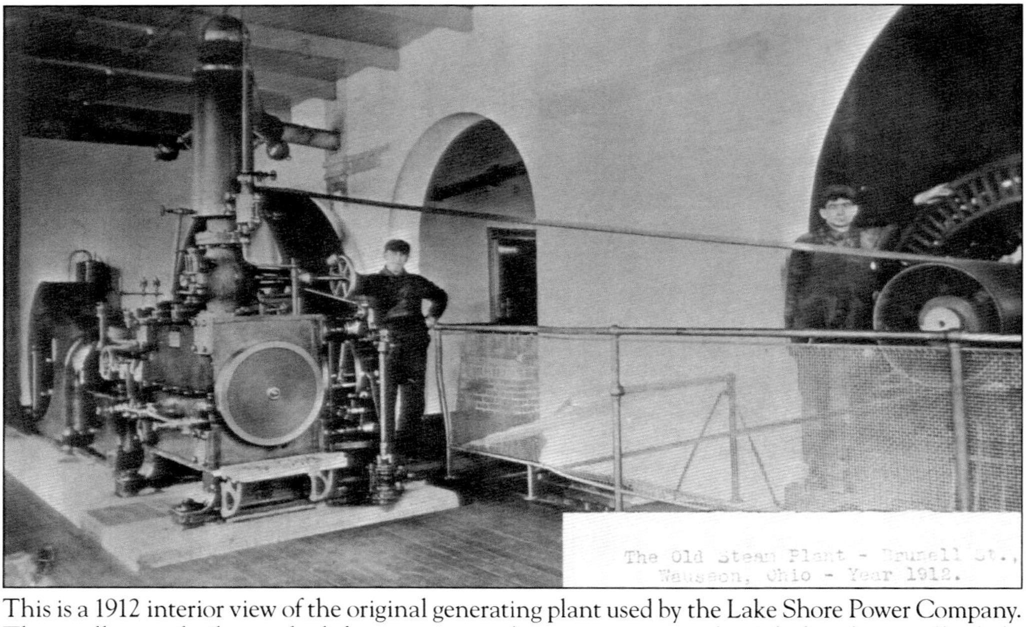

This is a 1912 interior view of the original generating plant used by the Lake Shore Power Company. The small steam boiler on the left was connected to a generator on the right by a large pulley belt. While not as efficient as today's systems, this electrical plant was one of the first in the nation to provide local power to residents. At midnight, the power was shut off, and residents would rely on kerosene and candlelights.

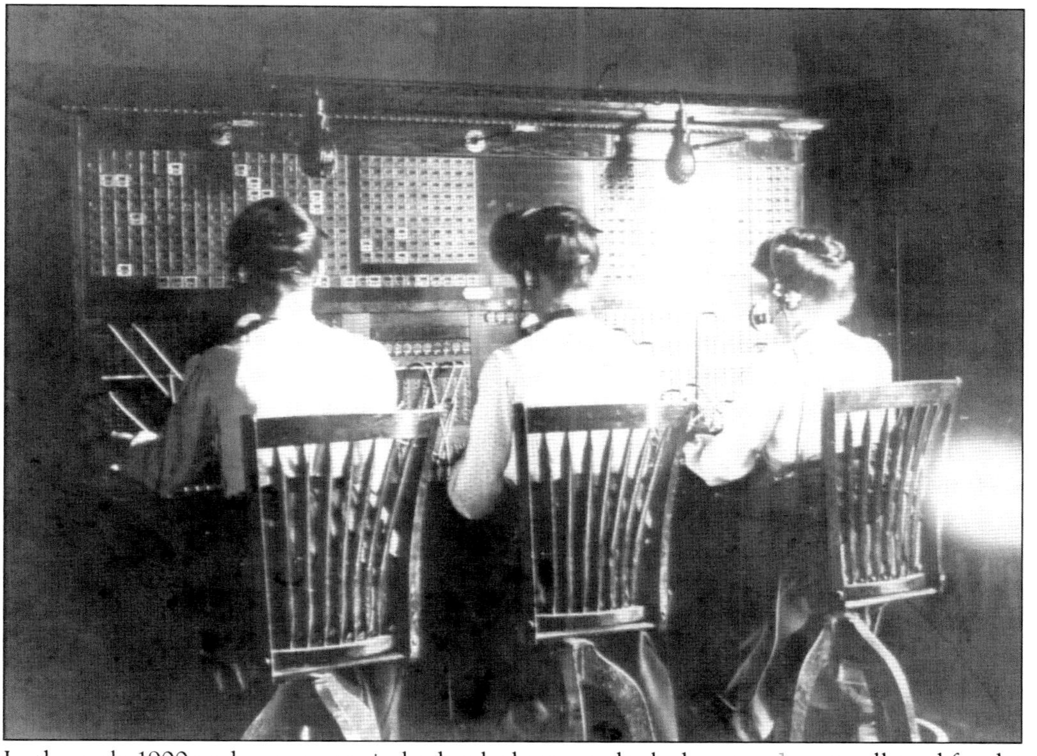

In the early 1900s, advancements in both telephones and telephone exchanges allowed for the introduction of phone services in rural areas, including Wauseon. Private ownership of the village's first system led to its acquisition by the Bell system, which connected independent switchboard operations together to form a nationwide calling system.

Local physician Dr. P.J. Lenhart was president of the town's first phone company. The use of automated switchboards became common in the 1960s, rendering the position of operators, such as August Sonnenburg, obsolete.

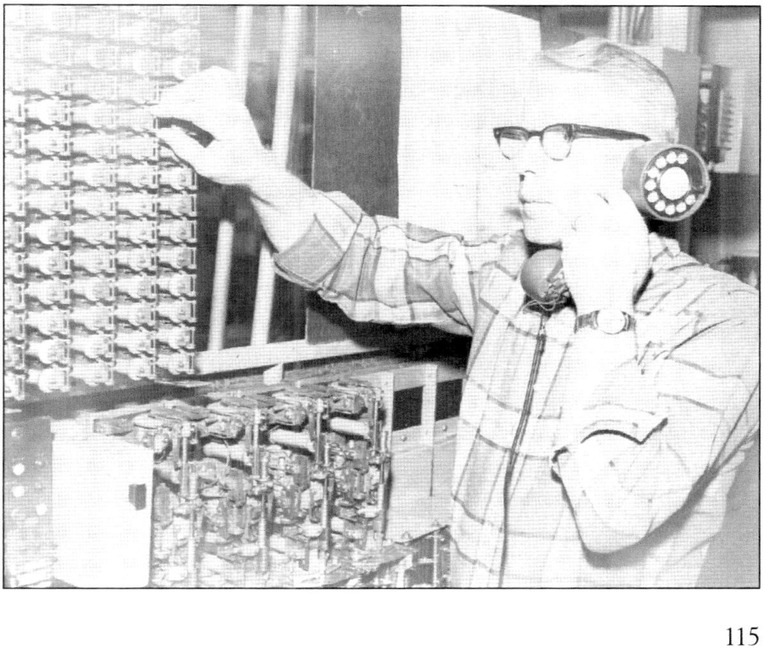

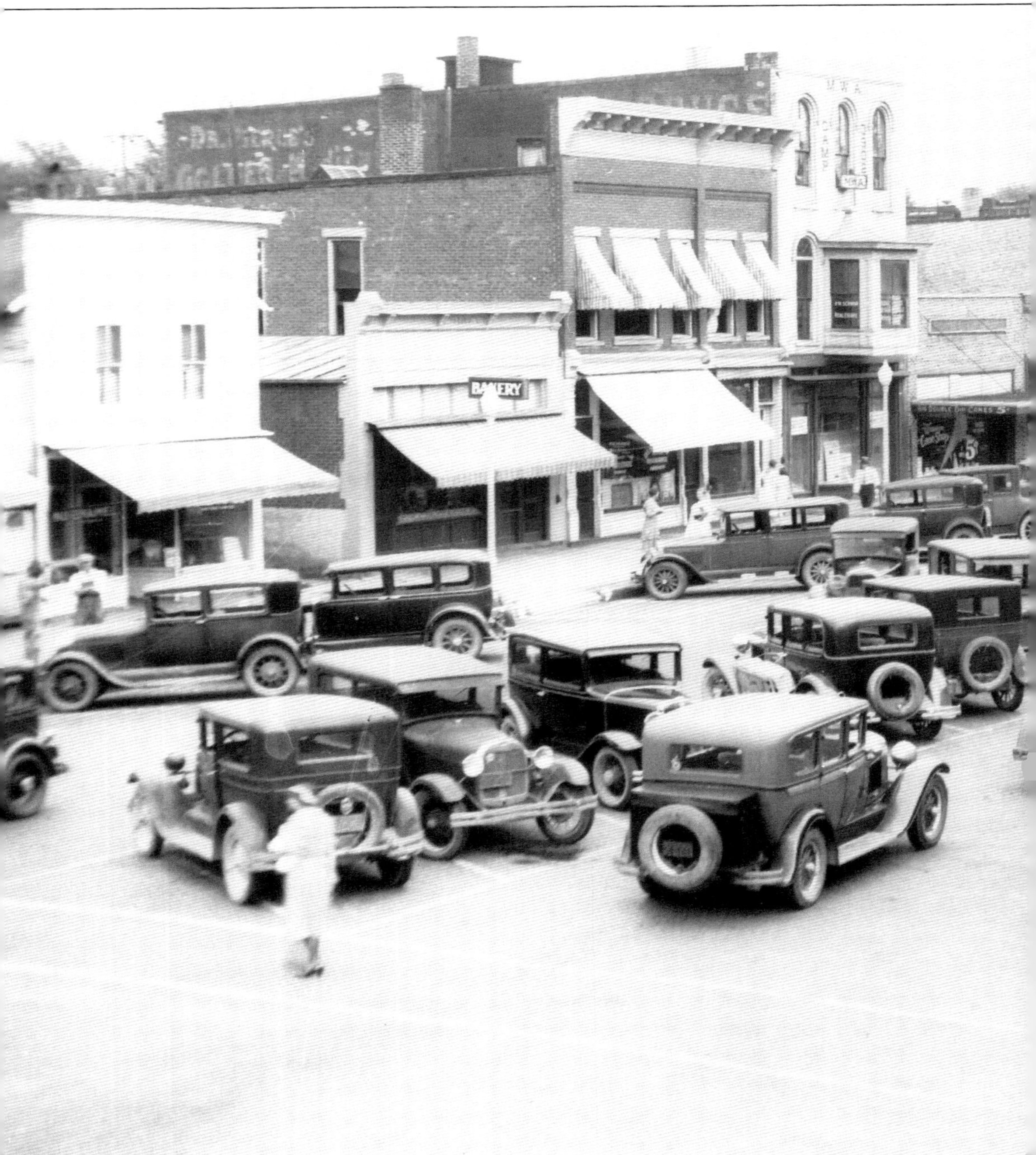

Both retail and manufacturing were still going strong in the early 1930s. Despite obstacles created by the Great Depression, which began in 1929, Wauseon remained the county center for both commercial and retail trade during this period. As a result, this photograph, taken from atop the newspaper building in the early 1930s, shows a very bustling and vibrant North Fulton Street, filled with vehicles. There are three items worth noting about this scene. The most obvious is the center-of-the-street parking, which was accomplished because the main thoroughfare

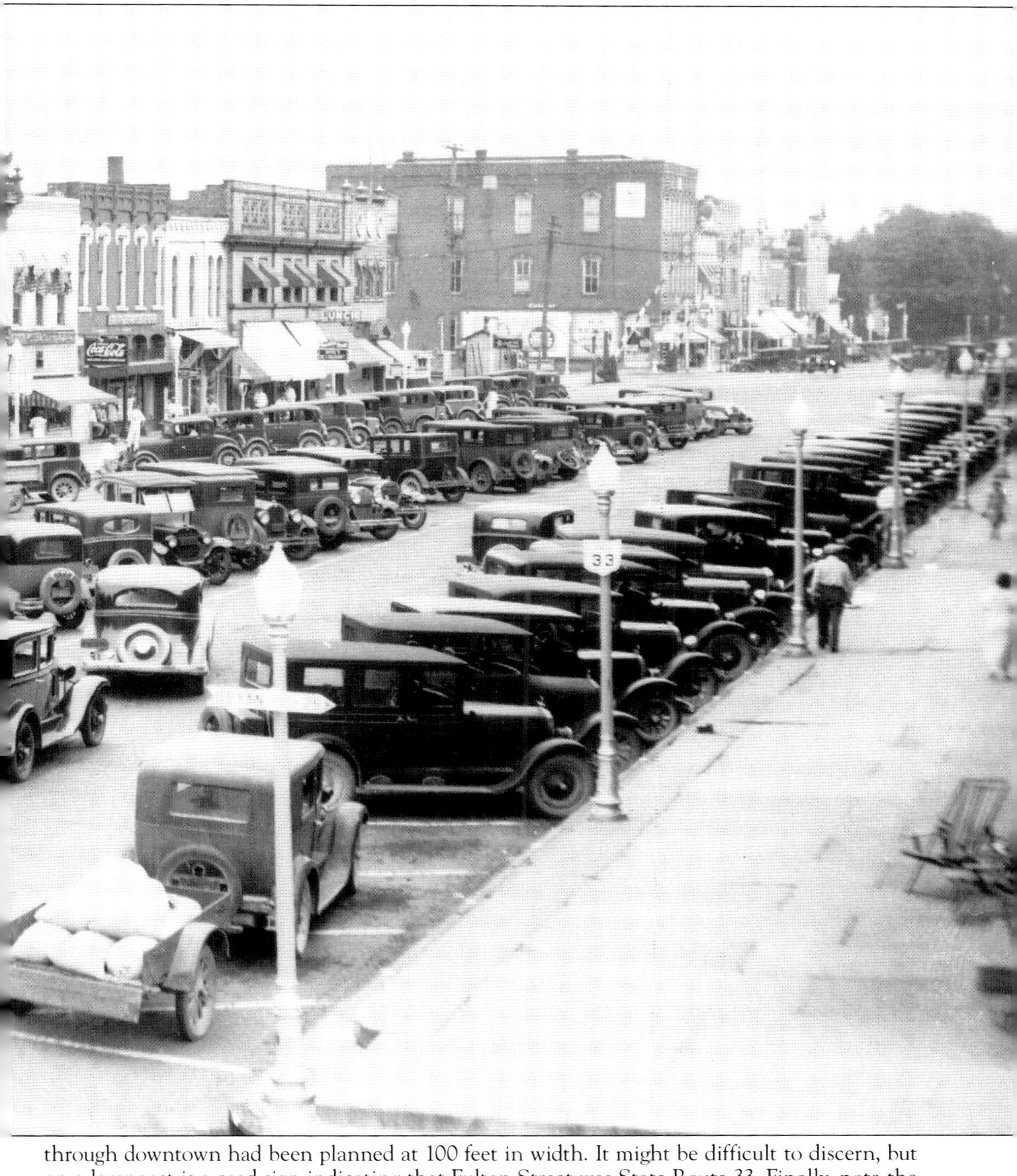

through downtown had been planned at 100 feet in width. It might be difficult to discern, but on a lamppost is a road sign indicating that Fulton Street was State Route 33. Finally, note the step needed for pedestrians to step from street level to the sidewalks. Sidewalks were particularly wide, enabling business owners to display merchandise outside during warmer weather and the city's popular sidewalk sale events.

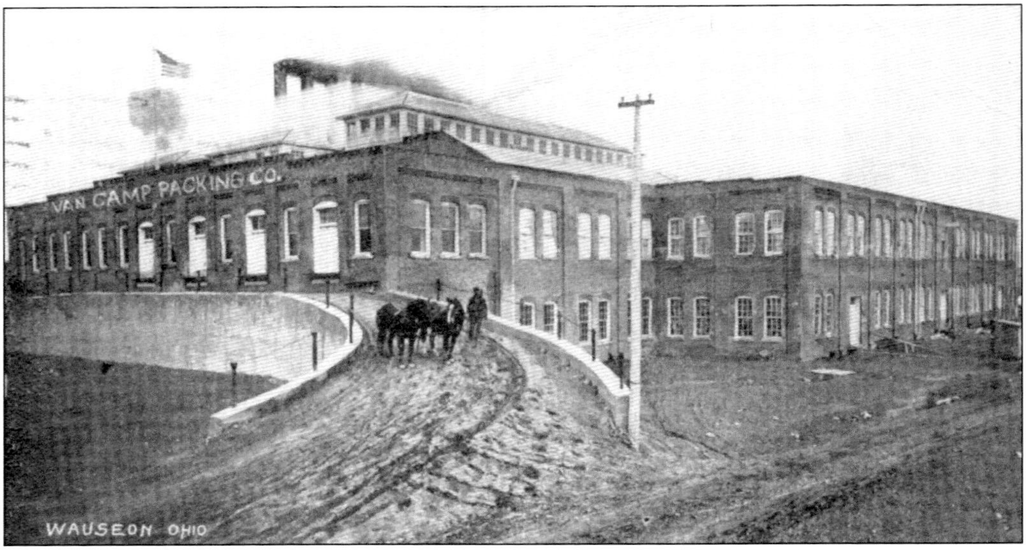

Before widespread refrigeration became common, the shelf life of dairy products, especially milk, was short-lived. Many relied upon condensed milk for their baking needs. The Van Camp Packaging Company established a milk-condensing plant in about 1905 on the east side of Shoop Avenue, situated near the railroad tracks. Other plants were located in Delta and Bryan. World War II created a huge demand for canned milk for troops stationed overseas. The Pet Milk Company bought the facility in 1944 and expanded manufacturing for several years. Declining sales led to it discontinuing production in the 1970s.

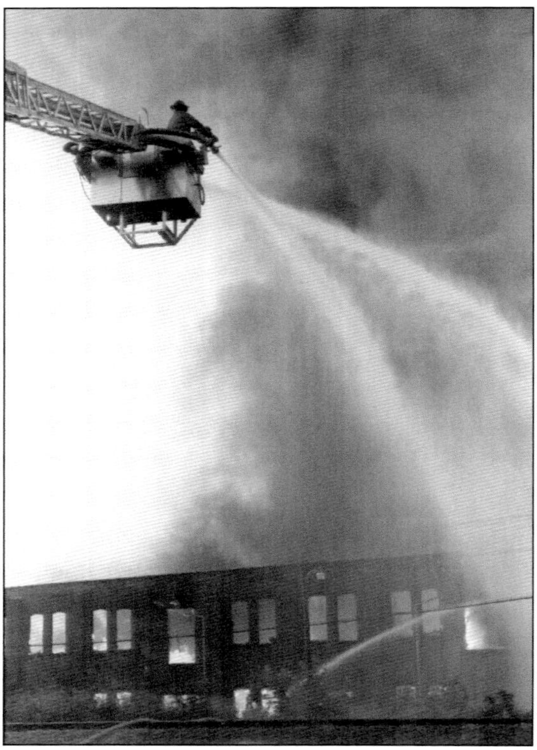

In 1980, the Wauseon Fire Department responded to a fire that had broken out at the old Pet Milk facility. Other area fire departments were also called to the blaze, which completely destroyed the plant. The cause of the fire was never determined. This was one of the most costly fires in the village's history, causing an estimated loss of $1.3 million. (Courtesy of the Wauseon Fire Department.)

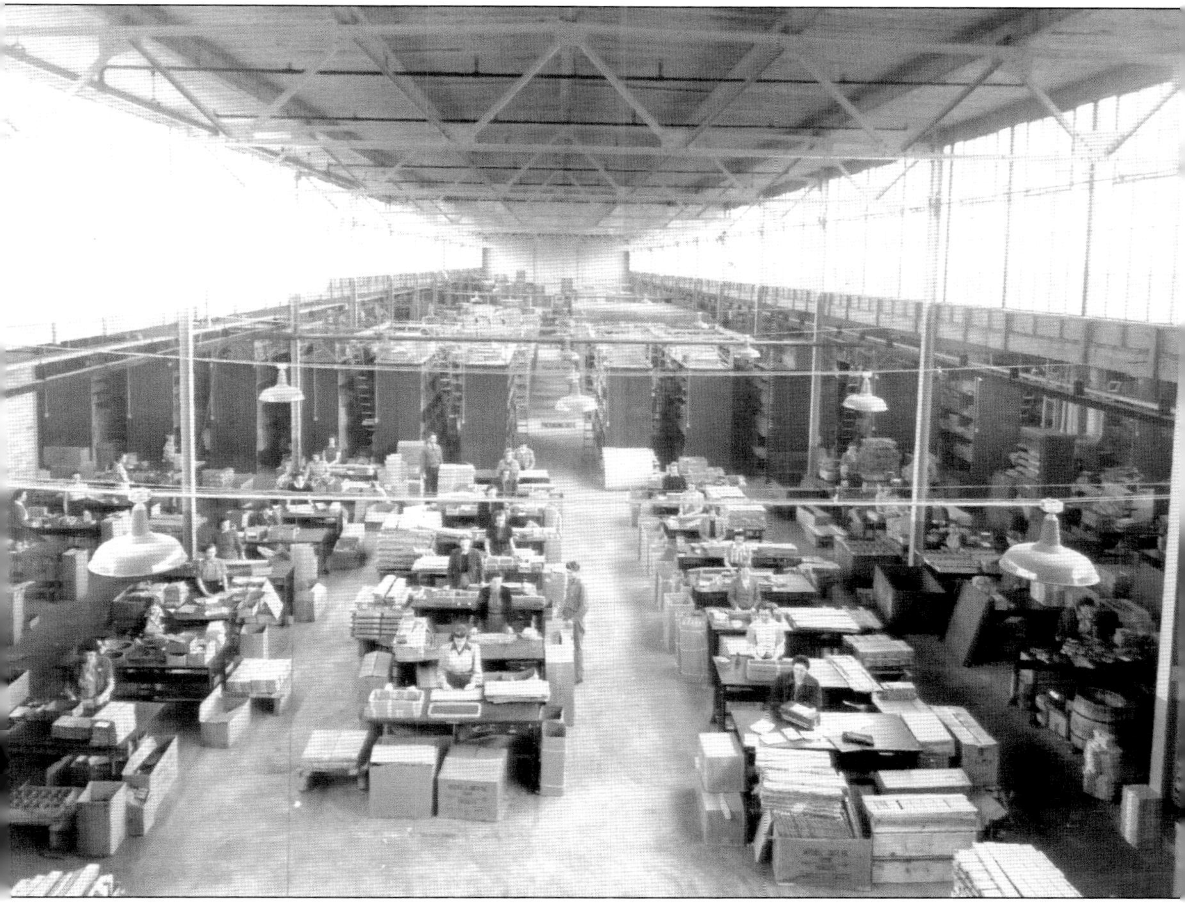

This is a scene from the packaging floor of the former McCord Radiator Company facility in the 1980s. The company employed about 100 people, who packaged and distributed a wide variety of gaskets and other small engine parts across the country. Consolidation led to the plant's closure in the early 1990s. The empty facility was purchased by the Haas Door Company, which is currently manufacturing a variety of garage doors for residential and commercial use.

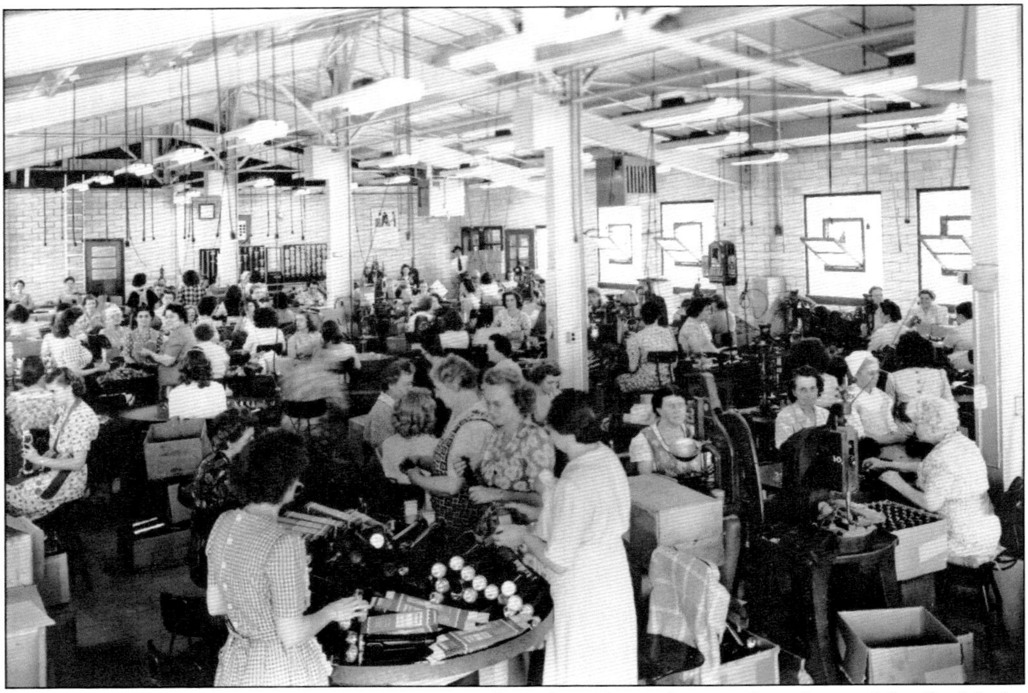

Fulton Industries was organized in 1939. Locally, it has always been referred to as "the flashlight factory." The company produces and distributes a wide variety of heavy-duty, industrial, consumer, government, and military flashlights. Its largest customer is the US military. As one of the largest flashlight manufacturers in the country, the plant, located on Linfoot Street, also produces safety-approved, waterproof, specialty inspection, and portable bow and stern lights for the marine market. Expertise gained in the manufacture of flashlights has also made the company specialists in deep-drawn stamping and assembly work, serving the automotive and appliance industry. This is a scene taken in about 1945, during World War II. In the 1960s, the company was selected by NASA to manufacture the flashlights that astronauts used on missions into space and to the moon.

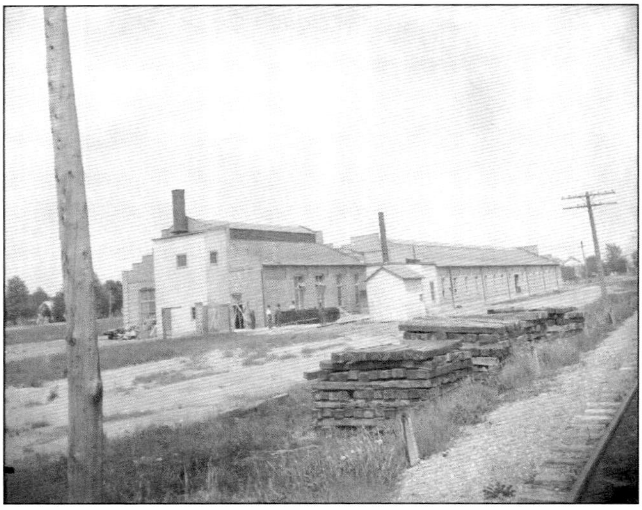

This Malleable Iron Works plant was located on North Ottokee Street, adjacent to the DT&I tracks. It was later purchased by the Winorr Canning Company and converted into a food processing plant. The company canned locally grown corn, beans, carrots, and tomatoes, providing seasonal employment for local workers. In 1982, it was destroyed in a fire causing damages of $1.1 million. A remnant of the building still remains, and it has been used in recent months by a trucking company.

Seven

Noteworthy Residents

Wauseon has been the home of many noteworthy residents. Three in particular have brought the community national recognition: race car legend Barney Oldfield, Civil War veteran Daniel Clingaman, and professional football standout Dick Volk.

Berna Eli "Barney" Oldfield was someone who enjoyed speed, albeit on bicycles and in early automobiles. Known as a daredevil racer, this Wauseon native also had a limited career as a stage and screen actor. Oldfield was born in a small farmhouse on the outskirts of Wauseon on June 3, 1878. Although his family moved to Toledo to operate a grocery store in 1883, he considered Wauseon his hometown, kept contact with family and friends here, and often visited when in the area.

Daniel Clingaman was Ohio's last surviving Civil War veteran and one of only seven veterans in the United States at the time of his death, on February 18, 1951. In 1853, Clingaman, along with his seven brothers and sisters, traveled from Seneca County to Fulton County in an oxen-pulled wagon. His father died soon after their arrival, and the family coexisted next to the last remaining Native Americans living in the county.

Near the end of the Civil War, at the age 18, Clingaman enlisted in the 195th Ohio Volunteer Infantry (OVI), Company D, with his older brother Andrew Jackson Clingaman. The 195th OVI fought in the Shenandoah Valley and near Richmond, Virginia, in 1865 under Gen. Phil Sheridan.

Richard Robert Volk was born on March 15, 1945, in Toledo, Ohio. While attending Wauseon High School, he was a three-sport star: an all-league basketball and baseball player and the quarterback on the football team. After graduation, the six-foot-three-inch-tall athlete went on to play football for the University of Michigan from 1964 to 1966, where he was a member of the 1964 team that won the Big Ten Conference championship and defeated Oregon State in the 1965 Rose Bowl. He played as a defensive back for Michigan's defensive unit and as a halfback and quarterback for the offensive unit.

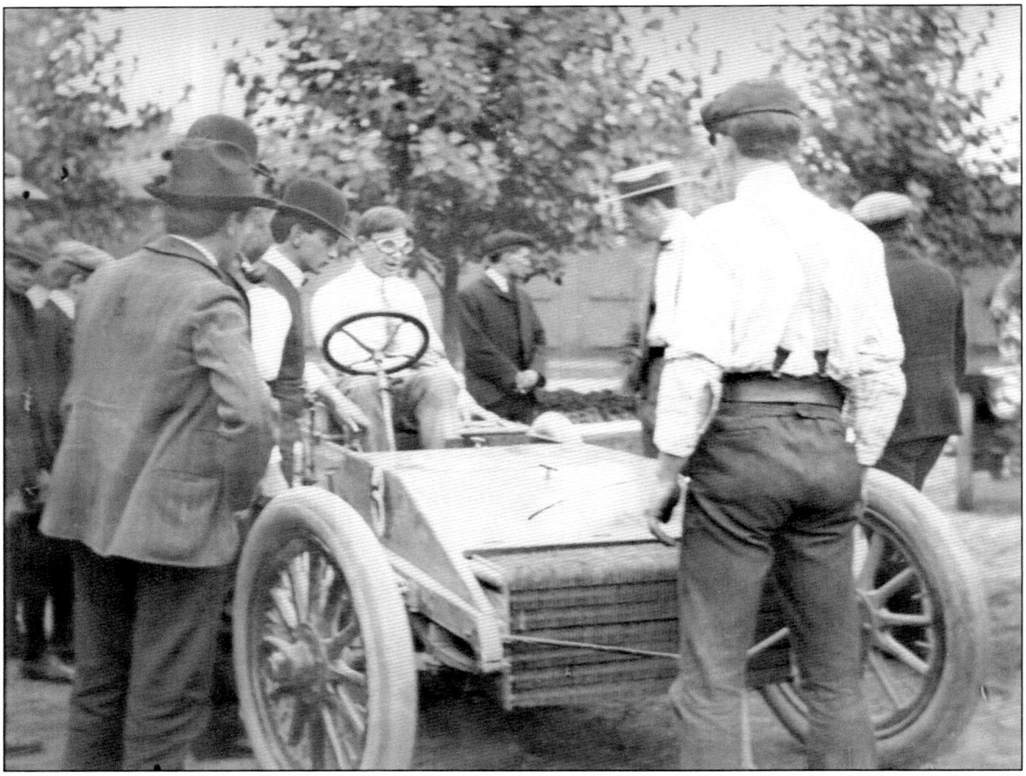

Most pictures of Oldfield show him with an ever-present cigar. He is seen here in the "Peerless Green Dragon" in about 1903. That year, Oldfield became the first driver to reach the speed of 60 miles per hour. In 1910, Oldfield hit 70 miles per hour and, several months later, 131 miles per hour. He continued setting speed records and was soon earning as much as $4,000 per appearance. After a suspension for recklessness, Oldfield returned to racing, retiring in 1918. Oldfield starred in the Broadway musical *The Vanderbilt Cup* in 1906 and in the silent film *Barney Oldfield's Race for a Life* in 1913, where he raced a train to rescue a heroine tied to the train tracks. He was featured in *The First Auto* in 1927 and later starred as himself in a racing film titled *The Blonde Comet*. Barney Oldfield died in 1946 and is buried in Culver City, California. A monument to his role in race car history stands in the Wauseon Union Cemetery. (Courtesy of Richard and Nan Zimmerman.)

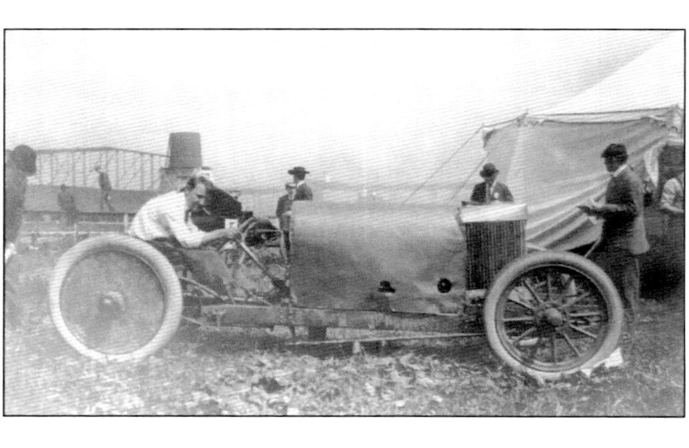

That race led to a meeting with auto pioneer Henry Ford. Although Oldfield had never driven an automobile, Ford asked him to test two of his race cars. Oldfield's success resulted in both him and Ford becoming household names. Pictured is Oldfield in the "Baby Bullet" at the Glenville Track in Cleveland in 1903. (Courtesy of Richard and Nan Zimmerman.)

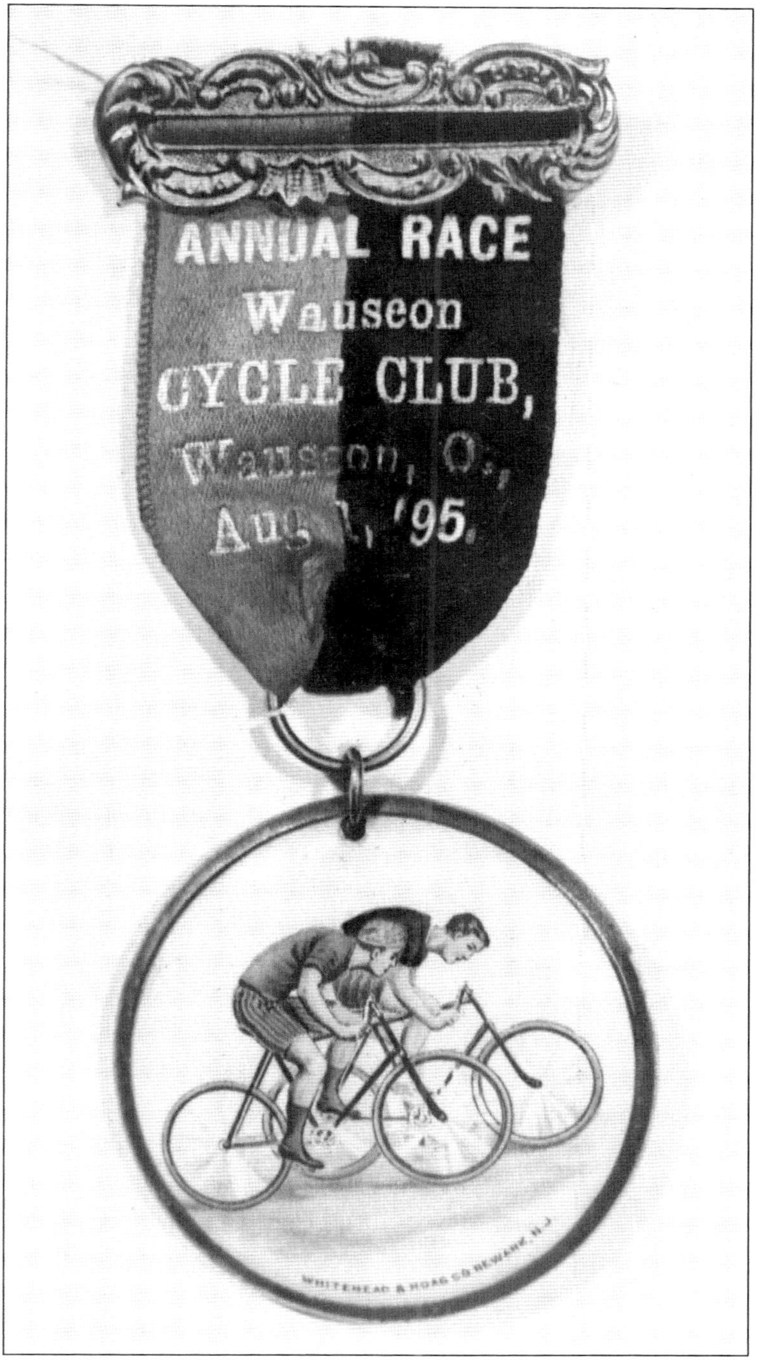

At the age of 16, Barney Oldfield began racing bicycles, winning silver medals and, once, even a gold watch. He competed in and won several bicycle races held on the dirt track at the Fulton County Fairgrounds. His successes led to lucrative contracts with several manufacturers. Pedal power soon led to gas power, and Oldfield was loaned a motorized bicycle, an early version of a motorcycle, during a race in Salt Lake City.

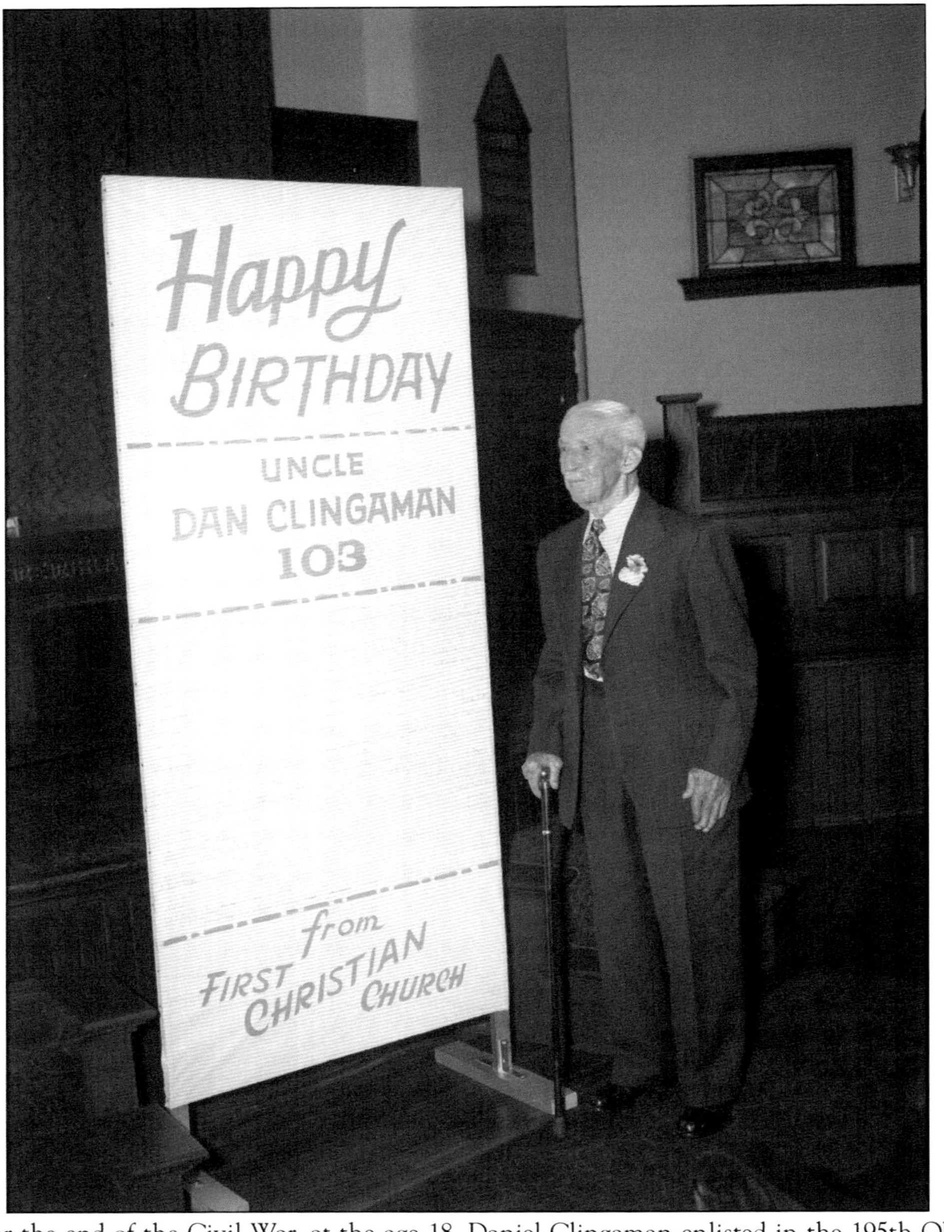

Near the end of the Civil War, at the age 18, Daniel Clingaman enlisted in the 195th Ohio Volunteer Infantry (OVI), Company D, with his older brother Andrew Jackson Clingaman. They fought in the Shenandoah Valley and near Richmond, Virginia, in 1865 under Gen. Phil Sheridan. While passing through Washington, DC, Clingaman reported seeing Pres. Abraham Lincoln strolling along a street. After the war, Clingaman was a blacksmith near Wauseon, but he later sold his business and began farming. In 1938, the Clingaman brothers attended the last bivouac held at Gettysburg, Pennsylvania. The New York Central Railroad made a stop in Wauseon to pick them up. Daniel Clingaman was 104 years, 4 months, and 23 days old when he passed away on February 18, 1951. He is interred in the Wauseon Union Cemetery. Clingaman is pictured here at party held for him at the First Christian Church on his 103rd birthday.

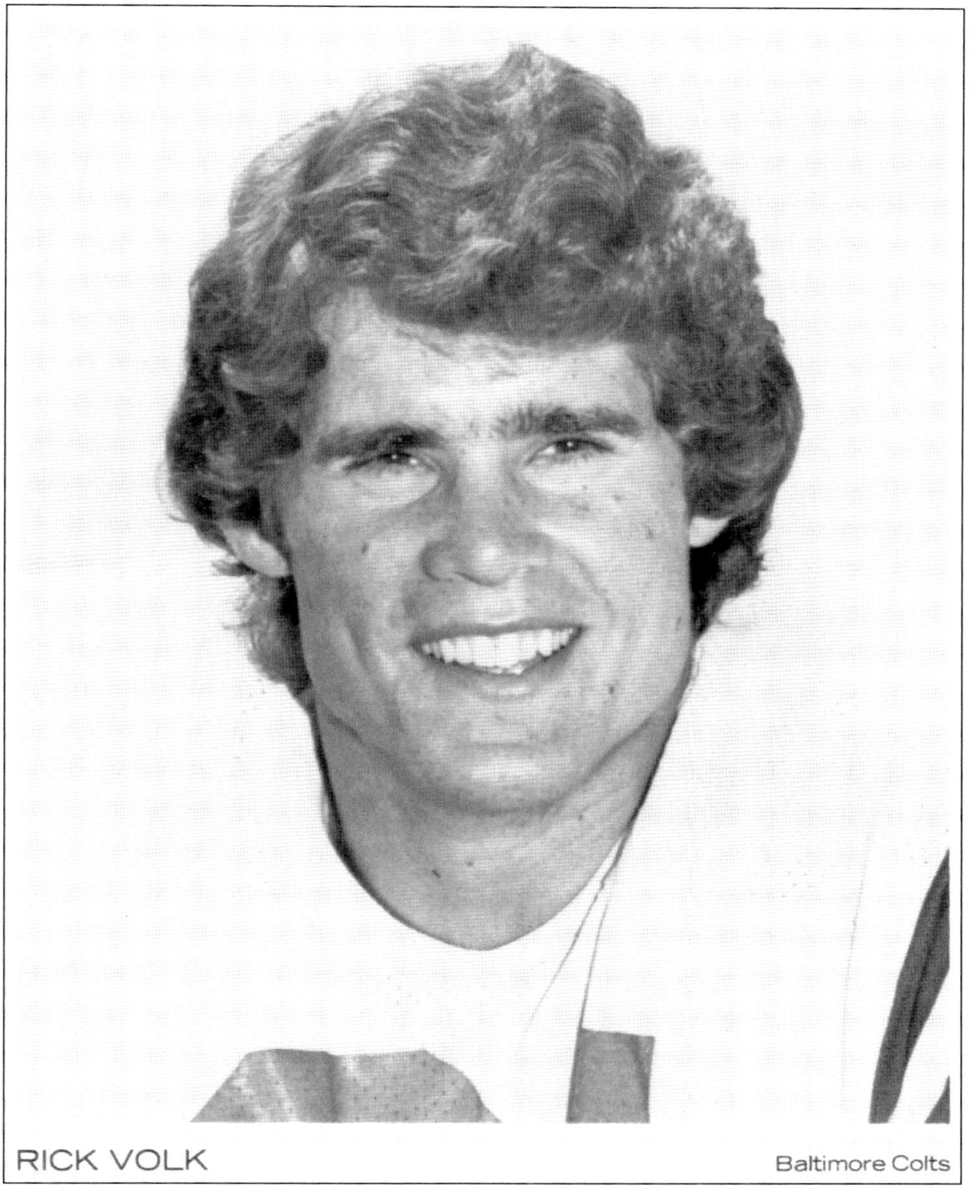

This is a publicity photograph of Richard Volk that was taken when he played for the Baltimore Colts, which he did for eight years, starting in 1967. He was a member of the Colts team that won Super Bowl V against the Dallas Cowboys. Volk was selected by the *Sporting News* as a first-team All-American in 1967. He had a successful 12-year career as a safety in the National Football League (NFL). Volk was selected as an NFL all-pro four times in a row from 1968 to 1971 and played in three Pro Bowls, in 1967, 1969, and 1971. After being released by the Colts in 1976, Volk concluded his impressive career with the New York Giants in 1976 and the Miami Dolphins from 1977 to 1978. In 1977, Volk was selected by Baltimore fans as a starter for the Colts' 25th-anniversary team. In 1989, he was inducted into the University of Michigan Athletic Hall of Honor. Volk has returned to Wauseon many times for visits and to support fundraisers, such as the former Perry-Krauss Memorial Golf Tournament and Auction.

BIBLIOGRAPHY

Fulton County Historical Society. *Fulton County Ohio, 1850–1976*. Wauseon, OH: Fulton County Historical Society, 1976.

Hamilton, James McClellan. *History of Montana, From Wilderness to Statehood*. Portland, OR: Binfords & Mort, 1970.

Hurt, R. Douglas. *The Ohio Frontier: Crucible of the Old Northwest, 1720–1830*. Bloomington, IN: Indiana University Press, 1996.

Miller, Larry L. *Ohio Place Names*. Bloomington, IN: Indiana University Press, 1996.

Nolan, William F. *Barney Oldfield: The Life and Times of America's Legendary Speed King*. Carpinteria, CA: Brown Fox Books, 2002.

Reighard, Frank H. *A Standard History of Fulton County, Ohio*. Vol. 1. Fulton County, OH: The Lewis Publishing Company, 1920.

About the Fulton County Historical Society

Napoleon wrote, "History is the version of past events that people have decided to agree upon." While there are conflicting versions explaining several of Wauseon's most important events, there is one thing most of us can agree on: our history is the result of tenacious pioneers who overcame tremendous challenges to transform this area into a wonderful place to raise families.

This retrospective is based largely on the photographic collection of the Fulton County Historical Society. This is far from a comprehensive history of Wauseon and is not intended as such. This book provides glimpses into the city's past as recorded by available sources.

The Fulton County Historical Society, founded in 1883, is the 13th-oldest historical society in Ohio. It maintains several historic buildings, including a blacksmith shop, a log cabin, and Swan Creek Township Hall, at the Fulton County Fairgrounds. It also manages the Lake Shore & Michigan Southern depot, on Depot Street in Wauseon, which houses artifacts relevant to the history of the railroads that once traversed the county. A restored Baltimore & Ohio caboose is located on this site. Most important is the society's extensive collection of rare artifacts and photographs, in the Monroe Street Museum in Wauseon. The mission of the society is to "collect, preserve, and interpret artifacts and written records pertaining to Fulton County."